Lecture Notes in Artificial Intelligence 2155

Subseries of Lecture Notes in Computer Science
Edited by J. G. Carbonell and J. Siekmann

Lecture Notes in Computer Science

Edited by G. Goos, J. Hartmanis, and J. van Leeuwen

W0245742

Springer

Berlin
Heidelberg
New York
Barcelona
Hong Kong
London
Milan
Paris
Tokyo

Harry Bunt
Robbert-Jan Beun (Eds.)

Cooperative Multimodal Communication

Second International Conference, CMC'98
Tilburg, The Netherlands, January 28-30, 1998
Selected Papers

 Springer

Series Editors

Jaime G. Carbonell, Carnegie Mellon University, Pittsburgh, PA, USA
Jörg Siekmann, University of Saarland, Saarbrücken, Germany

Volume Editors

Harry Bunt
Tilburg University, Computational Linguistics and AI Group
P.O. Box 90153, 5000 LE Tilburg, The Netherlands
E-mail: Harry.Bunt@kub.nl

Robbert-Jan Beun
Utrecht University, Department of Information and Computing Science
P.O. Box 80.089, 3508 TB Utrecht, The Netherlands
E-mail: rj@cs.uu.nl

Cataloging-in-Publication Data applied for

Die Deutsche Bibliothek - CIP-Einheitsaufnahme

Cooperative multimodal communication : second international conference ;
revised papers / CMC '98, Tilburg, The Netherlands, Januar 28 - 30, 1998.
Harry Bunt ; Robbert-Jan Beun (ed.). - Berlin ; Heidelberg ; New York ;
Barcelona ; Hong Kong ; London ; Milan ; Paris ; Tokyo : Springer, 2001
    (Lecture notes in computer science ; Vol. 2155 : Lecture notes in
    artificial intelligence)
    ISBN 3-540-42806-2

CR Subject Classification (1998): I.2, H.5.3, H.5, D.2, I.5, K.4

ISBN 3-540-42806-2 Springer-Verlag Berlin Heidelberg New York

This work is subject to copyright. All rights are reserved, whether the whole or part of the material is
concerned, specifically the rights of translation, reprinting, re-use of illustrations, recitation, broadcasting,
reproduction on microfilms or in any other way, and storage in data banks. Duplication of this publication
or parts thereof is permitted only under the provisions of the German Copyright Law of September 9, 1965,
in its current version, and permission for use must always be obtained from Springer-Verlag. Violations are
liable for prosecution under the German Copyright Law.

Springer-Verlag Berlin Heidelberg New York
a member of BertelsmannSpringer Science+Business Media GmbH

http://www.springer.de

© Springer-Verlag Berlin Heidelberg 2001

Typesetting: Camera-ready by author, data conversion by Christian Grosche, Hamburg
Printed on acid-free paper   SPIN: 10845541   06/3142   5 4 3 2 1 0

Preface

The chapters in this book are revised, updated, and edited versions of 13 selected papers from the Second International Conference on Cooperative Multimodal Communication (CMC'98), held in Tilburg, The Netherlands, in 1998. This was the second conference in a series, of which the first one was held in Eindhoven, The Netherlands, in 1995. Three of these papers were presented by invited speakers; those by Donia Scott (co-authored with Richard Power), Steven Feiner (co-authored with Michele Zhou), and Oliviero Stock (co-authored with Carlo Strapparava and Massimo Zancanaro). The other ten were among the submitted papers that were accepted by the CMC'98 program committee. The editors contributed an introductory chapter to set the stage for the rest of the book.

We thank the program committee for their excellent and timely feedback to the authors of the submitted papers, and at a later stage for advising on the contents of this volume and for providing additional suggestions for improving the selected contributions. The program committee consisted of Nicholas Asher, Normann Badler, Don Bouwhuis, Harry Bunt, Walther von Hahn, Dieter Huber, Hans Kamp, John Lee, Joseph Mariani, Jean-Claude Martin, Mark Maybury, Paul Mc Kevitt, Rob Nederpelt, Kees van Overveld, Ray Perrault, Donia Scott, Jan Treur, Wolfgang Wahlster, Bonnie Webber, Kent Wittenburg, and Henk Zeevat.

We thank the Royal Dutch Academy of Sciences (KNAW) and the Organization for Cooperation among Universities in Brabant (SOBU) for their grants that supported the conference.

July 2001

Robbert-Jan Beun
Harry Bunt

Table of Contents

Part 3: Multimodal Interpretation

Part 4: Multimedia Platforms and Test Environments

Multimodal Cooperative Communication

Robbert-Jan Beun[1] and Harry Bunt[2]

[1] Department of Information and Computing Science
University of Utrecht, Utrecht, The Netherlands
rj@cs.uu.nl
[2] Computational Linguistics and AI Group
Tilburg University, Tilburg, The Netherlands
bunt@kub.nl

1   Introduction

When we interact with computers, we often want them to be endowed with similar characteristics as we find in human communication, and that we are familiar with. One of these characteristics is the ability to use a combination of various communication modalities. In everyday conversation, people effortlessly combine modalities such as speech, gestures, facial expressions, touch and sounds to express meaningful conversational contributions. Since the perceptual, cognitive and motor abilities of humans are well adapted to the real-time processing of these various modalities, we expect that including the possibility to use various modalities in interfaces may contribute to a more efficient and satisfactory human-computer interaction.

It was only twenty years ago that interaction with computers was for the most part only possible through symbols that could be understood exclusively by expert users. Today we can hardly imagine that the interface once did not include the graphical apparatus of icons, buttons, pictures and diagrams that we have become so accustomed to. Clearly, the visual interactive qualities of interfaces have improved a lot, but they are still unable to utilise and integrate communication modalities in a similarly powerful way as we find in human communication. Commercially available interfaces are still unable to integrate speech and gestures, to adapt the modality to the circumstances of the communicative setting, or to decide in an intelligent manner whether particular information should be presented in a pictorial or textual format, spoken or written, or both.

In general, the term 'modality' refers to an attribute or circumstance that denotes the mode, manner or form of something. In the context of human-computer interaction, the modality of a message usually pertains to particular aspects of the surface structure or form in which information is conveyed. Message forms can be organised into a variety of physical, spatial and temporal structures. Depending on the nature of these structures, messages can, for instance, be volatile or have a more permanent character and can be received by a particular perceptual channel. Speech and gestures, for instance, are evanescent and, if not recorded, disappear the moment they are performed; written messages, on the

H. Bunt and R.-J. Beun (Eds.): CMC'98, LNAI 2155, pp. 1–10, 2001.
© Springer-Verlag Berlin Heidelberg 2001

other hand, may persist over hundreds or even thousands of years. A user interface designer must be aware of at least some of these properties, since they may have important consequences for the quality of the communication process.

Modality should not be confused with medium. Although both notions are related to the form of the message, a medium usually refers to the various physical channels and carriers that are used to transfer information, ranging from the human perceptual channels to carriers such as coaxial cable and radio waves. A modality, on the other hand, often refers to a particular communicative system, i.e. conventions of symbols and rules to use these symbols and to express messages. Language, for instance, can be conceived as a modality, not as a medium. In some cases, however, the distinction between the two notions is rather ill-defined. Speech is in some of the literature considered a different modality than written language, where the main difference is the medium used to transfer the messages. By contrast, a particular modality is sometimes considered to derive its character from different communication forms that make use of the same medium, e.g. written language and pictures.

Systems that combine different modalities in communication are usually called 'multimodal'. This book focuses on the use of multimodality in interface design and broaches topics such as the interpretation and production of multimodal messages by computer systems. Multimodal systems seem to derive their character from the possibility that different messages sent through two or more channels or by means of different communication forms can be integrated into a single message. For instance, the combination of pointing to a particular object and speaking the words *Put that in front of the TV* contains two different messages that can be integrated into a single one where the word *that* is assigned to the referred object.

Multimodality often involves several media, but since a transmission medium is not always a determining factor of the modality, multimodality can also be achieved through the same medium. When different messages are transferred through different media, as in pointing and speaking, we use the term 'diviplexing', following Taylor (1989); if the same medium is used, for instance in written text and pictures, we use the term 'multiplexing'. In the latter case, the two signals that carry the information of the separate messages are multiplexed into one signal, i.e. parts of one of the messages are interleaved with parts of the other message (time-division multiplexing) or the messages are simultaneously carried over different partitions of the channel (frequency-division multiplexing). Note that in order to reconstruct the original message in a multiplexed signal, the two signals first have to be separated at the receiver's side before they can be integrated again.

Developments in interaction technology and the resulting expansion of bandwidth of interactive systems enable designers to incorporate a variety of media and modalities in the computer interface. But merely adding amazing technological feats or increasing bandwidth does not necessarily improve the communication process. A signal has to be tuned to the many aspects that play a role in the interaction, such as the characteristics of the user's information processes, the content of the message, the task, or the communication channel. In many cases, a picture tells us more than a thousand words, but it is difficult, or even impossible, to put an abstract message such as *It is possible that John walks* in a picture without using symbols. A warning signal that indicates a fire in the building should be different from the signal that indicates the daily receipt of our electronic mail, and in a noisy environment, a visual signal may be preferred over an auditory one.

The use of more than one modality is often a cause of redundancy, which can be exploited to maximise the effectiveness of communication, as in the case of lip-reading. Perhaps even more important is that the efficiency of communication can be maximised by using different modalities simultaneously for different aspects of information. For example, when we use language to exchange information, we often do not express our emotional reactions explicitly in the language, but use gestures and facial expressions diviplexed with the language, or intonation patterns and other prosodic features in a multiplexed fashion. Feedback and other forms of dialogue control in face-to-face dialogue, such as attention monitoring, are only partly expressed linguistically, and often take a diviplexed form by nodding and looking at the dialogue partner. In written text, topic changes are often multiplexed with the spatial organisation of the words in paragraphs and sections. And pointing to an object can be much more efficient than using a complex linguistic description. The diviplexed and multiplexed use of different modalities and media is a fundamental feature of natural communication; the 'Multimax Principle' (Bunt, 1998) claims that people do not leave modalities unused that are available and useful in the given communication situation. (For instance, in face-to-face communication it would be very strange not to make any gestures or to keep one's facial expression exactly the same all the time.) Since the integration of various modalities is such a prominent characteristic of the human information process, the inclusion of integrated multimodality in human-computer interfaces opens the way for more effective and efficient forms of communication.[1]

Taking care of the appropriate combination of modalities can be considered a feature of cooperativeness. In general, cooperation involves joint activity and mutual consideration of goals. Focusing on conversational contributions, cooperation is often analysed in terms of the Gricean maxims (Grice, 1975), which roughly state that speakers have substantial evidence for their statements (maxim of quality), make their contributions as informative as required for the purpose of the conversation (maxim of quantity), are relevant (maxim of relevance) and behave perspicuously and economically (maxim of manner). The first

---

[1] Speaking of '*integrated* multimodality' may seem pleonastic, since the integration of information that is exchanged using different modalities may be considered to be inherent to multimodal communication. In their seminal discussion of the concepts of multimodality and multimedia, Nigay and Coutaz (1993) take the integration of information from different channels to be one of the defining characteristics of multimodality. A case of unintegrated multimodal communication could perhaps be said to occur when one speaks to one person and winks at someone else.

three maxims usually refer to the content of the contributions, while the last one concerns the form of messages.

Grice's maxim of manner can in fact be seen as tying together the concepts of cooperation and multimodality. Given a particular content, a speaker is supposed to present his utterances in an effective and efficient form that supports the addressee's understanding of the meaning of the sender's contribution for the ongoing conversation. Hence, the sender avoids, for instance, ambiguities and obscurities, because otherwise the addressee is unable to identify the original message. Avoiding ambiguities tends to lead to articulate, explicit utterances of considerable length. On the other hand, the maxim says that the sender should be as brief and efficient as possible, so that the decoding and encoding processes of the signal can be optimised. Multimodality not only enables the sender to choose the most efficient form for a particular piece of information, it also allows the sender to transfer different pieces of information simultaneously. Participants in a cooperative dialogue may be said to pursue several goals simultaneously: on the one hand the concrete goal(s) that motivate the dialogue, and at a meta-level also the general goal of communicating successfully, which entails such subgoals as being understood correctly, obtaining reliable and relevant information, and so on, much in the spirit of the Gricean maxims. These goals can be pursued simultaneously by performing multimodal communicative acts that are multi-functional,[2] and exploit the use of different modalities among other things to convey different information, relating to goals at different levels.

2   Multimodal Generation, Interpretation, Collaboration, and System Design

The chapters in this book have been grouped in four parts, which are concerned with the generation of multimodal dialogue contributions, with cooperativeness in multimodal communication, with interpretation in multimodal dialogue, and with multimodal platforms and test environments.

2.1   Multimodal Presentation and Generation

The first chapter by Donia Scott and Richard Power, *Generating Textual Diagrams and Diagrammatic Texts,* is concerned with the automatic coordination of diagrams and texts in electronic document generation. Scott and Power argue that there is no sharp division between text and diagrams, since texts are presented diagrammatically and, vice versa, most diagrams contain textual elements. In their paper, they take the position that diagrams can be conceived as texts with a rich graphical layout. Therefore, the production of the two communication forms is integrated and generated from a common architecture. In their approach, they extend a proposal by Nunberg who makes a distinction between

---

[2] See Allwood (2000) and Bunt (2000) for discussions of the multifunctionality of dialogue contributions.

text structure, realised by layout and punctuation, and the syntactic structure of sentences. Power and Scott postulate an intermediate abstract data structure that captures those features of layout and punctuation that interact with meaning. A feature that admits vertical lists, called 'Indentation', extends Nunberg's text-grammar. The results are applied in the ICONOCLAST system where the abstract data structure mediates between rhetorical/semantic structures and the details of the graphical layout and punctuation.

Susanne van Mulken in Chapter 2, PEDRO: *Assessing Presentation Decodability on the Basis of Empirically Validated Models,* describes an empirical study to test hypotheses that follow from a model about the decodability of pictorial presentations of object references. The model, which is implemented in a multimodal presentation system called 'PEDRO', exploits Bayesian networks to make predictions about the decodability of the user. Three independent variables were defined: a. Similarity Advantage, concerning the resemblance of antecedent and the presentation, b. Relative Salience, i.e. the perceptual salience of the object with respect to its surrounding, and c. Domain Expertise, which relates to the user's knowledge of names and sizes of components in a technical device. In general, the results of the experiment strongly supported the hypothesis that the number of correct responses decreases with decreasing levels of the independent variables. It was found, however, that Relative Salience only plays a role in case of complete ambiguity, i.e. if the object could not be determined by similarity and user knowledge, and that similarity only played a role if expertise was low. The outcome of the experiment had no impact on the model that was originally implemented in PEDRO.

In Chapter 3, IMPROVISE: *Automated Generation of Animated Graphics for Coordinated Multimedia Presentations,* a generation system that automatically creates sequences of animated graphical illustrations, called IMPROVISE, is presented by Michelle Zhou and Steven Feiner. Four features are discussed that facilitate coordinated multimedia design: a semantic model of the input data, a temporal model of visual techniques, an action based inference engine and an application independent visual realiser. In order to create a wide range of visual presentations, the semantic data model contains a taxonomy of application independent properties, such as 'type', 'attribute' and 'relation'. Visual techniques are used to assemble a new visual presentation or to modify an existing one; in IMPROVISE, visual techniques are extended with temporal constraints to coordinate animated graphics with other temporal media. Finally, Zhou and Feiner present the inference engine that creates the design specifications rendered by the visual realiser. In their paper, the generation and modification processes of animated visual narratives are illustrated by two examples. In the first example, a narrative is generated and combined with spoken sentences to present a hospital patient's information to a nurse; in the second example, an existing presentation of a computer network is modified.

In Chapter 4, *Multimodal Reference to Objects: An Empirical Approach,* Robbert-Jan Beun and Anita Cremers present an empirical study about object reference in task dialogues. A dialogue experiment was carried out where both participants had visual as well as physical access to a shared task domain where objects, consisting of coloured Lego blocks, had to be manipulated. Communication about these objects was possible by uttering linguistic expressions and/or non-verbal references, such as pointing. Main question was how people refer to a particular target object and why a specific surface structure was chosen. Several hypotheses were formulated on the basis of the principle of minimal cooperative effort and the assumption that dialogue participants establish different kinds of focus spaces. Beun and Cremers showed that in the dialogues obtained in the experiment most referential expressions were ambiguous with respect to the domain of discourse and that focus was an important factor in disambiguating these expressions. Also, references to objects outside the focus area were significantly more redundant than references inside the focus area. It was found that in a multimodal environment focus is not only a discourse-related phenomenon, but also depends on particular properties of the domain of conversation combined with the perceptual abilities of the dialogue partners.

2.2 Multimodal Cooperation

One of the key concepts in modelling cooperation in communication, is that of *communicative action*. The four chapters in this part of the book are all concerned with certain aspects of the planning, expression, and interpretation of actions in multimodal communication.

Oliviero Stock, Carlo Strappavara, and Massimo Zancanaro in their chapter, *Augmenting and Executing SharedPlans for Multimodal Communication*, propose the adoption of an extended form of the concept of *shared plans*, as developed by Grosz and Kraus (1993). The theory of shared plans (and their technical form, 'SharedPlans') is based on distinguishing between the plans that an agent 'knows' (recipes for actions) and the plans that an agent constructs and adopts. The theory of shared plans attempts to model interaction as a joint activity in which the participants try to build a plan in the latter sense; the plan is shared in the sense that the participants have compatible beliefs and intentions. Stock et al. take the view that the interface in multimodal interaction has a double nature: some of the actions are intended to augment the current SharedPlan, whereas others are intended to execute the related recipe. The authors therefore propose an extension to the model of plan augmentation as put forward by Lochbaum (1994), where SharedPlans are meant not only to be augmented, but also executed. They discuss and illustrate their proposal with examples from the prototypical multimodal systems they are developing, building on the ALFRESCO system (Stock et al., 1993).

With the advent of multimodal cooperative systems, a lasting source of inspiration for the design of interactive systems will be the way multimodal cooperation is achieved in human-human dialogue. Jens Allwood's contribution, *Cooperation and Flexibility in Multimodal Communication* (Chapter 6) explores some of the ways cooperativeness is multimodally manifested in natural dialogue with a view to the design of future cooperative human-computer interfaces. After a discussion and characterisation of the notion of cooperation, he proposes to extend cooperation into a notion of 'mutual flexibility'. An empirical study is presented of how verbal and nonverbal gestural means are used to achieve flexibility in Swedish face-to-face conversation. Allwood discusses possible implications for the design of interactive systems, which concerns such questions as whether systems should be friendly; should sometimes be non-serious or vague; should be non-imposing; should give and elicit supportive or other types of feedback; should show consideration and interest; and should be able to invoke mutual awareness and belief. If the answer to any of these questions is positive, then we are well advised to look at the ways in which these features are achieved in natural human communication, in order to know what means to use for making this happen in human-computer interaction.

In Chapter 7: *Communication and Manipulation in a Collaborative Dialogue Model,* Martine Hurault-Plantet and Cecile Balkanski present a dialogue model that has been developed and tested in an application that simulates a telephone switchboard, with data drawn from human-human dialogues recorded at a telephone switchboard in an industrial setting. This model rests on a theory of collaborative discourse based on the mental states of dialogue agents. The theory establishes conditions on the beliefs and intentions of the agents for them to be able to cooperate. The authors show how their model allows for the treatment of both communicative acts and manipulation acts. The model is thus equipped to model cooperative human-machine communication in a multimodal context, where natural language (in this case typed rather than spoken) is used in combination with direct manipulation.

In a multimodal user interface where language plays an important part, user requests for actions to be performed by the system may conveniently take the form of an imperative expression. Moreover, in a 'user-friendly' interface the user should be allowed to formulate logically complex requests such as *Do A_1 or A_2,* or *Do A if B.* From a semantic point of view, such logically complex imperatives can lead to strange results if they are interpreted as communicative acts, aiming at a situation where their propositional content is true. For instance, an implication *A if B* is logically equivalent to a disjunction *¬B or A*; therefore an interpretation of a request like *Hit the* Enter *key if you see the symbol '@'* could be interpreted as *Hit the* Enter *key or do not see the symbol '@'* – which is intuitively wrong. Paul Piwek, in his contribution *Relating Imperatives to Action,* provides an analysis of the use of complex imperatives which avoids such problems by taking the influence of background information into account. The analysis is carried out within a model of communicating agents in which imperatives modify their commitments, construed in terms of beliefs combined with plans for action. This analysis explicates what it means for an agent to have a successful policy for action with respect to satisfying his commitments, where some of these commitments have been introduced as a result of imperative language use. The work reported in this chapter was carried out within the framework of the DENK multimodal dialogue project (see also Chapter 11).

2.3   Multimodal Interpretation

In Chapter 9, *Interpretation of Gestures and Speech: A Practical Approach to Multimodal Communication,* Xavier Pouteau discusses the notion of a 'semantic frame' to integrate the interpretation of gestures and speech in multimodal interfaces. Pouteau distinguishes three functions of gestures: a. the epistemic function, which refers to the sense of touch, b. the ergative function, which pertains to the manipulation of objects, and c. the semiotic function, which concerns the information content of the gesture. It is argued that contemporary interfaces only use the first, i.e. touch, through the contact with keyboard and mouse, and that the other functions are neglected. In order to combine gestures with speech, Pouteau focuses on the semiotic functions of gesture, in particular the notion of *demonstratum* for pointing. In the semantic frame, Pouteau abstracts from the actual devices that support pointing and only registers the visual elements possibly pointed at during the interaction supplemented, with information about time and coordinates of the pointing act. This information is integrated with semantic information from the speech signal. Feedback messages are generated in case of interpretation failures.

Michael Streit in his chapter *Why are Multimodal Systems so Difficult to Build? - About the Difference between Deictic Gestures and Direct Manipulation,* addresses the question of synchronisation in diviplexed messages. Streit concentrates on the synchronisation of speech and gestures and argues that there is a gap between empirical findings and our expectations about natural conversation. Close observations of users interacting with the multimodal systems MOFA and TALKY has shown that, in contrast with human-human communication, long delays may exist between gestures and accompanying parts of the speech. Since the linguistic part of the message may help the disambiguation of the meaning of the gesture, these long delays may cause important problems for the interpretation process. Streit calls this the 'wait problem' and shows that the problem has no unequivocal solution. Therefore, several approaches to solve the problem are discussed, depending on the type of pointing, the pointing device, the verbal expressions and the type of object referred to. It is argued that appropriate feedback in combination with suitable pointing devices and gesture forms may reduce the problem.

In Chapter 11, *Multimodal Cooperative Resolution of Referential Expressions in the* DENK *System,* Leen Kievit, Paul Piwek, Robbert-Jan Beun and Harry Bunt describe a module of the DENK system, that finds the antecedents for referring expressions. The DENK system reflects a multimodal dialogue situation where users have direct access to a domain (by pointing and direct manipulation) or indirect access through natural language utterances. In the DENK system different types of context are distinguished, for instance the perceptual context (what the user can see in the application domain), the private context (the system's knowledge of the application), the common context (beliefs shared by system and user) and the dialogue history. The question arises, first, in which context to look for a referent and second, which object the user meant if more

than one object satisfies the conditions of the expression. The resolution process is guided by the type of definiteness of the expression. For instance, the
antecedent of a pronominal expression is first looked up in the dialogue history
and, if no fitting antecedent can be selected, the process takes another context
to find one or more suitable candidates. Within a particular context, objects
have some degree of saliency, and given the semantic agreement of the object
and the linguistic description, only salient objects are potential candidates. An
evaluation of the resolution process showed that the algorithm failed in only 5%
of the cases in a corpus of 523 referential acts that were taken from various dialogue corpora. The system is furthermore equipped with mechanisms to provide
clarification questions and to re-evaluate ambiguous utterances on the basis of
the user's reply.

2.4   Multimodal Platforms and Test Environments

In Chapter 12, *The IntelliMedia WorkBench - An Environment for Building Multimodal Systems,* Tom Brøndsted, Paul Mc Kevitt and others present a generic
multimedia platform, called CHAMELEON, that can be tailored to various applications and distributed over various hardware and software platforms. An
initial application of CHAMELEON is the IntelliMedia Workbench which inte-
grates modules such as a blackboard, a dialogue manager, a domain model and
various input and output modalities. The blackboard keeps a history of the interaction in terms of frames that are coded as predicate argument structures.
The dialogue manager decides which actions the system has to perform and,
subsequently, sends the information to the output modules, i.e. a speech synthesiser and a laser pointer. The current domain model contains information about
the architectural and functional layout of a building. Input modules consist of a
gesture recogniser and a speech recognition system. Since different modules may
be running on separate machines, modules are integrated by the so-called DACS
system, which supports communication facilities, such as synchronous and asynchronous remote procedures, by means of a demon that acts as a router for all
internal traffic and that establishes connections to demons on remote machines.

In the last chapter, *A Unified Framework for Constructing Multimodal Experiments and Applications,* Adam Cheyer, Luc Julia and Jean-Claude Martin
discuss a prototype system that enables users to interact with a map display
by means of a combination of pen and voice input. The system, which will be
used as a platform for Wizard-of-Oz (WOZ) experiments, offers facilities for
a multimodal interface on which the user may draw, write or speak about a
travel-planning domain. The approach employs an agent-based framework to
coordinate distributed information sources that work in parallel to resolve different types of ambiguities in the interpretation process. Since multiple users are
allowed to share a common workspace and the interface can be configured on a
per-user basis to include more or fewer GUI controls, the system already offers
important facilities for a fully automated application function part of a WOZ
experiment. The idea is that the Wizard will use the full functionality of the automated system, while the user interacts in an unconstrained manner. Hence, in

the same experiment, information will be collected about both the most natural way to interact and the performance of the real system. It is expected that the data can be applied directly to evaluation and improvement of the system.

References

Allwood, J. (2000) An activity-based approach to pragmatics. In: H.C. Bunt and W.J. Black (eds.) *Abduction, Belief and Context in Dialogue. Studies in Computational Pragmatics*, Benjamins, Amsterdam, 47–80.

Bunt, H.C. (1998) Issues in Multimodal Human-Computer Communication. In H.C. Bunt, R.-J. Beun and T. Borghuis (eds) *Multimodal Human-Computer Communication*. Springer Verlag, Berlin, 1–12.

Bunt, H.C. (2000) Dialogue Pragmatics and Context Specification. In: H.C. Bunt and W.J. Black (eds.) *Abduction, Belief and Context in Dialogue. Studies in Computational Pragmatics*, Benjamins, Amsterdam, 81–150.

Grice, H.P. (1975) Logic and Conversation (From the William James Lectures, Harvard University, 1967). In P. Cole and J. Morgan (eds.) *Syntax and Semantics 3: Speech Acts*. Academic Press, New York, 41–58.

Grosz, B. and Kraus, S. (1993) Collaborative plans for group activities. In *Proceedings of the 19th International Joint Conference on Artificial Intelligence*, Chambéry, 367–373.

Lochbaum, K. (1994) *Using Collaborative Plans to Model the Intentional Structure of Discourse*. PhD thesis, Harvard University, Cambridge, MA.

Nigay, L. and Coutaz, J. (1993) A Design Space for Multimodal Systems: Concurrent Processing and Data Fusion. *Proceedings INTERCHI'93*, 172–178.

Stock, O. and the ALFRESCO Project Team (1993) ALFRESCO: Enjoying the combination of NLP and hypermedia for information exploration. In M. Maybury (ed.) *Intelligent Multimodal Interfaces*. MIT Press, Cambridge, MA., 197–224.

Taylor, M.M. (1989) Response Timing in Layered Protocols: A Cybernetic View of Natural Dialogue. In: M.M. Taylor, F. Néel, and D.G. Bouwhuis (eds.) *The Structure of Multimodal Dialogue*. North-Holland, Amsterdam, 159–172.

Part 1:

Multimodal Generation

Generating Textual Diagrams
and Diagrammatic Texts

Donia Scott and Richard Power

ITRI, University of Brighton, Brighton, UK
{Donia.Scott,Richard.Power}@itri.brighton.ac.uk

Abstract. There are obvious ways in which text and diagrams within a document should be coordinated: for instance, the placement of a diagram might influence the wording of the text. However, there is a more subtle interaction between text and diagrams, which has emerged from work on generating technical documents that make extensive use of layout. Constituents that would normally be classified as textual may contain diagrammatic features (e.g., when multiple indenting is used); conversely, non-pictorial diagrams usually contain short strings of text (e.g., labels within boxes). We argue that text and diagrams really lie on a continuum, and that for generating documents of this kind we need a descriptive framework that combines linguistic and graphical features in the same representation.

1 Introduction

In many genres it is normal for documents to contain diagrams as well as text. (By 'diagrams' we mean schematic illustrations in which logical relationships are expressed graphically — for instance, tables, networks, or embedded boxes; we are not concerned here with pictures or photographs.) Obviously, any system that automatically produces documents in such genres must go beyond the normal capabilities of Natural Language Generation (NLG) programs, not only by generating diagrams and placing them appropriately, but by adapting the wording of the text (McKeown et al., 1992, André and Rist, 1995, van Deemter and Power, 2000). However, there is a more subtle sense in which text and diagrams have to be coordinated. If we look closely, we find that document parts that would normally be labelled 'text' often employ techniques of graphical organization typical of diagrams; conversely, document parts that would normally be labelled 'diagrams' make essential use of text.

Our interest in this field dates from the DRAFTER[1] and GIST[2] projects (Paris et al., 1995, Power and Cavallotto, 1996), which began in 1993. In both projects, the aim was to develop an NLG system that would allow an author

---

[1] *A Drafting Assistant for Technical Writers.* EPSRC project J19221, 1993–1996. http://www.itri.bton.ac.uk/projects/drafter.

[2] *Generating Instructional Texts.* European Commission project LRE 062-09, 1993–1996. http://ecate.itc.it:1025/projects/gist.html.

H. Bunt and R.-J. Beun (Eds.): CMC'98, LNAI 2155, pp. 13–29, 2001.
© Springer-Verlag Berlin Heidelberg 2001

to define the content of instructional texts, which were generated in several languages; in this way, experts on the relevant domains could produce documentation even in languages that they did not know. For DRAFTER the domain was software manuals, specifically for word processors and diary managers; for GIST, the domain was social security forms. During the early stages of these projects we studied wide-ranging examples of actual manuals (Paris and Scott, 1994, Hartley and Paris, 1996) and forms (Scott et al., 1995), and were struck in each case by the prevalence of diagrams and graphical layout, and their close integration with the content and syntax of the text. In software manuals, diagrams of interface objects (icons or buttons) were sometimes inserted directly into sentences as the subject or object of the verb; in social security forms, whole sections of text might be organized as an indented tree representing dependencies among questions (examples will be given later).

Within DRAFTER and GIST there was no provision for addressing these issues, but a lesson drawn from both projects was that in many genres it makes no sense to generate a text without specifying as well how the text should be laid out, and which diagrams (if any) should accompany it. It might seem at first sight that a text could be generated as a punctuated string, the layout and illustrations being added later as a formatting task, but this overlooks the essential contribution of layout and illustrations to meaning. Since 1997 we have been exploring the interaction between wording and layout in the ICONO-CLAST project[3] (Bouayad-Agha et al., 2000b); in addition, our colleague Markus Fisher has investigated the automatic generation of diagrams for user interfaces (Fischer, 1998, Fischer, 1999). In both these more recent projects, we used the technique of constraint logic programming, expressing interactions between graphical organisation and wording by means of constraints defined on linguistic and graphical features. By treating generation as a constraint satisfaction problem (Hentenryck, 1989), we were also able to produce multiple solutions, and so to consider the stylistic criteria by which one potential solution might be preferred to another.

In this chapter we describe an approach to document generation that has grown from all these projects. In what follows, we give examples suggesting that there is no sharp divison between text and diagrams; these concepts actually represent vaguely defined stretches along a continuum, and many document genres contain hybrid passages exhibiting a mixture of textual and diagrammatic features. The prevalence of such passages suggests that textual and diagrammatic features should be merged in a common descriptive framework; we will argue that this can be done through a level of representation called *abstract document structure* which has emerged from our work on ICONOCLAST (Bouayad-Agha et al., 2000a), and on the project RAGS[4], which aims at developing a reference architecture for NLG (Mellish et al., 2000). We finally describe

---

[3] *Integrating constraints on layout and style*, EPSRC Project L77102, 1997–2000. http://www.itri.bton.ac.uk/projects/iconoclast.

[4] *A Reference Architecture for Generation Systems*, EPSRC projects GR/L77041 and GR/L77102, 1998–2001. http://www.itri.bton.ac.uk/projects/rags.

an application demonstrating the generation of text and diagrams from rules defined in the same representational framework, and mention plans for future work.

2   Text and Diagrams

We will argue here that the distinction between text and diagrams is not as straightforward as it is often conceived to be: few documents are purely textual and most diagrams have a critical textual element (apart from their captions).

2.1   Diagrammatical Features within Texts

It is not simply the case that some texts *contain* diagrams: many texts are *presented* diagrammatically, with their linguistic and graphical elements jointly contributing in rather crucial ways to their meaning. Let us look at some fairly common examples.

Forms. Figure 1 shows a simplified section in the style of the form BR1 for retirement pensions, produced by the Document Design Unit of the British Department of Social Security. It belongs to a series of forms that has won awards for clarity and approachability. Compared with a conventional text, the outstanding feature of the section is its layout, obviously designed to express dependencies among questions. The placement of the second question 'Has your spouse applied for a pension before' shows that it is relevant only if the reply to the first question is 'Yes'. Unmarried users, having answered 'No' to the first question, can see immediately from the layout that *there is no need to read the second and third questions at all*, let alone answer them.

Are you married? No   □
                  Yes   □   Has your spouse
                             applied for a
                             pension before?   No   □
                                               Yes   □   State the pension number
                                                          _____

Fig. 1. Part of a Social Security Form (British Version).

To describe the structure of Figure 1 formally, the conventional textual hierarchy of sentence, paragraph, subsection, section, is plainly inadequate. At a superficial level, the section might be regarded as a table, with seven points of vertical alignment; at a deeper level it might be regarded as a binary tree which the user can navigate by following either the 'Yes' arc or the 'No' arc at each decision point. Layout apart, it also differs from conventional texts through the inclusion of ticking boxes next to the 'Yes' and 'No' answers. Is it a text or a diagram? Rather than refining the definitions of these informal terms, we would prefer to classify it as a hybrid, containing both textual and diagrammatic features.

Are you married? (Yes or No) _____

If *YES*, has your spouse applied for a pension before? (Yes or No) _____

If *YES*, state the pension number. _____

Fig. 2. Part of a Social Security Form (Italian Version).

Interestingly, we came across an Italian version of the form (including English translations), produced by a publisher that for one reason or another preferred a more conventional layout. Figure 2 gives the section of this form corresponding to Figure 1; again the content has been simplified, but the style remains faithful to the original. As can be seen, information previously shown by layout is now shown by additional wording. Instead of representing alternative answers by vertically aligned ticking boxes, the Italian version explicitly states 'Yes or No'. Instead of showing dependencies among questions by a graphical relationship to the ticking boxes, it words all follow-up questions in the conditional form — thus perhaps introducing ambiguities: is the third question conditional on the second question, or perhaps on the first? (Working this out is not too difficult, but we have to read the questions.) Whichever version is preferred, the important point is that each version adapts wording to layout: information expressed graphically in Figure 1 is expressed linguistically in Figure 2.

Tables. We normally think of text as a linear sequence, so that each unit has a single successor. A table, instead, is organized in two dimensions, so that each cell has two successors — the cell on the right if we follow rows, or the cell underneath if we follow columns. Some tables are not text-like: a table of numerical data, for example, would typically serve as an illustration, intended for reference rather than exhaustive reading; such tables are usually given a label and a caption, allowing them to float in relation to the text. However, in instructional documents we have often found tables in which the cells contain paragraphs of text, the columns of the table representing a repeated rhetorical relationship. Figure 3 shows an example from a patient information leaflet explaining how to use an insulin pen (ABPI, 1997pg. 535).

Problem	Action
Insulin is not appearing.	The needle may be clogged. Change the needle.
The dose window only shows half a number.	The pen was not reset to ⋆ before you dialled the dose. Reset to ⋆.
You cannot reset to ⋆.	Hold the pen firmly around the white cylinder ...

Fig. 3. Section from a Patient Information Leaflet.

The actual table contains several more entries, and makes up the whole of a section called 'Hints and tips'. It has no label and no caption, and clearly does not float in relation to the surrounding text. In short, apart from its organisation into rows and columns, it behaves like a conventional section of text.

From analysis of a corpus of over 500 patient information leaflets in (ABPI, 1997), we have observed that 'tables of text' are employed most commonly when there is a list of points with a parallel semantic or rhetorical structure. For example, in Figure 3 each point comprises a problem and a remedy, and by using tabular form the author is able to mark this rhetorical relationship just once, in the column headings. Even when a relationship is marked repeatedly, we have seen examples such as Figure 4 in which an informal tabular layout is still used in order to emphasize the parallelism.

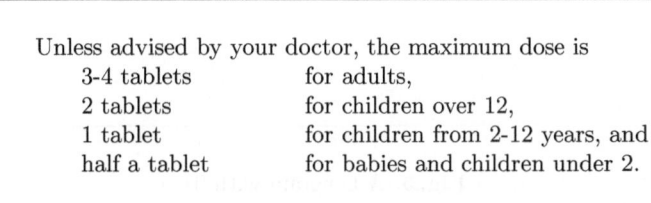

Fig. 4. Informal Tabular Layout.

Icons within Sentences. The '⋆' icon in Figure 3 illustrates the practice of integrating a small picture into a sentence in place of a descriptive noun phrase; the star sign here refers to a marking on the actual insulin pen. We have also noticed this intrusion of diagrams into syntax in software manuals, where a schematic drawing of a button or icon may be employed instead of a noun phrase like 'the Cancel button'

Click on Cancel if you want to close the dialogue box without performing an action.

2.2   Text within Diagrams

Most diagrams contain strings of text which contribute essentially to the meaning. Entity-relationship diagrams, for example, typically have labels on the nodes and arcs; trees have node labels; tables have alphanumerical characters (words or numbers) within the cells. We have been emphasizing the contribution of layout to the meaning of text, *but the contribution of text to the meaning of diagrams is often far more important.* Strip the labels from the system architecture diagram shown in Figure 5, and the result is virtually meaningless (Figure 6). Similarly, separating the labels from their diagrammatic context may leave some important relationships unexpressed, but in most cases it will be easier to reconstruct the meaning from the text alone than it would be from just the graphics.

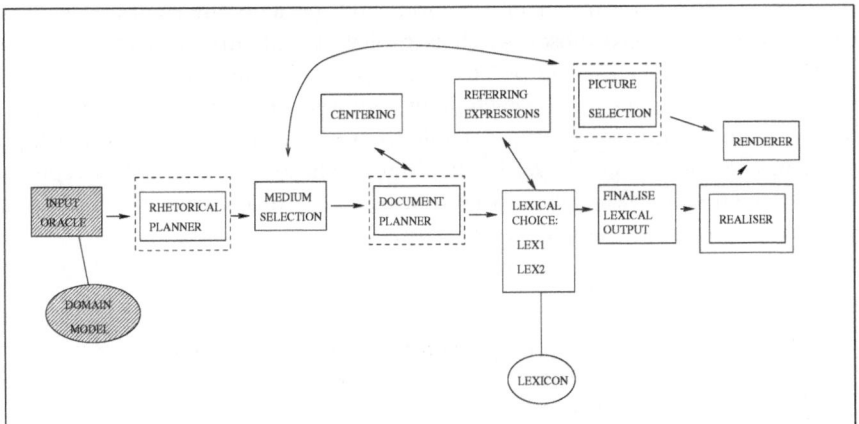

Fig. 5. A Diagram with Text.

3   Abstract Document Structure

The examples that we have discussed suggest the following radical conclusion: *diagrams are texts with rich layout.* This may be an exaggeration, especially for some types of diagram (e.g., ones containing schematic pictorial elements), but it is far nearer the truth than an approach that regards diagrams and text as

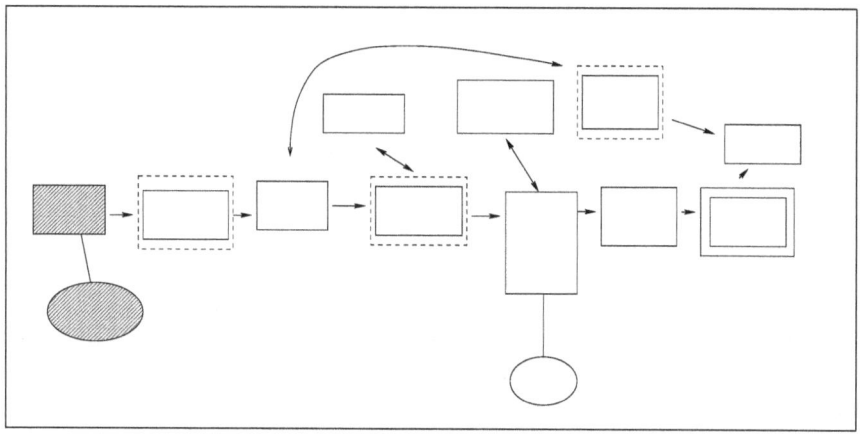

Fig. 6. A Diagram without Text.

distinct presentational forms. Let us adopt this idea provisionally and see how far it can be pushed.

As a foundation, we need a conceptual framework for describing the structure of plain text; with this foundation in place, we can extend the framework so that it covers more and more advanced layout features, leading eventually to diagrams. The most useful starting point, we believe, is the theory of text structure proposed by Nunberg (Nunberg, 1990) in his book 'The Linguistics of Punctuation'. This book introduces two crucial clarifications. First, it distinguishes *text structure*, which is realised by punctuation and layout, from *syntactic structure*. Secondly, it distinguishes *abstract* features of text structure from the *concrete* (or graphical) features by which they are expressed.

The distinction between text structure and syntax can be explained by considering two interpretations of the word 'sentence'. In linguistics, 'sentence' is used mainly as a syntactic category, defined by phrase-structure rules such as $S \rightarrow NP + VP$. However, a sentence can also be viewed as a portion of text starting with a capital letter and ending in a full stop; to distinguish this from the syntactic category, Nunberg calls it a 'text-sentence'. Sometimes the two categories of sentence coincide, but often they do not. Thus in the following passage:

He entered the office. Disaster. The safe was open and the money had gone.

the first text-sentence is also a syntactic sentence, but the second is merely a noun, while the third comprises two syntactic sentences (or three if we count the whole as well as its parts). Nunberg argues that if we have two kinds of category, then we need *two kinds of grammar*: he calls them the 'lexical' grammar (we prefer 'syntactic') and the text-grammar. In addition to text-sentence, the text-categories include 'text-clause', 'paragraph', and 'section', and the text-grammar allows us to formulate constituent structure rules such as

$$S_t \rightarrow C_t^+$$

meaning that a text-sentence comprises one or more text-clauses.

In introducing the concepts 'text-sentence', 'text-clause', etc., it is convenient to explain them in terms of their realisation in punctuation and layout: thus a text-sentence starts with a capital letter and ends in a full stop; a text-clause ends in a semicolon; a paragraph begins on a new line with a tab. However, this is not strictly correct. In Nunberg's theory, these concepts represent *abstract* structural properties of the text which may be realised differently according to context or convention. In the case of 'paragraph' this distinction is obvious, since we are all familiar with several devices for expressing paragraph boundaries: instead of a new line with a tab, for example, an editor might prefer two new lines (or some other vertical space) with no tab. However, the abstract/concrete distinction also applies to the other text-categories. For example, the passage

The safe was open; the money had gone.

contains two text-clauses, but the second has no semicolon because its ending coincides with the closure of a larger unit, a text-sentence, which is marked by a full-stop. Similarly, the stop at the end of a text-sentence is often dropped when the sentence is an item in a vertical list, for instance in a sequence of instructions:

To save the file:
1. Open the Save dialogue-box
2. Enter the filename
3. Click on the Save button

Thus text structure is *realised* by punctuation and layout, but the two are not equivalent.

The relationship between text structure and syntax is a difficult issue, but to simplify a complex story we can assume that syntactic relations hold only within text-clauses. It is easy to find exceptions, for instance in an informal style of writing

He felt beaten. Battered. And bewildered.

but in most cases this assumption holds. Within text-clauses, then, the structural features guiding interpretation are mainly syntactic; at higher levels, this role is taken over by the text structure.

Since his book is about punctuation, Nunberg focusses on text-categories like text-clause and text-sentence which are realised by marks like semicolon and full-stop. In ICONOCLAST, our aim has been to extend the concept of text grammar so that it covers all significant higher-level structure found in documents, including pictures and diagrams as well as layout patterns like bulleted lists. On this wider interpretation, the term 'text-structure' becomes misleading, so in the RAGS guidelines the term 'document structure' is preferred.

The significance of abstract document structure in ICONOCLAST (and RAGS) is that it mediates between rhetorical/semantic structure and the details of graphical layout and punctuation. As a simple illustration, consider the concept of 'emphasis'. On a rhetorical/semantic level, this concerns the information structure of the message: perhaps a particular element is focussed, as in the following formula:

$$contrast(likes(john, meat), ordered(john, \overline{fish}))$$

in which focussing is marked by an overline. At a later stage of generation, this message has been realised by an abstract document structure, perhaps comprising two text-clauses, and the focus on the element $fish$ has been realised by an emphasis feature on the word 'fish'. In XML notation, this abstract document structure could be represented as follows:

```
<text-sentence>
  <text-clause>
    John likes meat
  </text-clause>
  <text-clause>
    but he ordered <emphasis>fish</emphasis>
  </text-clause>
</text-sentence>
```

Finally, in the concrete document structure, these features of abstract document structure are realised by punctuation and formatting decisions. Since emphasis can be shown in several ways, the same abstract structure can be realised by a number of different concrete structures, depending on which convention is preferred:

John likes meat; but he ordered *fish*.
John likes meat; but he ordered **fish**.
John likes meat; but he ordered FISH.

Why postulate an intermediate abstract document structure, rather than passing directly from rhetorical structure to detailed layout and punctuation? The answer, we believe, is that through the concept of abstract document structure *we can capture those features of layout and punctuation that interact with meaning, and hence with wording.* Having decided to put focus on *fish*, the first issue that arises in expressing the message is whether to express this focus by wording (e.g., 'what he ordered was fish'), or by emphasis expressed through formatting. At this stage it does not matter whether the emphasis will be marked by italics, bold face, or capital letters: the choice of wording will remain the same no matter which of these alternatives is eventually used.

3.1 Advanced Layout

The implication of our argument is that a common architecture can be used for generating text and diagrams — or at least, some kinds of diagrams. Indeed, we have suggested that such an architecture is not only possible, but desirable, since the 'text' and 'diagrams' really lie on a continuum, with many hybrid forms. Minimally, this common architecture envisages two stages, although these could be further divided:

1. Starting from a rhetorical/semantic input, the wording and abstract document structure of the text/diagram is selected.
2. The output document is fully specified by decisions about punctuation, formatting, and graphical layout, which are guided by the abstract document structure.

In such a system, wording is adapted to layout through *co-occurrence constraints on syntax and abstract document structure*. Thus, if focus is to be expressed through a cleft construction, an 'emphasis' feature in abstract document structure might be ruled out (unless a redundant style was preferred). Or if an entity was to be expressed in abstract document structure by a node in an entity-relationship diagram, its syntactic realisation might take the form of a concise label rather than a full noun phrase (e.g., 'company location' rather than 'the location of the company').

If this approach is viable, the crucial next step is to extend Nunberg's text-grammar so that it encompasses the abstract forms of a wider range of layout patterns. Our first move in this direction has been to admit vertical lists through a new abstract feature called INDENTATION. In Nunberg's text-grammar, the categories form a hierarchy ordered by size: sections contain paragraphs, paragraphs contain text-sentences, text-sentences contain text-clauses, and so forth. Vertical lists complicate this picture because *lower units may contain higher units*, provided that the higher units are indented items. In the following passage, for example, a text-clause contains indented paragraphs (coordinated syntactically with the subordinating conjunction 'since'):

> In rare cases the treatment can be prolonged for another week; however, this is risky since
> – The side-effects are likely to get worse. Some patients have reported severe headache and nausea.
> – Permanent damage to the liver might result.

To formalise this extension, the ICONOCLAST system represents document units by two features called TEXT-LEVEL and INDENTATION. TEXT-LEVELs are represented using the familiar hierarchy from section to text-phrase; INDENTATION is represented by integers in the range $0..N$, so that for example an indented item within an indented item would have INDENTATION=2. For short, we can write for example Sen_0 for an unindented text-sentence and Par_1 for an indented paragraph. Within the same level of indentation, Nunberg's constituent structure rules hold good; thus we can write

$$Par_i \rightarrow Sen_i{}^+$$

meaning that a paragraph with indentation i may comprise one or more text-sentences also with indentation i. This rule (with $i = 1$) exactly describes the first indented item in the above passage. However, the children may also be indented one degree higher than the parent, in which case the usual constraint on TEXT-LEVEL hierarchy no longer applies. Thus we have for example:

$$Phr_i \rightarrow Par_{i+1}{}^+$$

meaning that a text-phrase (the constituent of a text-clause) may comprise one or more paragraphs at a higher indentation; with $i = 0$ this describes the whole indented list.

To specify abstract document structure for tabular layouts is more difficult, since it is unclear what is the right level of abstraction. Our first experiments have been based on the concepts 'row', 'column' and 'cell' that are used for defining tables in HTML and CLIM (Common Lisp Interface Manager); these define the schematic structure of a table, the exact spacing being determined by graphical features (e.g., distance between cells) which can be regarded as part of concrete document structure. Thus an abstract document structure for Figure 1 (the excerpt from a social security form), encoded in XML, might run as in Figure 7.

4 Applications

In the DRAFTER system, which generates instructions for using word processors and diary managers, the user specifies the desired content by interacting with a diagrammatic representation of the instructional procedure. The diagram is made up of a number of embedded boxes (Figure 8), orange boxes representing actions, defined by labels in the upper left, and violet boxes representing methods for achieving them; since a method includes a sequence of sub-actions, these violet boxes will contain smaller orange boxes in their turn.

Originally, we did not regard the production of diagrams like Figure 8 as a NLG problem. The diagram belonged to a user interface for creating and maintaining a knowledge base, from which output texts in natural languages (English and French) would then be generated. However, as pointed out in Section 2, strings of text play a vital role in such diagrams, and we had to implement at least a rudimentary syntax in order to produce action labels like 'Enter document name'.

Thus DRAFTER paradoxically had *two* NLG systems, not one. The knowledge-editing interface was able to produce diagrams (similar to Figure 8) from a knowledge-base in any state of completion; as well as indicating the current state of the knowledge, these diagrams could be manipulated interactively in order to perform editing operations — for instance, by adding further sub-actions to a sequence. In a way, the production of the diagrams was a more impressive application of NLG than the production of the output texts: the syntax may have been impoverished, but the use of layout was far more complex, the generator worked even when the knowledge was only partly specified, and the generated diagram showed extra information — not only the existing content, but the options for adding further content.

```
<section>
  <row>
    <text-sentence force=question>
      are you married
    </text-sentence>
    <column>
      <row>
        <text-sentence>no</text-sentence>
        <ticking-box/>
      </row>
      <row>
        <row>
          <text-sentence>yes</text-sentence>
         <ticking-box/>
        </row>
        <row>
          <text-sentence force=question>
            has your spouse applied for a pension before
          </text-sentence>
          <column>
            <row>
              <text-sentence>no</text-sentence>
              <ticking-box/>
            </row>
            <row>
              <row>
                <text-sentence>yes</text-sentence>
                <ticking-box/>
              </row>
              <text-sentence>
                state the pension number
              </text-sentence>
            </row>
          </column>
        </row>
      </row>
    </column>
  </row>
</section>
```

Fig. 7. Abstract Document Structure.

From this experience we drew two lessons. Firstly, if we could support knowledge editing through a generated diagram, why not support it through a generated *text*, thus freeing the user from any need to learn new diagrammatic conventions? Secondly, if the tasks of generating text and diagrams had considerable overlap, why not approach them by applying the same methods and resources? The first conclusion led to the development of the WYSIWYM[5] technique of knowledge editing (Power et al., 1998, Scott et al., 1998), which depends on interaction with a *feedback text* which plays the same role as the diagram in Figure 8. The second conclusion led to the attempt, in the ICONOCLAST project, to unify the generation of text and diagrams by treating diagrams as an enhancement of normal textual layout.

Fig. 8. Diagrammatic Representation of Instructions.

To express the point schematically, the two generators in DRAFTER produced presentations of the knowledge base which differed on two dimensions: *purpose*, and *appearance*:

Purpose. Presentations in the user interface served the purpose of *supporting editing*, by providing feedback on the current state of the knowledge base, along with options for editing. The texts produced by the English and French generators served the purpose of system output, to be incorporated into manuals. For short, we call these purposes *feedback* and *output*.

Appearance. Presentations in the user interface had a highly *diagrammatic* appearance; the output texts had a predominantly *textual* appearance.

Accordingly, in the first prototype of the ICONOCLAST system, we aimed to build a unified generator with all these properties: it could generate both output and feedback documents (thus allowing WYSIWYM editing), and it could produce both DRAFTER 'diagrams' and DRAFTER 'texts' (as well as various hybrids in between the two).

---

[5] WYSIWYM stands for "What You See Is What You Meant". A demonstration of how it works can be found at
http://www.itri.bton.ac.uk/projects/WYSIWYM/wysiwym.html.

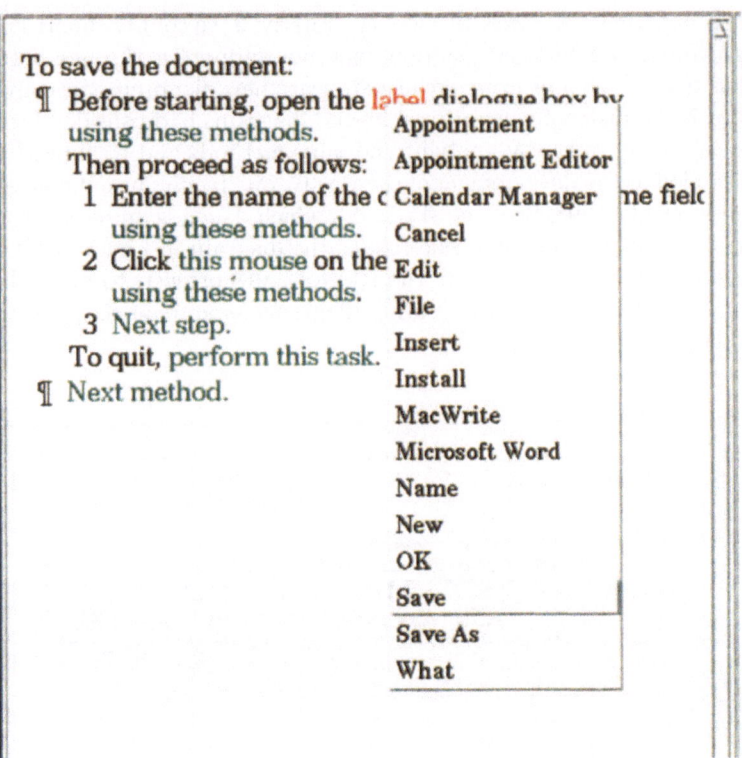

Fig. 9. WYSIWYM Editing.

Figure 9 shows a snapshot of the system during WYSIWYM editing of a procedure. As can be seen, the goal of the procedure (saving a document) has been fully defined, and some sub-actions of a method have been nearly defined: all that remains is to specify the label on a dialogue-box (i.e., the *Save* dialogue-box). The feedback text shows options for adding further information either by green 'anchors' (e.g., *Next step*) or by red anchors (*label*). These anchors are mouse-sensitive, and by clicking on the coloured spans the author can obtain a menu listing the types of object that may be inserted at that location. Red anchors signal that the insertion operation is obligatory; green anchors signal that it is optional. Insertion might appear to be an operation on the feedback text, but actually it is an operation on the underlying knowledge base; the feedback text is then completely regenerated, and might in some cases need to be re-organized (e.g., because information previously conveyed by a single sentence has become too voluminous). In Figure 9, the author has opened in the menu listing the options for the label on the dialogue-box, and is about to choose 'Save'.

Having obtained a complete knowledge base (i.e., having made all obligatory insertions), the author can switch the purpose setting to 'output' rather than

To save the document:
Before starting, open the Save dialogue box.
Then proceed as follows:
  1 Enter the name of the document in the Name field.
  2 Click on the Save button.

Fig. 10. Output with Textual Appearance.

'feedback'. The result will be a text which conveys the instructional procedure defined in the knowledge base, without signalling options for editing the knowledge (Figure 10). The difference that hits the eye is that the green anchors have gone, but of course this does not mean that the output text was derived merely by deleting the anchors from the feedback text. It is completely regenerated with a different pragmatic purpose setting; again, in some cases, this could lead to radical differences in text structure and syntax.

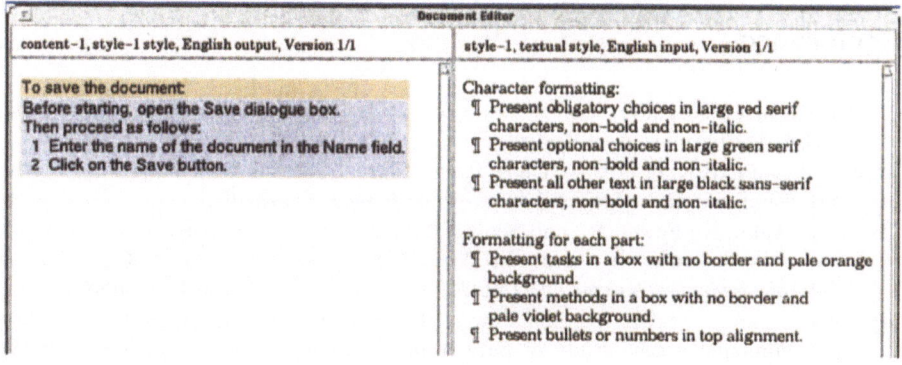

Fig. 11. Output with Hybrid Appearance.

A final novelty of the ICONOCLAST prototype is that it allows the author to edit the *presentational style* of the instructional text/diagram as well as its content. This is done through a style profile, presented in an accompanying pane, which can be modified in the usual way through WYSIWYM editing. In Figure 11, the author has requested a basically textual appearance, except that whole procedures should be presented on an orange background, while their constituent methods (the actions for achieving a goal) should be presented on a violet background: we thus obtain a hybrid between the diagrammatic output of Figure 8, and the textual output of Figure 10.

5   Summary and Conclusions

We have argued that text and graphics are not as distinct as they are generally conceived to be. While we would agree that speech and graphics are clearly discrete categories, we do not believe this to be the case for text and diagrams. Certainly, within the context of documents, these two media are very closely related. If clear categorisation is what we seek, then this is more likely to be between linguistic material – not text – and graphics. A given text or diagram will fall somewhere on a continuum ranging from the purely linguistic to the purely graphical. Texts will tend to fall closer to the linguistic end, and diagrams to the graphical end, clearly some textual genres (e.g., letters) are more purely 'linguistic' than others (e.g., instruction manuals), just as some diagrams (e.g., Venn diagrams) are more graphical than others (e.g., maps). Applying these insights to natural language generation systems, we have shown that these two media can be generated from a common architecture.

If we want to describe (or generate) documents, we have to use a framework that goes beyond purely linguistic features and includes graphical ones. In doing so, we obtain a framework applicable to presentations that would normally be thought of as multimedia, including graphical user interfaces.

References

ABPI, editor (1996–1997). *Compendium of Patient Information Leaflets.* Association of British Pharmaceutical Industry.

André, E. and Rist, T. (1995). Generating coherent presentations employing textual and visual material. *Artificial Intelligence Review,* 9:147–165.

Bouayad-Agha, N., Power, R., and Scott, D. (2000a). Can text structure be incompatible with rhetorical structure? In *Proceedings of the International Conference in Natural Language Generation (INLG-2000),* pages 194–200, Mitze Ramon, Israel.

Bouayad-Agha, N., Scott, D., and Power, R. (2000b). Integrating content and style in documents: a case study of patient information leaflets. *Information Design Journal,* 9(2–3):161–176.

Fischer, M. (1998). A framework for generating spatial configurations in user interfaces. In *Proceedings of the 1998 meeting of Design, Specification and Verification of Interactive Systems,* pages 225–241.

Fischer, M. (1999). *Automatic Generation of Spatial Configurations in User Interfaces.* PhD thesis, University of Brighton. Also available as ITRI Technical Report ITRI-99-02.

Hartley, A. and Paris, C. (1996). Two sources of control over the generation of software instructions. In *Proceedings of the 1996 Meeting of the Association for Computational Linguistics,* Santa Cruz, California, USA.

Hentenryck, P. V. (1989). *Constraint Satisfaction in Logic Programming.* MIT Press, Cambridge, Mass.

McKeown, K., Feiner, S., Robin, J., Seligman, X., and Tanenblatt, Y. (1992). Generating cross-references for multimedia explanation. In *Proceedings of the Tenth National Conference on Artificial Intelligence (AAAI'92),* pages 9–16.

Mellish, C., Evans, R., Cahill, L., Doran, C., Paiva, D., Reape, M., Scott, D., and Tipper, N. (2000). A Representation for Complex and Evolving Data Dependencies in Generation. In *Proceedings of the 6th Applied Natural Language Processing Conference (ANLP 2000)*, pages 119–126.

Nunberg, G. (1990). *The Linguistics of Punctuation*. Number 18 in CSLI Lecture Notes. CSLI Publications, Stanford, CA.

Paris, C. and Scott, D. (1994). Intentions, structure and expression in multilingual instructions. In *Proceedings of the Seventh International Workshop on Natural Language Generation*, pages 45–52, Kennebunkport, Maine. Also available as ITRI Technical Report ITRI-94-2.

Paris, C., Vander Linden, K., Fischer, M., Hartley, A., Pemberton, L., Power, R., and Scott, D. (1995). A support tool for writing multilingual instructions. In *Proceedings of the 14th International Joint Conference on Artificial Intelligence*, pages 1398–1404, Montreal, Canada.

Power, R. and Cavallotto, N. (1996). Multilingual generation of administrative forms. In *Proceedings of the 8th International Workshop on Natural Language Generation*, pages 17–19, Herstmonceux Castle, UK.

Power, R., Scott, D., and Evans, R. (1998). What you See Is What You Meant: direct knowledge editing with natural language feedback. In *Proceedings of the 13th Biennial European Conference on Artificial Intelligence (ECAI'98)*, pages 677–681.

Scott, D., Gorman, L., Hartley, A., Paris, C., Pemberton, L., Power, R., and Vander Linden, K. (1995). Characteristics of good administrative forms. Technical Report ITRI-95-3, Information Technology Research Institute, ftp://ftp.itri.bton.ac.uk/reports/ITRI-95-3.ps.gz.

Scott, D., Power, R., and Evans, R. (1998). Generation as a Solution to its own Problem. In *Proceedings of the 9th International Workshop on Natural Language Generation*, pages 256–265.

van Deemter, K. and Power, R. (2000). Authoring multimedia documents using WYSI-WYM editing. In *Proceedings of the 18th International Conference on Computational Linguistics (COLING 2000)*, pages 222–228.

PEDRO: Assessing Presentation Decodability on the Basis of Empirically Validated Models

Susanne van Mulken

German Research Center for Artificial Intelligence (DFKI) Saarbrücken, Germany*
mulken@dfki.de

Abstract. This chapter describes a psychological experiment performed in the framework of a user modeling component that makes use of Bayesian networks to anticipate the decodability of presentations planned by a multimedia presentation system. The goal of this empirical study was to test the validity of the assumptions contained in a decodability model postulated for the problem of reference resolution. This paper briefly introduces the user modeling component and describes the experiment.

1 Introduction

In order to determine whether a presentation will be effective and efficient for a particular user, a multimedia presentation system needs to consider several factors. These include: 1) the type of information, 2) the type of media available, 3) the goal of the presentation, and 4) the characteristics of the individual user.

Many research groups in the field have focussed on the use and coordination of multiple media. For *media allocation*, they generally take into account the factors type of information, available media, and – although to a lesser extent – the user's task.

Also, several projects have started to integrate user modeling techniques to adapt presentation contents to the individual user, thus trying to ensure that a presentation is effective in the sense that it lies within the user's understanding capabilities. However, this type of adaptation only concerns the contents of the presentation. Therefore, one could regard this not to be really characteristic of automatic multimedia presentation but rather of automatic presentation in general (e.g. also of purely textual presentations).

However, also at the surface level of generation, the user's familiarity with the particular code used is important. Graphics, for instance, can be regarded as a language itself with each element having a specific meaning. Here, the effectiveness and efficiency of a presentation depend not only on the type of information and the user's task, but also on the individual's knowledge with regard to the specific graphical language used. So far, adaptation to the *individual* user has

---

* This work was carried out while the author was a member of Cognitive Science Program at the University of Saarbrücken and funded by the German Science Foundation (DFG).

H. Bunt and R.-J. Beun (Eds.): CMC'98, LNAI 2155, pp. 30–42, 2001.
© Springer-Verlag Berlin Heidelberg 2001

been more or less neglected (see van Mulken, 1997; 1998). Neglecting the characteristics of the individual user may render invalid the system's estimate of what would constitute an effective and efficient presentation for a given communicative goal.

This paper therefore advocates an approach implemented in the system PE-DRO[1] that explicitly takes into account the specific characteristics of the user while estimating whether a planned (textual or graphical) presentation will be effective and efficient for a particular individual. PEDRO was built with an orientation toward the hypermedia system PPP (see e.g. André et al., 1996; André and Rist, 1996; Wahlster et al., 1993).

PEDRO exploits Bayesian networks to make *predictions* about the decodability of a presentation and to *interpret* evidence received from user input. The Bayesian networks represent the variables and their interrelations that play a role in decoding presentations. Some of the models – that is, the specific variables and their relationships – were investigated empirically in psychological experiments.

In the following, it is first pointed out how the systems PPP and PEDRO can interact with each other so as to raise effectiveness and efficiency. Then, an empirical study that examined the validity of one of the models is described.

2 Approach

As it is impossible to anticipate every possible decoding problem beforehand, the strategy adopted in this work is that of an anticipation feedback loop (AFL) (Jameson and Wahlster, 1982). In the present work, AFL means that the presentation system plans a presentation as usual, but that before outputting this presentation, it is evaluated with regard to decodability for the intended user. Not until the planned presentation is rated as decodable is the presentation actually output.

Using an AFL in this manner, the decodability of a presentation can be taken into account on-line. Thus, also decodability problems that are hard to anticipate – and that are therefore hard to specify design rules for – can be considered. The problem then comes down to predicting how likely a user is to decode a presentation as intended. This in turn comes down to a prediction of whether the user will draw particular inferences required by the presentation. For this reason, the system needs to have a representation of what causes a particular inference to be more or less easy to draw.

PEDRO represents its decodability knowledge using Bayesian networks (BNs). BNs are directed acyclic graphs whose nodes represent chance variables. The edges in the networks represent the (causal) relationships between the variables. The nature of the relationships between the variables are represented in conditional probability tables. In such a table, for each combination of values (e.g., true or false) of a child and parent variable, a conditional probability is stored.

---

[1] PEDRO stands for PrEsentation Decodability pRedictOr.

By propagating the probabilities over the edges of the network (essentially based on Bayes' rule), the system can reason about the respective variables. Downward propagation yields a prediction, whereas upward propagation yields an interpretation of given evidence (see e.g. Charniak, 1991, for a short introduction and see Pearl, 1988, for a thorough discussion of BNs).

3   Example: Resolution of Pictorial Referring Expressions

As an example of one of the inferences that a user must often make when reading multimodal presentations, consider the one induced by a referring expression in which both the antecedent and the anaphor are presented graphically. Figure 1 shows such an expression in the context of instructions for an espresso machine.

Expressed verbally, the communicative goal of the presentation is to explain to the user how she should put the cover on the container and make sure that the mark is between "min" and "max". The inference the user has to draw here is what object in the main frame the cover depicted in the inset refers to. Unfortunately, the different perspective taken in the inset leads to greater perceptual similarity between this object and the switch in the front panel of the espresso machine. Thus, the user may become confused as to what the object in the inset refers to.

Fig. 1. Part of the Instructions for an Espresso Machine.

Several factors are important in the correct resolution of a pictorial referring expression. Our hypotheses are partly based on psychological research on visual search and inference processes and partly on psycholinguistic research with respect to anaphora resolution.

> ▷ *Relative perceptual salience.* Perceptual salience refers to an object's conspicuousness with respect to colour, brightness, size, and position in the graphic relative to other objects. In psychological experiments on visual search processes, it has been found that if a target object has particular

features that the surrounding objects (distractors) do not have – e.g. a particular colour or orientation – it can be found extremely fast. In such cases, the target objects appear to pop out (e.g. Treisman and Gelade, 1980). Furthermore, in research on the psychology of thinking and reading, it has been found that the more salient an object in comparison to another object, the more likely it will be involved in inferences (see e.g. Manktelow and Jones, 1986, concerning the concept of *salient task features*).

▷ *Relative perceptual similarity.* A well established finding concerning linguistic anaphora resolution is that the parallelism between antecedent and anaphor with respect to syntax and semantics plays an important role in the ease of resolution (see e.g. Garnham, 1987; Huls et al., 1995). In analogy to this, we assume here that the user will be more likely to regard an object as a potential antecedent, the greater its relative perceptual similarity.

▷ *Domain knowledge.* The user's domain knowledge plays a role inasmuch as it can help her locate the intended object – for instance because she has seen such an object before and remembers where this type of object is generally located in the device.

Figure 2 shows how these dependencies are represented in the Bayesian network that PEDRO constructs for the prediction of whether a particular user, $\mathcal{U}$, will be able to infer the intended antecedent of the cover shown in the inset in the instructions of Figure 1. The node RELATIVE PERCEPTUAL SALIENCE OF TARGET represents the perceptual salience of the target relative to other possible candidates. Its values range from VERY LOW to VERY HIGH.

The node to its right, SIMILARITY ADVANTAGE OF TARGET, represents the difference in the degree of similarity between the referring object and the target on the one hand and that between the referring object and the next most similar object on the other hand. The values of this variable range from VERY LOW to VERY HIGH as well.

As a rough approximation, we assumed that the relationship between RELATIVE PERCEPTUAL SALIENCE OF TARGET (X), SIMILARITY ADVANTAGE OF TARGET (Y), and their child node, OBVIOUSNESS OF TARGET AS ANTECEDENT (Z), can be described as follows:

$$P(Z = z | X = x, Y = y) = f\left(z - \frac{g(x) + g(y)}{2}\right),$$

where f is the density function of a normal distribution with mean 0 and standard deviation 1.0, and the function g maps the values of X and Y onto $[0, 1]$.

The node on the left, KNOWLEDGEABILITY OF $\mathcal{U}$ ABOUT DOMAIN represents $\mathcal{U}$'s domain expertise. We assume that the influence of KNOWLEDGEABILITY OF $\mathcal{U}$ ABOUT DOMAIN (X) on the resolution of the anaphor will be relatively small if OBVIOUSNESS OF TARGET AS ANTECEDENT (Y) is high: The probability that a layperson will be able to associate anaphor and antecedent correctly is still high. However, if the OBVIOUSNESS OF TARGET AS ANTECEDENT is low, then KNOWLEDGEABILITY OF $\mathcal{U}$ ABOUT DOMAIN can play a much bigger role, because it can

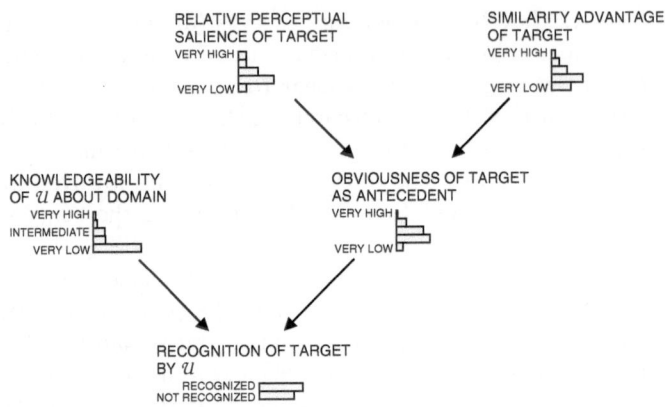

Fig. 2. Bayesian network for the prediction of whether $\mathcal{U}$ will be able to correctly resolve the pictorial anaphor in Figure 1. The histogram for each node represents PEDRO's belief about the node in question before any evidence from user input has become available.

help her to infer the correct association, for instance, on the basis of previous experience with espresso machines. Formally, the relationship between the variables KNOWLEDGEABILITY OF $\mathcal{U}$ ABOUT DOMAIN (X), OBVIOUSNESS OF TARGET AS ANTECEDENT (Y), and RECOGNITION OF TARGET BY $\mathcal{U}$ (Z) can be described by the following equation:

$$P(Z = \text{RECOGNIZED}|X = x, Y = y) = 1 - (1 - f(y))(1 - f(x)),$$

where f is a linear function that maps the values of X and Y onto $[0, 1]$.

As can be seen from the network, for this user (having little domain knowledge) and this presentation, PEDRO predicts that the user will probably be able to infer the correct antecedent (see the histogram for the node RECOGNITION OF TARGET BY $\mathcal{U}$). However, it is quite uncertain about this.

If requested, PEDRO can give a recommendation for improvement, which is based on a search through the BN (see van Mulken, 1998). The recommendation is fed back to PPP, which can now decide either to accept the risk of possibly being unclear or to restart the planning process to find an alternative way to present its message and so improve the presentation.

As indicated above, the postulated relationships on which PEDRO based its reasoning were regarded as rough approximations. In order to investigate our hypotheses about the relationships between the variables, we carried out the experiment described in the following section.

4   Empirical Investigation of the Postulated Model

An experiment was designed in which subjects had to identify objects of which short descriptions were given. Each item consisted of textual and graphical instructions about a component for a particular type of equipment and a display of the equipment itself. The task of the subject was to identify by mouse click the component they thought was referred to in the short description.

Three independent variables were defined: Similarity Advantage (S), Relative Salience (R), and Domain Expertise (D). The dependent variable was Correctness of the Response (C).

4.1   Hypotheses

To investigate the hypothesis that with a rise in an object's Relative Salience, it is increasingly likely that the object is considered as a possible target, we defined three variations of Relative Salience: *low*, *intermediate*, and *high*. These levels were operationalized through the saturation of the objects. We expected that the probability of a Correct Response should decrease with decreasing levels of Relative Salience.

Similarity Advantage was operationalized through the size of the objects to be identified. Again, we defined three variations: Similarity Advantage (S) could take on the values *low*, *intermediate*, or *high*. We expected that the higher Similarity Advantage, the more likely $\mathcal{U}$ is to consider an object as a possible target of a referring expression. In particular, the probability of a Correct Response in the condition S=*low* should be smaller than that in the conditions S=*intermediate* and S=*high*. Moreover, the probability of a Correct Response should be smaller in the condition S=*intermediate* than in the condition S=*high*.

Finally, Domain Expertise was operationalized through the knowledge of the names and sizes of particular components in a technical device. It was assumed that the more knowledge a user has about the domain of the instructions, the greater the probability of correct reference resolution should be, as this knowledge may restrict the number of possible candidates for a referring object. Again, to test this hypothesis, we made three variations of Domain Expertise: *low*, *intermediate*, and *high*. As above, we expected the probability of Correct Response to be smaller with decreasing levels of Domain Expertise.

Furthermore, it was expected that there should be a compensating relationship between Similarity Advantage and Domain Expertise (cf. section 3). Thus, the difference in Correctness of Response between the levels of Similarity Advantage should become smaller as the level of Domain Expertise increases. A similar interaction was assumed between Domain Expertise and Relative Salience. It was expected that Relative Salience would have a greater effect with low Domain Expertise than with intermediate or high levels of Domain Expertise.

4.2   Method

Subjects and Design.   Subjects were 45 students from the University of Saarbrücken. The three independent variables Relative Salience, Similarity Advantage, and Domain Expertise were all manipulated within-subjects. The variable Domain Expertise was varied over three experimental phases. The order of these phases was completely counterbalanced, and they were assigned to the subjects randomly. For each level of Domain Expertise (i.e. in each experimental phase), three levels of Similarity Advantage and three levels of Relative Salience were realized (i.e. a 3 × 3 × 3 design).

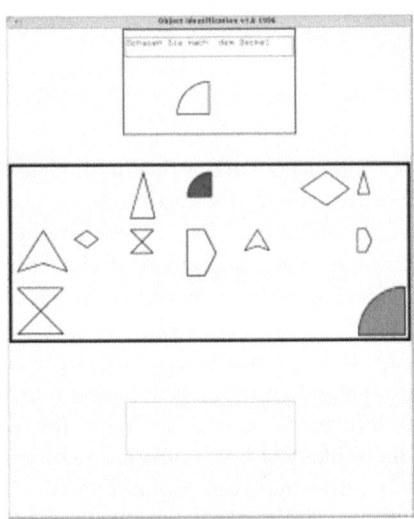

Fig. 3. An example item from the experiment. In this item, the pie-shape in the lower right corner is the intended object (in preceding study sessions, subjects could learn that the *Deckel* (cover) is the big one of the two pie shapes). Here, Relative Salience is *plus* (it has a higher saturation); Similarity Advantage is *zero* (the referring object is of medium size).

Materials. The 162 items[2] presented to the subjects consisted of instructions such as shown in Figure 3. Each item consisted of a referring expression. This referring expression was composed of a graphically presented component of a technical device and a textual expression naming the intended component in the context of a request, such as *Take a look at the cartridge* or *Check the on/off switch*. In the middle of the screen appeared (the top-view of) the technical device, in which the intended component was to be identified by mouse-click. The technical devices were all fictitious and presented in stylistic form – that is, the components had the shape of simple geometric figures. They concerned two network computers (two different versions) and a laser printer.

---

[2] In each of the three experimental phases, the subjects were presented with 54 items: Each of the nine S-R combinations was tested six times.

Operationalization of Independent Variables. The variable Similarity Advantage was operationalized through the size of the objects. It was assumed that objects of the same size are more similar to each other than objects of different sizes. Three objects were relevant for the definition of each particular level of Similarity Advantage: the referring object, the target object, and the distractor object. The size of the target and distractor objects was either small or big. The size of the referring object was either small, big, or medium. The size of the medium objects was such that they appeared to be exactly half-way in size between the small and the big objects.

Three levels of Similarity Advantage were implemented: *minus*, *zero*, and *plus*.[3] The level *minus* was defined as a referring object with a size equal to that of the distractor object but different from that of the target object. For instance, if the referring object was small then the target object was big, and the distractor object was small. The level *zero* was defined as a referring object of medium size, either with a big target object and a small distractor object or with a small target and a big distractor object. The level *plus* was defined as a referring object and target object of equal size and a distractor object of a different size.

The variable Relative Salience was operationalized through saturation. It was assumed that generally a colour with high saturation is more salient than a colour with low saturation. The relative salience of a target object depends on the degree of saturation in comparison to the distractor object. Thus, for the definition of the different levels of Relative Salience two objects were relevant: the target object and the distractor object. Target and distractor objects could take on one of two values: red with low saturation or red with high saturation.

Again three levels *minus*, *zero*, and *plus* were defined. The level *minus* was defined as a combination with a distractor object in red with high saturation and target object in red with low saturation. The level *zero* was defined as a combination with a distractor object and a target object with equal saturation. Finally, *plus* was defined as a combination with a distractor in red with low saturation and a target object in red with high saturation.

In each item, the two possible candidates were filled with the colour red, whereas the remaining components of the device were unfilled. The two possible candidates were always of the same shape as the component mentioned and shown in the referring expression.

Examples of the definitions of the levels of Relative Salience and Similarity Advantage are shown in Figure 4.

Domain Expertise (D) was defined as knowledge about the names and the sizes of the components. In the condition D=*low*, subjects were given no such knowledge. In the conditions D=*intermediate* and D=*high*, subjects were given a study session in which they were presented with the technical device in question along with a legend revealing the names of the components. Subjects had to learn

---

[3] These levels correspond to *low*, *intermediate*, and *high* as defined in the hypotheses, respectively.

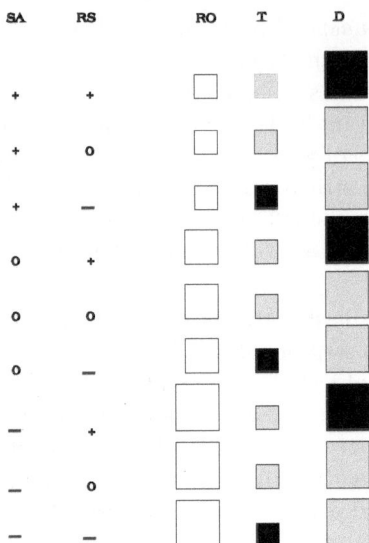

Fig. 4. Definition of the levels *minus*, *zero*, and *plus* for the factors Similarity Advantage (SA) and Relative Salience (RS). The third column depicts the size of the referring object (RO); the fourth column shows the target object (T); the last column shows the distractor object (D). The lighter squares are the ones with higher saturation.

the names and the sizes of the components.[4] On subsequent tests, they were tested on their knowledge. The criteria for these tests were 50 percent and 80 percent correctness for the condition D=*intermediate* and the condition D=*high*, respectively. Subjects only proceeded from the study phase to the experimental phase if they had passed the respective tests.

4.3   Results

The relative frequency of a Correct Response was calculated separately for each treatment combination. For the following analyses an α level of .05 was chosen.

To determine the effects on Correct Responses, the data were subjected to a repeated measures Analysis of Variance (ANOVA). Results indicated significant main effects for all independent variables, Domain Expertise ($F(2,88)=147.84$; p<.05), Similarity Advantage ($F(2,88)=116.0$; p<.05), and Relative Salience ($F(2,88)=12.94$; p<.05). In addition, the two-way interaction between Similarity Advantage and Relative Salience ($F(4,176)=10.46$;p < .05) and the interaction between Similarity Advantage and Domain Expertise ($F(4,176)=28.95$; p < .05) were significant. The two-way interaction between Domain Expertise and Relative Salience was not significant. Finally, the three-way interaction between

---

[4] In the study sessions, subjects had 1 and 2 minutes time, respectively.

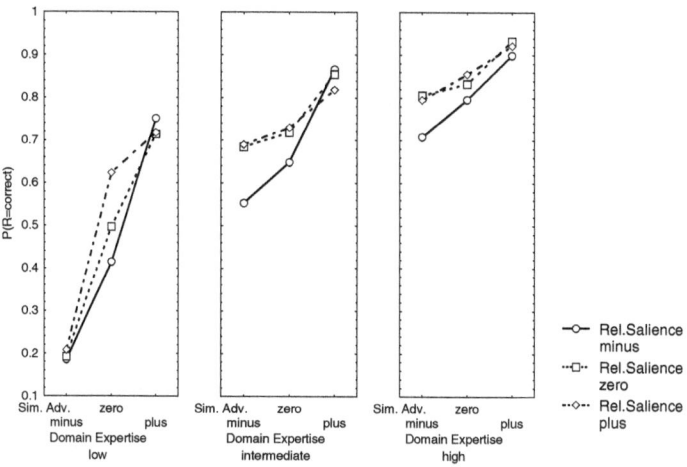

Fig. 5. Correct Responses as a function of Domain Expertise, Similarity Advantage, and Relative Salience.

Domain Expertise, Similarity Advantage, and Relative Salience achieved significance (F(8,352)=3.46; p < .05).

As post hoc Sheffé tests (which are more conservative) revealed, the three-way interaction was caused by a difference between R=*minus* and R=*plus* in case D=*low* and S=*zero* (see the left panel in Figure 5). The difference between D=*intermediate* and D=*high* was not significant.

Thus, the main effect of Relative Salience as indicated by the ANOVA cannot be interpreted as such exactly because Relative Salience only has influence if D=*low* and S=*zero*. Main effects of Domain Expertise and Similarity Advantage, however, can still be interpreted as such, as both affect Correct Responses irrespective of the levels of the other independent variables.

In line with the results of the post hoc tests for the three-way interaction, the two-way interaction between Similarity Advantage and Relative Salience was not supported by post hoc tests: The tests did not reveal any differences between the different levels of Relative Salience.

The interaction between Similarity Advantage and Domain Expertise has its caused in extremely low performance for S=*minus* in case D=*low*. Compared to the other two levels of Similarity Advantage, this results in a steeper rise in Correct Responses for S=*minus* going from D=*low* to D=*intermediate*. Moreover, the effect of Similarity Advantage decreases as the level of Domain Expertise increases.

The Pearson product moment correlation between the postulated model and the data was r = .87 (p<.05).

4.4 Discussion

We expected main effects of Relative Salience, Similarity Advantage, and Domain Expertise. In addition, we expected two two-way interactions: one between Domain Expertise and Similarity Advantage and one between Domain Expertise and Relative Salience. Unexpectedly however, the data showed a three-way interaction between the three independent variables, which means that there is a more complex relationship between the variables. A closer examination of this interaction shows that Relative Salience apparently only plays a role in case of complete ambiguity, that is, if subjects had no domain knowledge (D=*low*) and if the size of the object to be identified was in between the size of the big and small objects in the equipment (S=*zero*). Thus, it seems that if subjects have no other cues, they rely on Relative Salience for their decision; if they do have other cues, they reside to these and disregard Relative Salience.

The data support the hypotheses concerning the main effects of Domain Expertise and Similarity Advantage. The higher levels of Similarity Advantage resulted in better performance than the low levels. With regard to Domain Expertise, the expectation concerning the difference between the two higher levels was not supported by the data. A reason for this may lie in the fact that, despite the results from pilot studies, the difference in training was insufficient: Apparently subjects were well capable of learning names and corresponding sizes within one minute. Thus, there was no further training effect *after* one minute.

As Relative Salience only appears to play a role in case of complete ambiguity with respect to the other variables, its main effect should not be interpreted as such. A reason for the lack of the effect may lie in the operationalization: Each item consisted of two candidate objects differing in saturation and differing from the rest of the objects in shape *and* colour (the objects that played no role in the definition of the S-R combination were not filled). This circumstance might have resulted in the two candidate components being salient to such an extent that the difference in salience *between* them was not influential.

We expected two two-way interactions: one between Similarity Advantage and Domain Expertise and another between Relative Salience and Domain Expertise. These interactions were expected because we assumed that higher levels of Domain Expertise would compensate for lower levels of both Similarity Advantage and Relative Salience.

Contrary to the expectations, the interaction between Relative Salience and Domain Expertise was not supported by the data. The lack of this interaction may be caused by the circumstance described above to account for the lack of the main effect of Relative Salience.

The hypothesis that Similarity Advantage affects the probability of a Correct Response to a greater extent in case Domain Expertise is *low* compared to when it is *intermediate* or *high* was supported by the data. The data show a much steeper increase in the first panel of Figure 5 than in the other two panels. If subjects have intermediate or high levels of Domain Expertise, they seem to rely progressively more on their Domain Expertise as a basis for their decision than on Similarity Advantage.

To summarize, the data show that Domain Expertise and Similarity Advantage affect performance most, and that mainly in case of complete ambiguity Relative Salience plays a role in the subjects' decision as to what object is the intended one in a multimodal referring expression. In addition, Similarity Advantage has a greater influence in case of little Domain Expertise than in case of intermediate or much Domain Expertise.

Consequence for the Postulated Model. As reported, Pearson's product moment correlation between the data and the postulated model was $r = .87$, which is quite high. This model differs from the data in that it does not reflect the fact that Relative Salience only plays a role in case D=*low* and S=*intermediate*.

A modification of the postulated model was made so as to reflect the independence between Relative Salience and the Probability of a Correct Response given D$\neq$*low* and S$\neq$*zero*. That is, in case D$\neq$*low* and S$\neq$*zero*, OBVIOUSNESS OF TARGET AS REFERENT was solely dependent on SIMILARITY ADVANTAGE OF TARGET; in case D=*low* and S=*zero*, the previously postulated model was used. This modification resulted in $r = .95$, p<.05.

The question is now whether we should leave the model as proposed or whether it is worthwhile to indeed take into account the fact that Relative Salience merely plays a role in case of complete ambiguity. In this work, we opted for the former solution, as we believe that the relatively small impact of Relative Salience is more likely to be due to the operationalization than to an actual absence of the effect: A red shape among unfilled shapes has a high level of salience regardless of its degree of saturation. Subsequent studies, however, need to reinvestigate the particular influence of Relative Salience.

5 Conclusion

We described an alternative approach to ensuring effectiveness and efficiency of presentations generated by multimedia presentation systems. We showed how the system PEDRO models the decodability of a planned presentation with Bayesian networks. An empirical study was described that was to examine the validity of the assumptions contained in the model for the resolution of pictorial referring expressions. The results of the study showed that the postulated model and the data correlated relatively strongly. This suggests that the model PEDRO relies on may be safely used to predict how likely a particular user is to resolve a pictorial referring expression.

Compared to rule-based approaches to effective and efficient presentation design, an advantage of the present approach is that, once an adequate underlying model of the problem domain has been found, many more (unforeseen) design problems can be accounted for. Furthermore, as PEDRO reasons from first principles, it will also be able to reason about the decodability of presentation techniques for which expert design knowledge is not available, such as, for instance, entirely novel presentation styles. Rule-based approaches on the other hand must necessarily rely on expert design knowledge so that they are likely to have difficulties in dealing with cases in which new presentation techniques are used.

Acknowledgments

The author wishes to thank the CMC/98 reviewers for valuable comments on an earlier draft of this paper.

References

André, E., Müller, J., and Rist, T. (1996). The PPP Persona: A Multipurpose Animated Presentation Agent. In *Advanced Visual Interfaces*, 245–247. New York: ACM Press.

André, E. and Rist, T. (1996). Coping with Temporal Constraints in Multimedia Presentation Planning. *Proceedings of the Thirteenth National Conference on Artificial Intelligence*, Portland, Oregon, 142–147

Charniak, E. (1991). Bayesian Networks Without Tears. *AI Magazine* 12 (4), 50–63.

Garnham, A. (1987). Understanding Anaphora, In Andrew W. Ellis (Ed.) *Progress in the Psychology of Language* 253–300. London: Lawrence Erlbaum.

Huls, C., Bos, E., and Claassen, W. (1995). Automatic Referent Resolution of Deictic and Anaphoric Expressions, *Computational Linguistics* 21, 59–79.

Jameson, A. and Wahlster, W. (1982). User Modelling in Anaphora Generation: Ellipsis and Definite Description. *Proceedings of the Fifth European Conference on Artificial Intelligence*, Orsay, France, 222–227.

Manktelow, K. and Jones, J. (1986). Principles from the Psychology of Thinking and Mental Models. In Margaret M. Gardiner and Bruce Christie (Eds.), *Applying Cognitive Psychology to User Interface Design*, 83–117. Chichester: John Wiley & Sons.

Pearl, J. (1988). *Probabilistic Reasoning in Intelligent Systems: Networks of Plausible Inference*. San Francisco, CA: Morgan Kaufman.

Treisman, A. and Gelade, G. (1980). A Feature Integration Theory of Attention, *Cognitive Psychology* 12, 97–136.

van Mulken, S. (1997). Inferenzen über die Verständlichkeit einer Präsentation: Benutzermodellierung für Multimedia-Präsentationssysteme. In Rainer H. Kluwe (Ed.) *Strukturen und Prozesse intelligenter Systeme*. Wiesbaden: DUV.

van Mulken, S. (1998). *User Modeling for Multimedia Interfaces: Studies in Text and Graphics Understanding*. Wiesbaden: DUV.

Wahlster, W., André, E., Finkler, W., Profitlich, H.-J., and Rist, T. (1993). Plan-Based Integration of Natural Language and Graphics Generation, *Artificial Intelligence* 63, 387-427.

IMPROVISE: Automated Generation of Animated Graphics for Coordinated Multimedia Presentations

Michelle X. Zhou[1] and Steven K. Feiner[2]

[1] IBM T.J. Watson Research Center, Hawthorne, NY, USA
mzhou@watson.ibm.com
[2] Department of Computer Science
Columbia University, New York
feiner@cs.columbia.edu

Abstract. In this chapter, we describe a graphics generation system, IMPROVISE (Illustrative Metaphor PROduction in VISual Environments), focusing on how it can be used to design coordinated multimedia presentations. IMPROVISE is a knowledge-based system that can automatically create sequences of animated graphical illustrations to convey a wide variety of data. Our emphasis here is on describing how four important features of IMPROVISE facilitate coordinated multimedia presentation design. These four features are: a knowledge-rich representation of input data, a fine-grained temporal model of visual techniques, an action-based inference engine, and a portable visual realizer.

1 Introduction

An automated visual presentation system should be able to communicate a set of data entities (e.g., database tables) to a specific user in a particular context (e.g., a user with a known set of skills, using a particular display device) in a way that fulfils a presentation intent (e.g., to *summarize* certain aspects of the data). To automatically create proper visual presentations, automated visual presentation systems are usually built using a knowledge-based approach (e.g., Seligmann and Feiner 1991; Roth and Mattis 1991). In other words, these systems have knowledge about the underlying data, users and their intents, and visual design. They are also powered by an inference engine to infer the proper visual design on the fly. Thus, all knowledge-based visual presentation systems must contain three main components: a knowledge base that stores various information about data to be presented and visual design, an inference engine that performs reasoning, and a visual realizer that transforms design specifications into human-perceivable pictures.

Following this view, we have developed IMPROVISE, a knowledge-based system that can automatically create visual presentations for a wide variety of data. IMPROVISE can be used stand-alone to create purely visual presentations or cooperate with other media generators (e.g., a spoken language generator) to create

H. Bunt and R.-J. Beun (Eds.): CMC'98, LNAI 2155, pp. 43–63, 2001.
© Springer-Verlag Berlin Heidelberg 2001

coordinated multimedia presentations. Unlike the work on automated generation of individual visual presentations (e.g., Mackinlay 1986; Roth and Mattis 1991) or sequences of discrete visual presentations (e.g., Seligmann and Feiner 1991; Andre and Rist 1993), IMPROVISE focuses on automatically creating coherent visual discourse. We use the term *visual discourse* to refer to an animated visual narrative expressed in the form of sequences of temporally-ordered, animated visual actions (Zhou and Feiner 1998a). For example, a narrative generated by IMPROVISE may start by displaying a set of objects, and then animate the highlighting of one object, followed by the generation of a cutaway view to reveal its internal structure.

To create a coherent, animated visual presentation and cooperate with other media generators, IMPROVISE has a well-formulated knowledge base, a sophisticated and efficient inference engine, and a portable visual realizer. IMPROVISE uses a knowledge-rich representation to express all input data, and has a fine-grained model for describing its visual design knowledge. These two features not only provide a foundation for automated graphics generation, but also make possible cooperative multimedia presentation design.

IMPROVISE uses a top-town, hierarchical-decomposition, partial-order planning-based inference engine to compose sequences of animated visual actions (Zhou and Feiner 1998b). As we describe later, the flexibility of this action-based approach greatly facilitates cooperative multimedia presentation design. Once the inference engine creates the design specifications, IMPROVISE's visual realizer interprets the meaning of the design while obeying the constraints specified in the design (e.g., temporal duration). Using a platform-independent multimedia authoring language and a precise action-execution scheduler, the visual realizer can render the design specifications on various platforms and faithfully maintain the specified temporal constraints among different actions.

Since we have described various features of IMPROVISE elsewhere (Zhou and Feiner 1998a, 1998b), here we focus on illustrating how four features of IMPROVISE facilitate coordinated multimedia presentation design: the representation of input data, the temporal model of visual techniques, the action-based planning engine, and the portable visualizer. After a brief discussion of related work, we give an overview of IMPROVISE's architecture and analyze two examples that are created by IMPROVISE. We then explain each of the four features in the context of designing coordinated multimedia presentations. Finally, we present our conclusions and indicate some future research directions.

2   Related Work

Unlike other automated graphics generation systems such as IBIS (Seligmann and Feiner 1991) and SAGE (Roth and Mattis 1991), IMPROVISE can generate sequences of coherent, animated graphical actions with fine-grained temporal constraints. In addition, IMPROVISE is capable of adjusting its constraints so that it can cooperate with other media components to produce a coordinated presentation.

IMPROVISE has been combined with a language generation system to produce an automated multimedia presentation system, called MAGIC (Multimedia Abstract Generation for Intensive Care) (Dalal et al. 1996). MAGIC can automatically generate multimedia briefings using two temporal media: speech and animated graphics. Compared to other multimedia presentation systems, MAGIC differs in two aspects. First, earlier multimedia systems (e.g., Feiner and McKeown 1991; Wahlster et al. 1993; Mittal et al. 1998) produce discrete multimedia presentations that do not involve temporal media, such as continuous speech or animated graphics. In these systems, media coordination tasks are relatively straightforward; for example, coordinating each picture with a text caption. In contrast, MAGIC deals with temporal media and requires that the order and duration of actions that occur in different temporal media be coordinated (Dalal et al. 1996).

Second, more recent multimedia presentation systems (e.g., Towns, Callaway, and Lester 1998; Andre, Rist, and Müller 1998; Noma, Zhao, and Badler 2000) that employ temporal media, including video clips, animated graphics, and speech, use preconstructed graphics objects, speech, or scripts to compose their presentations. In contrast, MAGIC's media-specific actions, such as speech and animation, are all generated dynamically with temporal constraints, and the coordination tasks are implicit. In other words, the decisions about coordinating the content and form of all media must be made at run-time. In addition, our media actions are specified at a more detailed level of representation, and require much finer-grained coordination. For example, temporal durations specified for words and phrases in speech must be coordinated with the durations of corresponding actions in graphics, such as displaying and highlighting objects.

3   System Architecture

IMPROVISE's cycle of presentation design, shown in Fig. 1, starts with a set of *presentation intents*, which usually describe domain-specific communicative goals. The *task analyzer* is responsible for formulating and translating presentation intents (e.g., to examine a network link structure) into corresponding visual tasks (e.g., Focus on the link and Expose its internals). To accomplish these visual tasks, the *visual presentation planner* starts the design process. In IMPROVISE, design is an interleaved process involving two submodules: the visual content planner and the visual designer. These two submodules work cooperatively, using the *inference engine* to access the *knowledge base* and infer a visual design. The *visual content planner* selects and organizes the content that needs to be presented, while the *visual designer* makes decisions about what visual cues to use and how to combine various visual elements into a coherent whole. Once the design is finished, it is written out in an intermediate presentation authoring language, and eventually converted to the target graphics language to be realized. IMPROVISE also has a simple *interaction handler* that processes *user events* and formulates new communicative goals (presentation intents), and these new goals are passed to the task analyzer where a new design cycle begins.

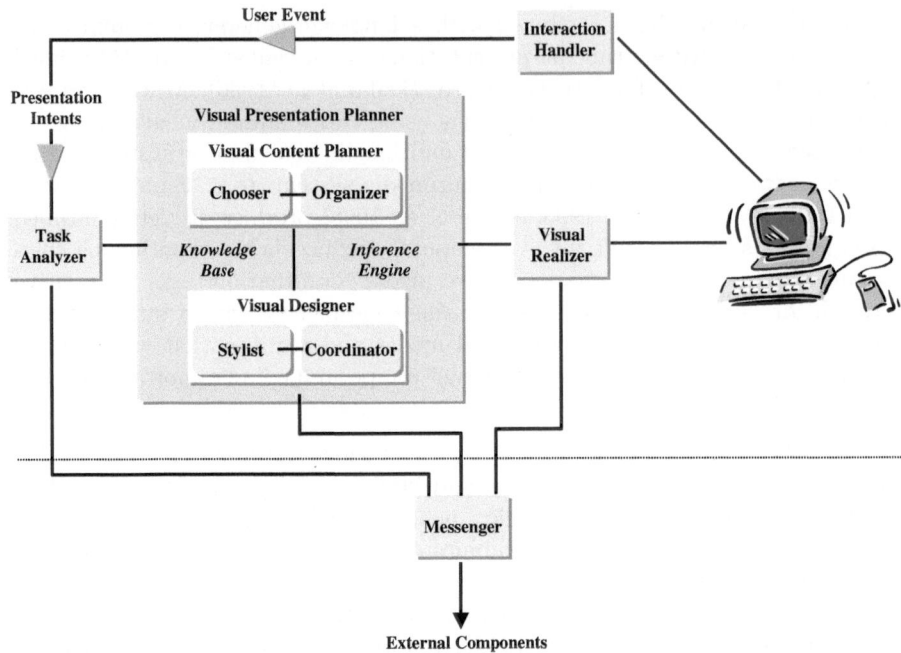

Fig. 1. IMPROVISE System Architecture.

When embedded in a multimedia system, such as MAGIC, IMPROVISE has an additional communication module, the *messenger*, which is responsible for exchanging information between other internal components of IMPROVISE and external components (e.g., a *media coordinator*, not shown here). IMPROVISE uses a task-based communication strategy for its internal components to exchange messages with external components, and to let the messenger deal with all low-level format transformation (e.g., converting the data to a format that can be understood by another system) and communication issues (e.g., establishing socket connections).

Currently, IMPROVISE supports four types of communication tasks: get-goals, get-action-orders, get-action-durations, and get-start-time. Using the first task get-goals, IMPROVISE's task analyzer can obtain the annotated communicative goals from MAGIC's media allocator. IMPROVISE's visual presentation planner employs the other three tasks to negotiate with the media coordinator for its visual actions' temporal orders, durations, and starting times.

4   Examples

Here we use two very different examples to demonstrate how IMPROVISE creates animated visual narratives in different situations. The first example shows how IMPROVISE generates a visual narrative from scratch to present a hospital patient's information to a nurse after the patient's coronary artery bypass graft (CABG) operation. In this case, the generated visual narrative is combined with generated spoken sentences to produce a coordinated multimedia summary (Fig. 2). In the second example, IMPROVISE modifies an existing visual presentation of a computer network (Fig. 4a), using a set of animated visual actions to gradually reveal the internal structure of a user-selected network link (Fig. 4b-d).

4.1   Presenting Information to a Nurse

In this task, IMPROVISE must accomplish two goals: creating an overview of patient information, and elaborating the patient information details based on that overview. To achieve the first goal, IMPROVISE plans to construct a *structure diagram* that organizes various information (e.g., IV lines) around a core component (the patient's body). This decision is made based on the fact that in this domain, the nurses with whom we worked prefer to see this information arranged relative to the patient's body. In a top-down design manner, IMPROVISE first creates an 'empty' structure diagram. This empty diagram is then refined through its individual components by recursively partitioning and encoding the patient information into different groups. For example, the patient's demographics, including name, age, and gender, are encoded as the *heading* of the diagram (the highlighted block at the top of Fig. 2a); a representation of the patient's physical body serves as the *core*, and the rest of the information is arranged around the core as diagram *elements*. To express the partial designs and their refinement, variables and constraints are used to represent the progressively refined diagram at different levels of detail. In addition, spatial constraints are formulated to help determine the sizes and locations of various diagram components (e.g., the length of various lines).

To accomplish the second goal, IMPROVISE plans a series of visual actions to allow certain information to be reinforced or revealed, based on the overview. For example, the pictures in Fig. 2(a-b) are created to reinforce the patient's demographics information and IV lines by using the visual action Highlight, while the pictures in Fig. 2(c-d) are planned to reveal the drip (intravenously administered drug) and lab report details.

The order and duration of these visual actions must also be coordinated with the order and duration of corresponding spoken references to produce a coherent multimedia narrative (Dalal et al. 1996). Fig. 3 shows a segment of coordinated media actions at the beginning of the presentation, where the patient's demographics are emphasized. Here, IMPROVISE highlights the leftmost portion of the patient's demographics first to coordinate with the first part of the spoken sentence. It then highlights the remainder of the demographics to synchronize with the rest of the spoken references. As we explain in Section 5, in this case IMPROVISE must adjust its own graphics constraints to cooperate with the speech generator.

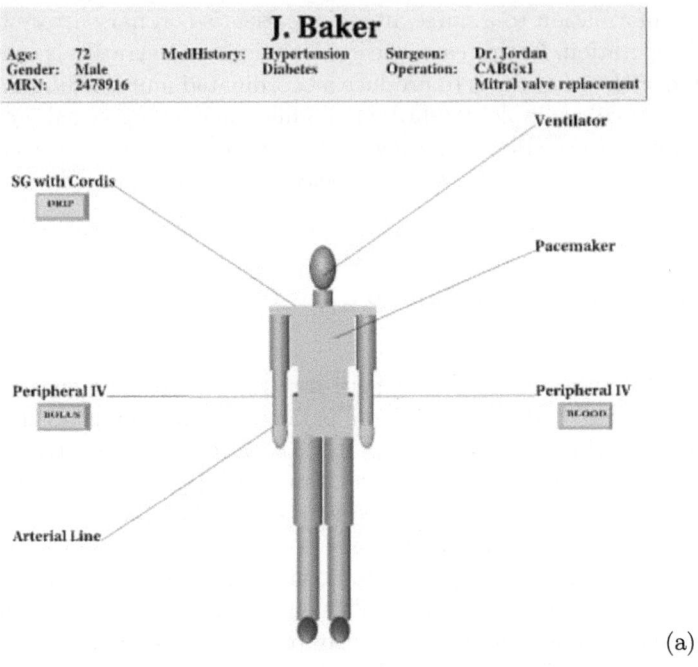

(a)

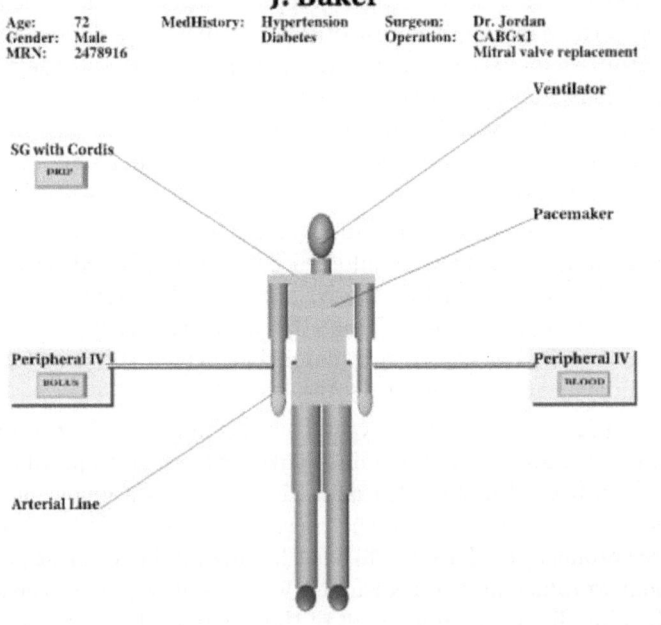

(b)

Fig. 2. Selected Keyframes Generated by IMPROVISE to Present a Patient's Information to a Nurse.

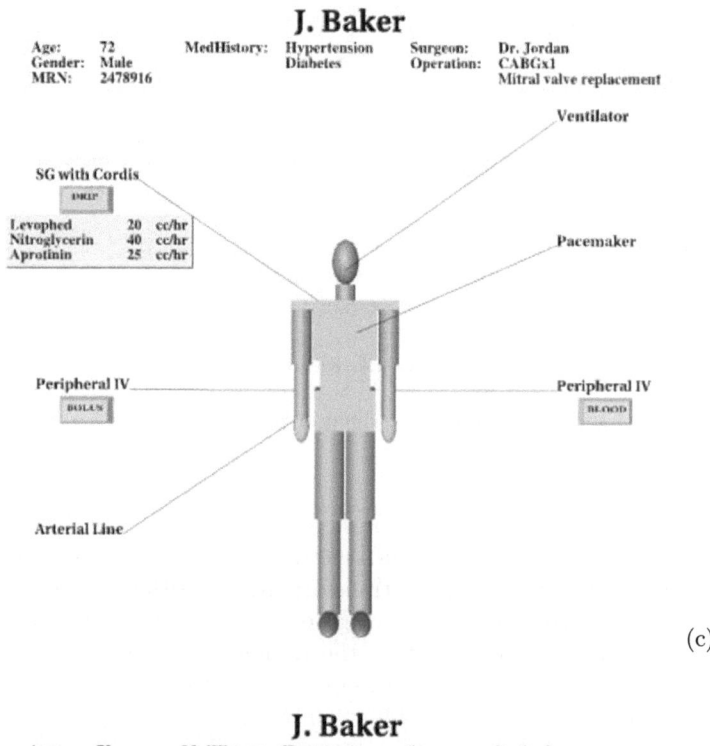

(c)

J. Baker

Age:	72	MedHistory:	Hypertension	Surgeon:	Dr. Jordan
Gender:	Male		Diabetes	Operation:	CABGx1
MRN:	2478916				Mitral valve replacement

Lab Report

Ca	30
K	45.0
HCT	*23*
PCO2	32
PO2	250

(d)

Fig. 2. (*continued*)

J. Baker

Age:	72	MedHistory:	Hypertension	Surgeon:	Dr. Jordan
Gender:	Male		Diabetes	Operation:	CABGx1
MRN:	2478916				Mitral valve replacement

Speech: Mr. Baker is a seventy-two-year-old, hypertensive, diabetic male patient . . .

J. Baker

Age:	72	MedHistory:	Hypertension	Surgeon:	Dr. Jordan
Gender:	Male		Diabetes	Operation:	CABGx1
MRN:	2478916				Mitral valve replacement

Speech: ... of Dr. Jordan undergoing CABG with mitral valve replacement

Fig. 3. Generated Coordinated Speech and Graphics.

4.2   Exploring a Computer Network

In this example, we show how IMPROVISE designs a new visual presentation by using sequences of animated visual transformations. Although these animations are currently used alone, the underlying design mechanisms and representation formalisms can be used to facilitate the design of a coordinated multimedia presentation (see Section 5). This example tackles the task of revealing the attributes of a user-selected network link. In a network management application, users often want to explore the internal structures of interesting network entities, such as links and nodes. For example, a link may contain a set of *virtual path segments* that have attributes such as capacity and utilization. Suppose that the user has selected link23, the link between Austin (node1), and Tucson (node5) in the network representation of Fig. 4(a).

IMPROVISE first formulates a communicative goal: Elaborate<link23>. Using a set of elaboration strategies and relevant data properties (e.g., that there are multiple links shown and this link has an internal structure), this communicative goal is then refined using two visual tasks (abstract visual actions): Focus<link23> (bringing the selected link into the center of focus) and Expose<link23> (revealing the link's internal structure). These two abstract visual actions are ordered to ensure the design's effectiveness. In particular, IMPROVISE will Focus on the selected object (link23) first and then Expose the object's internal structure.

Since Focus is a composite action, it is associated with a set of decomposition strategies. These strategies state that Focus may be achieved using one of three actions: Separate, Enlarge, and Highlight. In this case, IMPROVISE chooses to refine Focus with Separate (separating link23 from the rest of the network). The rationale behind this decision is that a link is likely to intersect with other objects and Separate pulls intersected objects away to prevent any potential intersection while achieving focusing. In contrast, focusing by Enlarge increases the intersection possibility, and focusing by Highlight does not fix or prevent any intersection. Similarly, another composite action, Expose, is replaced by the

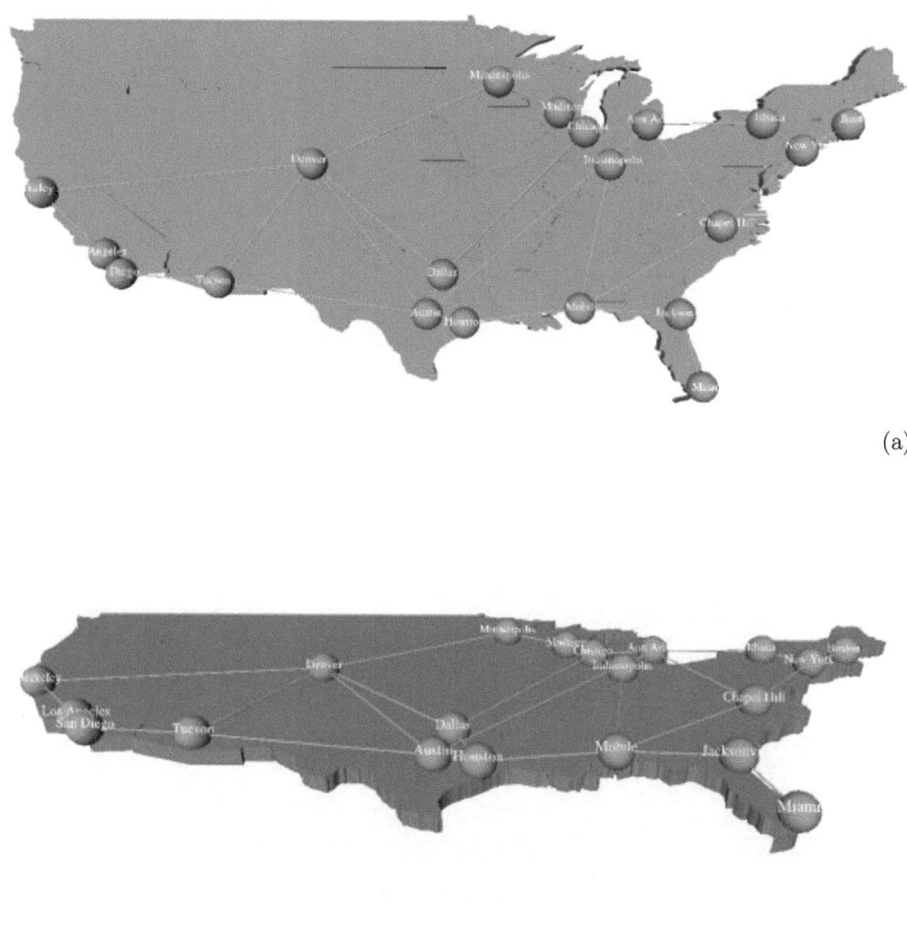

(a)

(b)

Fig. 4. Keyframes Generated by IMPROVISE to Reveal a Link's Internal Structure.

action Open (open link23), as the selected link is represented as a cylinder, which is a graphical object that IMPROVISE knows how to 'open'.

At this level of design, IMPROVISE needs to take care of the precondition of the action Expose. Expose requires that the visual representations of the internals must exist. Since the visual representation of the current link's virtual path segments does not yet exist, IMPROVISE needs to create one. As in the previous section's example, IMPROVISE generates the graphical representation for the virtual path segments.

When IMPROVISE advances to the next level of design, Separate, now the only remaining non-primitive action, needs to be decomposed. In this case, Separate is decomposed into two actions: Align and Move. Align rotates the whole network

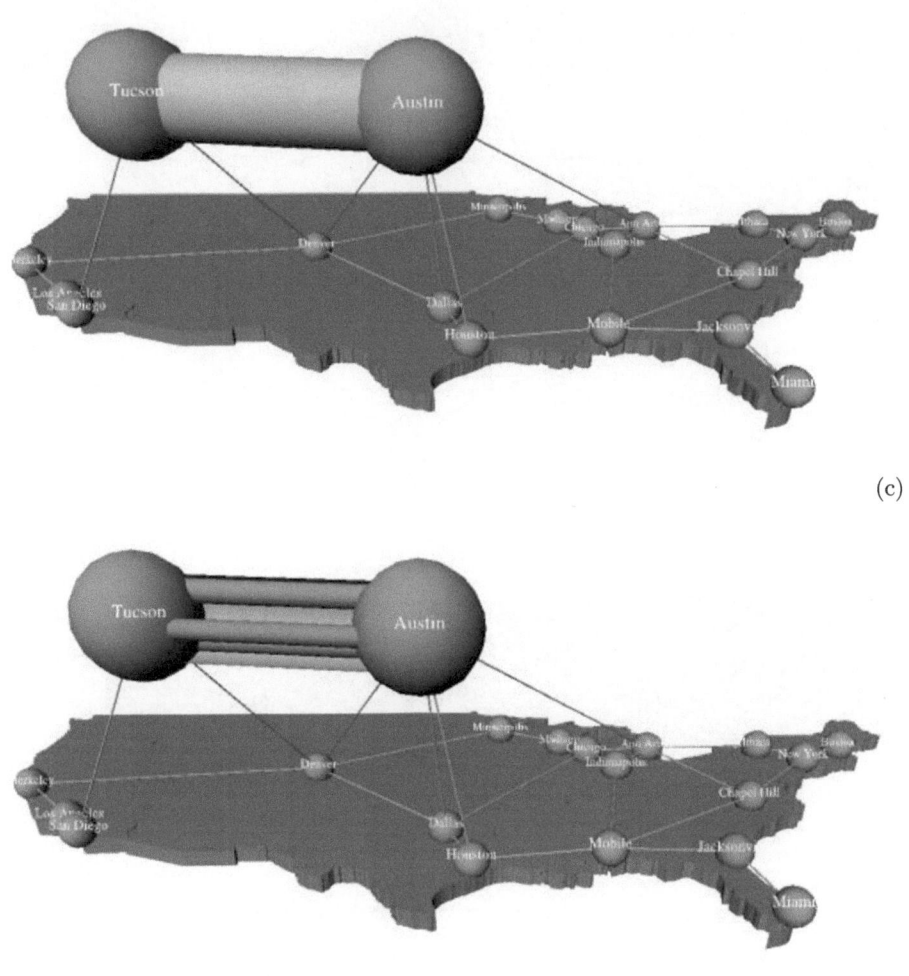

(c)

(d)

Fig. 4. (*continued*)

so it is laid down (Fig. 4b), while Move moves the link and its two end nodes away from the rest of the network (Fig. 4c). A partial order is also specified: executing Align before Move to ensure a coherent transformation. The action Open is already a primitive action. However, its precondition requires that the object be large enough so that the opening effect is recognizable. To establish this precondition for Open, IMPROVISE chooses the action Scale. This also means that Scale must be executed before Open to achieve its precondition first.

When the plan is complete, we have a global order among actions (the attached numbers represent an animation's starting and ending times in seconds):

Align(0, 3) → Move, Scale, . . . (3, 6) → Open(6, 9)

Note that such a global order is not necessarily a linear order; for example, actions Move and Scale are executed simultaneously here. Rendered images of several keyframes from the resulting design are shown in Fig. 4(b-d).

5 Designing Multimedia Presentations

Although the previous two examples are quite different, IMPROVISE uses the same set of design strategies and inference mechanism with two different domain models: one for hospital patients and one for computer networks.

Based on these two examples, next we explain in detail how four important features of IMPROVISE play key roles in the design of coordinated multimedia presentations. We first show how IMPROVISE's data representation formalism and temporal model of visual techniques help provide useful information to other media components in the course of designing a coordinated multimedia presentation. We then describe how IMPROVISE's action-based inference engine can cooperate with other media generators to produce desirable visual actions for a multimedia presentation. Finally, we discuss how IMPROVISE's visual realizer synchronizes the execution of multiple media actions.

5.1 Data Representation

IMPROVISE is built to create a wide range of visual presentations for conveying heterogeneous data that can include both quantitative and qualitative information. To achieve this goal, IMPROVISE has a rich data semantic model. In other words, IMPROVISE has a representation of the underlying meaning of its input data, and uses this information to create graphical representations that communicate the data.

As data semantics may vary greatly from one application to another, it is difficult to build a data model that captures all possible individual data features. Thus, we develop a knowledge-rich, data semantic model based on a set of meta information. The meta information is organized by a *data characterization taxonomy* that abstracts a set of common visual presentation-related data properties (Zhou and Feiner 1996). Our taxonomy describes data characteristics along six dimensions:

type:	atomic vs. composite data entities
domain:	semantic categories, such as temperature or mass
attribute:	meta attributes, such as ordering, form, and importance
relation:	data connections, such as has-part and attributive relations
role:	data function, such as being an identifier or a locator
sense:	visual interpretation preference, such as symbol or label

Not only do these meta properties help us formulate portable (application-independent) design rules, but IMPROVISE can also use them to coordinate its actions with other media generators.

Different media may be used to convey different data entities or to present the same data entities from different perspectives. For example, in the medical example given above, the speech component may be instructed to summarize the received therapy, while IMPROVISE is directed to emphasize the critical components of the therapy. Thus, speech may state that the patient "has received massive cardiotonic therapy" and graphics may pinpoint the individual components involved in this therapy by highlighting the drips, the ventilator, and the pacemaker. In this case, IMPROVISE fulfils its assigned task by creating a highlighting action:

```
Highlight <drips, Ventilator, Pacemaker>
    (style OUTLINE) (startTime ...)(endTime ...)
```

This action specifies the objects to be highlighted, the highlight style, and the associated temporal constraints. Similarly, the speech component produces a speech action:

```
Speak <cardiotonic-therapy>
```

Since both the highlighting and speech actions are associated with temporal constraints, they must be coordinated to produce a coherent presentation. This is different from other automated multimedia presentation systems, which focus on generating written text with static graphical illustrations (Feiner and McKeown 1991; Mittal et al. 1998) or composing preconstructed media actions with generated actions (Towns, Callaway, and Lester 1998; Andre, Rist, and Müller 1998; Noma, Zhao, and Badler 2000). In these systems, temporal coordination is either not required or the coordination task is explicit (e.g., coordinating a generated action, such as a gesture, with a pre-existing media action, such as playing a video clip).

To coordinate different media actions, MAGIC's media coordinator must first identify corresponding actions among the media actions that it has received; for example, from a set of actions, it needs to relate the highlighting with a specific speech action. One approach for the media coordinator to relate corresponding actions is to trace all media generation processes to find out whether different actions are related to the same goal. In our example, the highlighting and the speech actions are created to accomplish the same goal (conveying the therapy). Nonetheless, it is often too costly for the media coordinator to understand and keep track of the complete generation processes of all different media generators. Thus, in our approach, IMPROVISE provides the media coordinator with additional information by exploiting the data characteristics. In this case, relying on data semantic relations, IMPROVISE can inform the media coordinator that the drips, Ventilator, and Pacemaker, are parts of the cardiotonic therapy. The media coordinator can then relate the two actions based on this information.

Based on data characteristics, IMPROVISE can selectively inform the media coordinator about the rationale behind its design decisions to facilitate coordination. Suppose that there is a quantitative ordering among a set of data entities to be presented. To create an effective illustration, IMPROVISE decides to present the data entities one by one in a sorted order (e.g., a descending order). Assume that a series of spoken sentences is also generated to explain each data entity in the set. To coordinate the visual displays with the spoken sentences, the media coordinator must come up with a temporal order that is compatible across both media. Besides offering the graphics ordering information, in our case, IMPROVISE can better inform the media coordinator by indicating that its presentation order is in fact determined by the sortable quantitative ordering attribute.

IMPROVISE may also selectively inform other media components about its intermediate actions. This information could help other media components create cross-references to material that it has generated (McKeown et al. 1992). Suppose that IMPROVISE informs the speech component that the data entities have been sorted. Here, the sorting action is an intermediate graphics action and it is output by IMPROVISE with the data ordering property. This information could then be used to generate more informative speech: the speech could first refer to the data set being presented in a particular order, and then explain individual data entities in that order. This type of content cross-reference may not be achieved in other multimedia generation systems, as other components can only utilize information about finalized graphical actions. For example, in COMET, the graphics generator IBIS can inform the language generator about the graphical actions it has decided to use (e.g., the generation of a cutaway view; see McKeown et al. 1992). But without a deep semantic model, IBIS has no way of telling which one of its intermediate steps would be important for the language generator to know.

5.2 Visual Techniques

IMPROVISE uses a visual presentation language to specify and manipulate graphical presentations (Zhou and Feiner 1998a). We characterize visual design knowledge divided into three types: visual objects, visual techniques, and visual design principles. *Visual objects* are the syntactic, semantic, and pragmatic encoding of visual patterns. *Visual techniques* are procedures that describe a graphical synthesis or manipulation process. *Visual design principles* are sets of rules that guide the proper application of visual techniques. We concentrate here on describing visual techniques, since their representations are most useful in designing coordinated multimedia presentations.

Visual techniques are used by IMPROVISE to assemble a new visual presentation or to modify an existing one. IMPROVISE has two main types of visual techniques: formational and transformational. *Formational* techniques create visual objects from scratch. For example, the formational technique DesignStructureDiagram creates a structure diagram to encode a particular set of input data entities. *Transformational* techniques modify existing visual objects. For example, the transformational technique Move modifies the location of a visual object.

Unlike IBIS and SAGE, IMPROVISE can employ visual techniques with temporal constraints (Zhou and Feiner 1998b). Compared to other planning systems that handle temporal constraints (Wilkins and Myers 1995; André and Rist 1996), IMPROVISE uses multilevel topological and metric temporal constraints to specify visual actions at a finer granularity. This unique feature enables IMPROVISE to cooperate effectively with other media generators to produce fine-grained, coordinated multimedia presentations. Specifically, IMPROVISE can specify/modify visual techniques with both temporal order and duration constraints, since these two types of constraints are the basis for coordinating animated graphics with other temporal media (Dalal et al. 1996).

First, IMPROVISE can use qualitative temporal constraints (e.g., **before** and **after**) to specify the ordering between two visual techniques. For example, IMPROVISE may generate a set of highlighting actions to stress in sequence the individual drip items depicted in Fig. 2(c). These actions are ordered to produce a natural, top-to-bottom, highlighting effect. After receiving this graphical ordering information, the media coordinator can order the corresponding spoken references to produce a coordinated presentation. Note that, in this case, graphics is constrained by its spatial layout, but the speech does not have a preference as to the order in which the items should be spoken. As will be seen next, IMPROVISE can also adjust its constraints to cooperate with a speech action.

In addition to defining qualitative ordering constraints, IMPROVISE can also specify quantitative temporal durations within a visual technique (usually indicated in seconds). In particular, IMPROVISE can define up to four temporal durations within a visual technique: An absolute **startTime** and **endTime** define a total duration; **animDuration** is the time taken to turn on the desired visual effects (e.g., gradually changing the colour of an object to highlight it); **holdingDuration** is the time spent on keeping the effect on the screen (e.g., holding the highlighting effect); and **animOffDuration** limits the time taken to reverse the visual transformation (e.g., turning off the highlighting). These durations greatly simplify the definition of a complex animation without compromising its function. For example, we can reverse the animated effect easily without explicitly introducing an undo action (e.g., turning off highlighting without using a separate 'unhighlight' action).

More importantly, IMPROVISE's approach to temporal durations helps produce fine-grained temporal media coordination. For example, IMPROVISE does not have a rigid duration constraint as to how long the patient identification and medical history should stay highlighted (Fig. 3). Consequently, using speech's duration constraints, IMPROVISE can fine-tune its highlighting duration to ensure that the highlighting is turned on or off at the exact moment when the corresponding speech segment starts or finishes.

To facilitate temporal media coordination, IMPROVISE also uses flexible time-window constraints. For example, IMPROVISE may specify that a highlighting action needs a minimum of **1s** or maximum of **2s** to turn on the highlight, and another **3s** to **5s** to keep the highlighting. The media coordinator can use the time window to compute a time duration acceptable for both graphics and speech.

In our previous example of highlighting drip items, the media coordinator may compute an agreeable time duration to ensure that the duration of each spoken reference to these items is not too short to cause a blinking effect, and that the graphical highlighting is not too long to create an awkward silence.

5.3   Action-Based Inference Engine

To create coherent, animated graphical illustrations, IMPROVISE employs an action-based inference engine. Given a set of inputs, including the data to be conveyed, the presentation intent, and the relevant presentation context, our engine can automatically create animated illustrations using sequences of temporally-ordered visual actions (instantiated visual techniques).

The core of the engine is a top-down, hierarchical-decomposition, partial-order planner that employs visual techniques as planning operators and visual design principles as planning constraints. Using a top-down hierarchical-decomposition strategy (Young, Pollack, and Moore, 1994), IMPROVISE first sketches a visual design that is complete, but too vague to be realized; then it refines the vague parts of the design into more detailed subdesigns, until the design has been refined to sequences of visual actions that can be executed by a realizer. To facilitate this top-down hierarchical design process, we have the notion of primitive and abstract techniques. Primitive techniques, such as Move and Scale, are clearly defined by a parametrized visual procedure. In contrast, abstract techniques, such as DesignStructureDiagram, which may contain other abstract or primitive techniques, are only partially specified. Abstract techniques must eventually be decomposed into a set of primitive techniques to be carried out.

In keeping with this approach, IMPROVISE's design process includes an action-decomposition process, in which abstract visual actions are recursively replaced with a set of more specific, partially-ordered subactions. In the network example presented earlier, the Separate action is decomposed into two actions: Align and Move. In addition to action decomposition, IMPROVISE may also require object decomposition. For example, a DesignStructureDiagram action may be decomposed into a set of subactions that define individual diagram components, such as the header. Accordingly, the data input used to produce the diagram must also be decomposed into smaller units that can be used by the subactions. Similar to action decomposition, object decomposition also produces partially-ordered data subunits. Since we have described elsewhere how IMPROVISE handles action and object decomposition (Zhou1999), we focus here on how our inference engine uses action/object decomposition to produce flexible visual plans that benefit the design of a coordinated multimedia presentation.

Using a planning approach, our inference engine produces a visual plan. As the plan bears sequences of actions, IMPROVISE can communicate with the media coordinator to negotiate the ordering of these actions. In particular, visual actions in IMPROVISE are partially ordered only if there is insufficient information. Generating a partial order not only provides a negotiation ground for IMPROVISE to cooperate with other media generators by relaxing its constraints, but also helps improve the design efficiency by reducing unnecessary backtracking.

In the example shown in Fig. 3, IMPROVISE produces the following actions with two sets of possible partial orders to accomplish the task of emphasizing the patient's demographics information:

```
Action1: Highlight <demographics>
Action2: Highlight <mrn, age, gender>
Action3: Highlight <medhistory>
Action4: Highlight <surgeon operation>

Partial orders:
1. (contains Action1
        ((before meet) Action2 Action3 Action4))
2: (contains Action1
        (* Action2 Action3 Action4))
```

Here, using Allen's (1983) temporal relations, the first set of partial orders specifies that Action1 starts before and ends after all the other actions (contains); and that among the other three actions, each action (e.g., Action2) ends either before or at the same time that the next action (e.g., Action3) in the list starts (before or meet). The second set states the same relationship between Action1 and the other three actions, but there is no particular ordering among the rest of the three actions (* relation). After receiving the negotiation requests from the media generators, the media coordinator uses MATS (Kautz 1991) to compute a compatible order specified in terms of the objects (Dalal et al. 1996); in this example, the order returned to IMPROVISE is:

```
(contains demographics
    ((before equal meet) mrn age medhistory gender
                        surgeon operation))
```

By adapting this compatible order, IMPROVISE can then refine its own partial orders to produce a complete order of graphical actions. In this case, IMPROVISE must refine the second set of partial orders because the first set is incompatible with the negotiated results:

```
Complete order: (contains Action1
                    (meet Action5 Action4))
    Action5 = (merge Action2 Action3)
```

Here a new action Action5 is created by IMPROVISE to resolve the conflict between the negotiated order and the structure of current graphical actions. Specifically medhistory comes between age and gender, effectively breaking the structure of Action2. In this case, IMPROVISE is able to merge Action2 and Action3 together, because the two actions have similar goals (emphasizing part of demographics), the same type (highlighting), and the same constraints (e.g., colouring style). Thus, a new action is generated to replace Action2 and Action3:

```
Action5: Highlight <mrn age gender medhistory>
```

IMPROVISE can replan because our action-based inference engine maintains the history and state of actions as steps are begun and completed. As shown in this example, the complete history (e.g., goal association) and state of the actions (e.g., the constraints specified within actions) provide much-needed information for replanning.

In addition to partial-order planning/replanning, the top-down hierarchical design strategy employed by our inference engine also facilitates media coordination. Instead of waiting for all graphical actions to be fully specified near the end of the design process, IMPROVISE can incrementally provide other components with a set of visual actions at different levels of detail. For example, at a high level, IMPROVISE may inform other components about its decision to use two abstract actions Focus and Expose to gradually reveal the network link's internals (Fig. 4). At a lower level, IMPROVISE may advise other components that it chose the primitive action Open to achieve Expose.

By outputting these progressively refined visual actions at each level of planning, IMPROVISE can allow the media coordinator and other media components to know what can or cannot be done early on. As a result, critical design conflicts can be detected early, and timely remedies can be tried to avoid costly backtracking. Once learning that at a high level IMPROVISE must use Focus before Expose to gradually reveal the link's internals, the media coordinator could compute a compatible order at an early design stage to make sure that the order of corresponding speech actions matches the order used in graphics.

On the other hand, through the exchange of information, IMPROVISE could also cooperate with other media generators by gradually incorporating their feedback into its planning process. For example, at a high level, and with insufficient constraints, IMPROVISE may only know that it needs to emphasize the drip items as a whole (highlighting the entire list). Through the exchange of information, it may learn that the speech generator will enumerate the drip items in sequence. Using this information, IMPROVISE could refine its current visual emphasis plan by adding sub-highlighting, which would highlight each item in turn as the item is spoken.

5.4   Portable Visual Realizer

Once a visual plan is complete, it needs to be realized by a *realizer*. To make our realizer portable, we separate IMPROVISE's realization from its visual design process by employing an intermediate presentation authoring language (PAL). Similar to the node-based scene graph descriptions used in Open Inventor (Wernecke 1994), PAL is an object-oriented authoring language that represents every visual object and visual technique as a node (e.g., a material node). A complex node (e.g., a table chart node) may recursively consist of a collection of simpler nodes (e.g., text nodes). High-level design specifications, such as the temporal constraints among visual actions, and low-level graphics details, such as the geometric properties of visual objects, are all encapsulated in the nodes. Moreover, new media actions or design patterns can be easily added as new types of nodes. In fact, we have incorporated a speech action node in PAL and these speech actions can be treated as the same as visual actions. For example, using PAL, the set of coordinated graphical and speech actions depicted in Fig. 3 can be represented as four nodes:

```
DEF Act1 Highlight {
        operands demographics
        style MARKER        // change the background colour
        startTime 0.0
        endTime 7.66
        color 1.0 1.0 0.0  // use a yellow background
}
DEF Act2 Highlight {
        operands [mrn, age, gender, medhistory]
        style COLORING      // change the text colour
        startTime 0.0
        endTime 5.25
        color 1.0 0.0 0.0  // use red text
}

DEF Act3 Highlight {
        operands [surgeon, operation]
        style COLORING
        startTime 5.25
        endTime 7.66
        color 1.0 0.0 0.0
}
DEF Act4 Speak {
        operands [name, age, medhistory, gender,
                  surgeon, operation]
        startTime 0.0
        endTime 7.66
}
```

Once these actions are expressed using PAL, the realizer parses the PAL descriptions. The challenge now is to execute this set of actions while faithfully maintaining all temporal constraints. In our approach, we have implemented a time queue to schedule various actions and ensure that their temporal constraints are met. All actions are first entered in the time queue by their starting times. The scheduler then uses a global alarm clock to invoke actions when their starting times are reached. A local timer is also maintained within each visual action to signal its termination when its finishing time approaches.

This approach works fine until the following problem arises: Two closely scheduled actions (e.g., actions A and B in Fig. 5) may overlap because the scheduler cannot guarantee a full stop in a previous action (e.g., A) when its local timer expires. This can happen because the local timer does not account for the time spent for executing various implicit finishing acts. For example,

(< A B) & (Meet B C) & (Overlap C D)

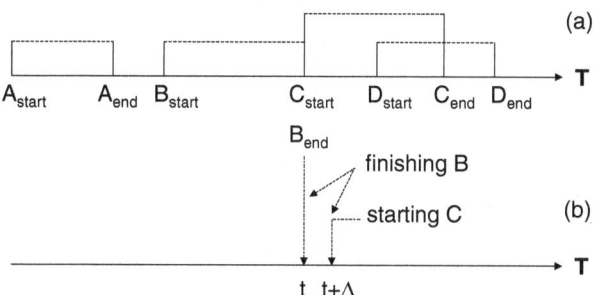

Fig. 5. Time Queue for Action Execution.

action A may call an instantaneous undo act (animOffDuration is 0.0s) when its local timer expires. Thus, there is no guarantee that A's undo act will be finished before B starts.

To fix this problem, each action is required to signal the scheduler when it is truly finished. In addition, we insert a dummy finishing act for each action in the time queue at its finishing time to ensure that the global clock will be stopped if the previous action has not finished. As shown in Fig. 5(a), when the global clock reaches the dummy act A_{end}, it will not be advanced to action B_{start} until it receives A's finishing signal.

The above approach fixes only half of our problem: it works for actions scheduled one after another (e.g., A and B in Fig. 5a), but not for actions scheduled right next to each other (e.g., B and C). In this case, the realizer is expected to execute two tasks simultaneously: finishing the previous action (B) and starting a new action (C). In our uniprocessor implementation, these tasks will be executed in a nondeterministic order. This may result in undesirable visual effects. Let B be Act2 and C be Act3 from the previous example; here B must unhighlight [mrn, age, gender, medhistory] before C starts to highlight [surgeon, operation]. Because of the nondeterministic execution order, C might start before B finishes, causing an undesired visual effect: two sets of objects highlighted at the same time instead of in sequence.

To ensure desired visual effects, we add sub-order temporal constraints to serialize simultaneous actions using heuristics. For example, one of IMPROVISE's heuristic rules asserts that all dummy finishing acts precede any other action scheduled at the same time. In the above example, the plan agent will process B_{end} before C_{start}, as if the time point t is expanded into a time interval $[t, t+\Delta]$ (Fig. 5b). This ensures that all objects in action B are unhighlighted before any object in action C is highlighted.

6 Conclusions and Future Work

In this chapter, we have presented IMPROVISE, an automated graphics generation system that can automatically create sequences of coherent, animated graphical illustrations to convey a wide variety of data. We explained how IMPROVISE facilitates the design of coordinated multimedia presentations, and examined IMPROVISE's knowledge-rich data representation model and its role in providing useful information for other components to make informative and cooperative design decisions. We introduced IMPROVISE's visual techniques and their temporal constraints, and explained how these temporal constraints facilitate temporal media negotiation. We also described IMPROVISE's action-based inference engine and demonstrated how its partial-order and hierarchical design approaches make it possible for IMPROVISE to negotiate incrementally with other media generators. Finally, we presented IMPROVISE's visual realizer, emphasizing its action-execution scheduler.

We are currently working on ways to improve IMPROVISE so that it can be used to create more sophisticated multimedia presentations. One approach that we are taking is to extend IMPROVISE to generate interactive graphical illustrations whose illustrative objects are also actionable. This would allow users to ask for new information (e.g., relevant details) or to manipulate the information already presented (e.g., to compare two data objects). By producing interactive illustrations, IMPROVISE could cooperate with other media components to create coordinated, interactive multimedia presentations.

Building upon current visual action manipulation strategies (e.g., the action merge strategy), another direction is to investigate additional strategies to augment IMPROVISE's replanning capabilities for situations when the compatible order returned by the media coordinator does not agree with IMPROVISE's graphical action structure. For example, the media coordinator may inform IMPROVISE that the devices and treatments (e.g., IV lines) illustrated in the patient example need to be presented sequentially, instead of together as they are now. In this case, a separation strategy is needed to effectively break the single display action into several display actions that handle one item or several relevant items at a time (e.g., to ensure that left and right IVs always appear simultaneously).

Acknowledgments

We thank Rahamad Dawood for implementing the scheduler, and Blaine Bell for porting the entire system from IRIX to Windows. This research was supported in part by DARPA Contract DAAL01-94-K-0119, the Columbia University Center for Advanced Technology in High Performance Computing and Communications in Healthcare (funded by the New York State Science and Technology Foundation), the Columbia Center for Telecommunications Research under NSF Grant ECD-88-11111, and ONR Contract N00014-97-1-0838.

References

Allen, J. (1983) Maintaining knowledge about temporal intervals. *Communications of the ACM*, 26(11):832–843.

André, E. and T. Rist (1993) The design of illustrated documents as a planning task. In M. Maybury, editor, *Intelligent Multimedia Interfaces*, Menlo Park, CA: AAAI Press/The MIT Press, 94–116.

André, E. and T. Rist (1996) Coping with temporal constraints in multimedia presentation planning. In *Proceedings AAAI '96*.

André, E., T. Rist, and J. Müller (1998) Webpersona: A life-like presentation agent for the world wide web. *Knowledge-Based Systems*, 11(1):25–36.

Dalal, M., S. Feiner, K. McKeown, S. Pan, M. Zhou, T. Höllerer, J. Shaw, Y. Feng, and J. Fromer (1996) Negotiation for automated generation of temporal multimedia presentations. In *Proceedings ACM Multimedia'96*, Boston, MA, November 18-22, 55–64.

Feiner, S. and K. McKeown (1991) Automating the generation of coordinated multimedia. *IEEE Computer*, 24(10):33–41.

Kautz, H. (1991) *MATS (Metric/Allen Time System) Documentation*. AT&T Bell Laboratories.

Mackinlay, J. (1986) Automating the design of graphical presentations of relational information. *ACM Transactions on Graphics*, 5(2):110–141.

McKeown, K., S. Feiner, J. Robin, D. Seligmann, and M. Tanenblatt (1992) Generating cross-references for multimedia explanation. In *Proceedings AAAI'92*, 12–17.

Mittal, V., J. Moore, G. Carenini, and S. Roth (1998) Describing complex charts in natural language: A caption generation system. *Computational Linguistics*, 24(3):431–467.

Noma, T., L. Zhao, and N. Badler (2000) Design of a virtual human presenter. *IEEE Computer Graphics and Applications*, 20(4):79–85.

Roth, S. F. and J. Mattis (1991) Automating the presentation of information. In *Proceedings IEEE Conference on AI Applications*, 90–97.

Seligmann, D.D. and S. Feiner (1991) Automated generation of intent-based 3D illustrations. *Computer Graphics*, 25(4):123–132.

Towns, S., C. Callaway, and J. Lester (1998) Generating coordinated natural language and 3D animations for complex spatial explanations. In *Proceedings AAAI '98*, 112–119.

Wahlster, W., E. André, H. Finkler, J. Profitlich, and T. Rist (1993) Plan-based integration of natural language and graphics generation. *Artificial Intelligence*, 63(12):387–427.

Wernecke, J. (1994) *The Inventor Mentor: Programming Object-Oriented 3D graphics with Open Inventor*. Reading, MA: Addison Wesley.

Wilkins, D. and K. Myers (1995) A common knowledge representation for plan generation and reactive execution. *Journal of Logic and Computation*, 5:731–761.

Young, R.M., M.E. Pollack, and J.D. Moore (1994) Decomposition and causality in partial-order planning. In *2nd Intern. Conference on AI Planning Systems: AIPS-94*, Chicago, IL, June 1994, 188–193.

Zhou, M. (1999) Visual planning: A practical approach to automated visual presentation. In *Proceedings IJCAI'99*, August 1999, 634–641.

Zhou, M. and S. Feiner (1996) Data characterization for automatically visualizing heterogeneous information. In *Proceedings IEEE InfoVis'96*, San Francisco, CA, October 1996, 13–20.

Zhou, M. and S. Feiner (1998) Automated visual presentation: From heterogeneous information to coherent visual discourse. *Journal of Intelligent Information Systems*, 11:205–234.

Zhou, M. and S. Feiner (1998) Efficiently planning coherent visual discourse. *Journal of Knowledge-Based Systems*, 10(5):275–286.

Multimodal Reference to Objects: An Empirical Approach

Robbert-Jan Beun[1] and Anita Cremers[*2]

[1] Institute for Information and Computing Science
Utrecht University, Utrecht, The Netherlands
rj@cs.uu.nl
[2] TNO Human Factors, Soesterberg, The Netherlands
cremers@tm.tno.nl

Abstract. In this chapter we report on an investigation into the principles underlying the choice of a particular referential expression to refer
to an object located in a domain to which both participants in the dialogue have multimodal access. Our approach is based on the assumption
that participants try to use as little effort as possible when referring to
objects. This assumption is operationalized in two factors, namely the
focus of attention and a particular choice of features to be included in a
referential expression. We claim that both factors help in reducing effort
needed to, on the one hand, refer to an object and, on the other hand, to
identify it. As a result of the focus of attention the number of potential
target objects (i.e., the object the speaker intends to refer to) is reduced.
The choice of a specific type of feature determines the number of objects
that have to be identified in order to be able to understand the referential
expression. An empirical study was conducted in which pairs of participants cooperatively carried out a simple block-building task, and the
results provided empirical evidence that supported the aforementioned
claims. Especially the focus of attention turned out to play an important
role in reducing the total effort.

1 Introduction

When two people discuss a task they are to perform together, they must indicate, among many other things, which of the available objects should be used.
If the task is carried out in a *shared domain* with multimodal access, i.e., a domain to which both participants have visual as well as physical access, they can
communicate these objects by means of *referential acts*, i.e., verbal referential
expressions and/or nonverbal references, such as pointing or other gestures. In
an actual interactive situation, the speaker may use one or more of the object's
features to indicate that particular object; for instance, the speaker may refer to

---

[*] This chapter is a slightly adapted version of: Beun, R.J. and Cremers, A.H.M. (1998)
Object Reference in a Shared Domain of Conversation. Pragmatics and Cognition
6(1/2), 121–152.

H. Bunt and R.-J. Beun (Eds.): CMC'98, LNAI 2155, pp. 64–86, 2001.
© Springer-Verlag Berlin Heidelberg 2001

a specific object by saying 'the red block' or 'the block left of the yellow one', possibly in combination with a pointing action.

The primary goal of this chapter is to present some fundamental cognitive concepts and pragmatic principles in object reference in a shared domain of conversation. More specifically, we will be concerned with the rules underlying the choice of a particular referential act to indicate an object that has been selected by the speaker. We will call this object the *target* object. Hence, the main questions to be answered in this chapter are *how* speakers refer to a specific target object and *why* speakers opt for a specific surface structure of the referential act, given the circumstances of the utterance.

Our analysis will be based on the *principle of minimal cooperative effort* (Clark and Wilkes-Gibbs, 1986); we will not only be concerned with the minimization of the effort to verbalize the expressions in a conversation, but also with a minimization of the effort to identify the relevant object(s) by the hearer. Hypothetically, this minimization can be established in at least two ways. First, central in our approach is the assumption that participants in a conversation establish some kind of focus space (see also, e.g., Grosz, 1977; Grosz and Sidner, 1986) that enables the speaker to use less information than actually needed when taking the complete domain of conversation into account. Second, we assume that by choosing a specific type of feature, a speaker can limit the number of objects that must be identified before the referential act can be understood.

Here we will focus on the part of the referential act that we call the *descriptive content*. This is the part where the speaker actually provides content information about the object to be identified, i.e., the entire referential act except the determiner and gestures. Since we are especially interested in the amalgam of the processes of object identification and object reference, we will restrict our analysis to first references to target objects. In these cases the descriptive content contains the maximal amount of information and the salience of the objects is not predominantly determined by the discourse.

To find evidence in real discourse for the hypotheses that we formulated on the basis of the principle of minimal cooperative effort, we conducted an empirical study where pairs of Dutch subjects had to carry out a specific task in a shared domain of conversation.

In Section 2, we define referential acts, focusing on the descriptive content of these acts. In Section 3, we introduce the principle of minimal cooperative effort, which we think is the basic underlying mechanism for object reference, and discuss two important notions: the focus of attention and the choice of features in the descriptive content. In these sections hypotheses are formulated about the choice of particular features in the descriptive content and the influence of the focus of attention on this choice. In Section 4, the setup of the empirical study that was carried out is described. Section 5 links the abstract notions used in the model to the properties of the domain used in the empirical study. In Section 6, the results are described and in Section 7 we will discuss how these results can be interpreted in terms of the model sketched in Section 3.

2   Form and Content of Referential Acts

An instance of a referential act may consist of a referential expression, possibly accompanied by a gesture. In this chapter we are only concerned with reference to single objects, so only singular expressions are considered. For our purposes, we assume a possible referential act to be constructed as in the following schema. The brackets in this schema indicate that the category is optional. However, at least one of the optional categories must be present in each rule. The star (*) indicates that the category can be used more than once. Gestures are indicated by a dagger †.[1]

referential act =   *(referential expression) (†)*
referential expression = (determiner) (descriptive content)
descriptive content =   (premodifier)* (head) (postmodifier)*

Examples of referential acts are:

1. $(het)_{det}((grote)_{premod}(rode)_{premod}(blok)_{head}(voor \ mij)_{postmod})_{descr.cont}$
   'the large red block in front of me'
2. $(een)_{det}((groot)_{premod} \ (blok)_{head} \ (dat \ achter \ de \ rode \ staat)_{postmod})_{descr.cont}$
   'a large block lying behind the red one'
3. $(die)_{det} \ ((grote)_{premod} \ (hier)_{postmod})_{descr.cont} \ (†)$
   'that large one here (†)'

The schema does not indicate that pronouns can also be used as a referential expression instead of a combination of determiner and descriptive content (e.g., 'het' ('it')). However, in this chapter we will not be concerned with pronouns, since we will concentrate on the analysis of the use of information in the descriptive content of the referential act. Pronouns, determiners and gestures will only be included in the analysis when necessary.

2.1   Descriptive Content

The descriptive content may consist of one or more *premodifiers*, a *head*, and one or more *postmodifiers*. Premodification is carried out by means of adjectives (e.g., 'groot' ('large'), 'rood' ('red')). In contrast to English, where 'one' can be used instead of the noun, the head is usually a noun in Dutch (e.g., 'blok' ('block')). If the noun is not used in Dutch, an ellipsis takes place and the noun is

---

[1] Actually, in English as well as in Dutch, the form of references can be more complicated (Quirk et al., 1972; Bennis and Hoekstra, 1983). A reference may be constructed of: *(predeterminer)(determiner)(postdeterminer)*(premodifier)* (head)(postmodifier)** or *pronoun*. However, we will only consider the simple form here. Moreover, although reference to objects can also be carried out by using *proper names*, such as 'De Nachtwacht' ('The Nightwatch'), in this chapter we will not be concerned with these. The referential process becomes easier if objects have names assigned to them, since then there is a one-to-one relationship between name and object, and no alternative objects need to be considered for identification.

omitted altogether (e.g., example (3)). Post-modification is expressed by means of a relative clause (e.g., 'dat achter de rode staat' ('that is lying behind the red one')) or a prepositional phrase (e.g., 'voor mij' ('in front of me')). We assume that predicates of the object are expressed in the pre- and post-modifiers and type information of the object in the head.

Semantically, we distinguish between *absolute* and *relative* features, both of which can be expressed in the descriptive content. Absolute features are features that can be identified without having to consider other entities; for instance, the feature 'color' and the type of the object (e.g., 'het rode blok' ('the red block')). Relative features can be either implicit or explicit. In both cases, though, other entities have to be identified to interpret the meaning of the expression. In the implicit case, the other entities are omitted from the surface structure of the descriptive content, e.g., 'the left block', 'the large one'. In these examples the omitted entities are, respectively, the participants in the dialogue and other objects. In the explicit case, other entities are always included in the surface structure (e.g., 'the block behind the red one'). Following Levelt (1989), we will call the entity involved as a reference object the relatum (in our example 'the red one').

3 Pragmatic Principles and Cognitive Concepts in Object Reference

3.1 The Principle of Minimal Cooperative Effort

Our analysis will be based on the *principle of minimal cooperative effort* defined by Clark and Wilkes-Gibbs (1986). They state that reference to objects can be seen as a collaborative process; the principle expresses the idea that there is a trade-off between the noun phrase that is uttered first and the possible additions or corrections to this utterance by the speaker or the partner. Hence, a speaker can decide to start by uttering an ambiguous expression, expecting the partner to make an educated guess about the intended referent or to ask for clarification if this was not possible. This results in a shared responsibility of both speaker and hearer for the establishment of the common knowledge that the expression is understood well enough for the current purposes.[2]

In this chapter, we will assume that the principle should be interpreted in a broad sense. In contrast to Clark and Wilkes-Gibbs, who focus on the linguistic and dialogue-related aspects of the referential process, we emphasize the process of identification by the hearer. The speaker and the addressee not only try to say as little as possible together, but they also try to do as little as possible and,

---

[2] In terms of Sperber and Wilson's theory of relevance this would probably mean that humans always try to maximize the relevance of the information that is being processed; in other words, they try to improve their knowledge of the world as much as possible given the available resources (Sperber and Wilson, 1986). However, the idea of relevance will not be pursued any further in this chapter.

as a result, try to minimize the amount of effort it takes to actually *identify* the target object.

A reduction in effort can be established in at least two ways. In the first place, the speaker can reduce the number of features in the description by trying to take as few potential target objects as possible into account. He can do this by making use of factors that are related to the focus of attention of the participants. In the second place, the speaker can try to involve as few objects as possible in the description itself, either implicitly or explicitly. He can do this by making use of absolute features that require the identification of only one object.

3.2   Focus of Attention

An important determinant of the ease with which an object is identified is its relative *salience* in the context of the domain at some point during the interaction. The concept of salience has a two-way relationship with the focus of attention of the participants. On the one hand, an object that is salient at some point can be said to attract the focus of attention of the participants. On the other hand, an object that is in some way in the focus of attention of the participants can be said to be more salient.

In our opinion, there are at least three ways in which an object can become salient and/or part of the current focus of attention. First, an object can acquire an inherent salience if at some point during the interaction it stands out in the context. Secondly, an object may be salient either if it has been mentioned recently, if it is related in some way to an entity that has been mentioned earlier, or if the attention has been pulled toward it in some other way. Thirdly, an object may become salient if it is functionally relevant in the current context. If an object is salient at some point during the interaction, and the speaker wants to refer to this object, then he or she will generally need less information to do this, because there are less other competing (i.e., salient) objects from which the target object has to be distinguished. Below, we will briefly discuss the first two types of focus.

Inherent Salience. Objects that are salient within the domain of conversation attract attention.[3] What salience means for the identification of objects was shown by Treisman and Gelade. They found that if a target item differed from the irrelevant items with respect to a simple feature such as orientation or color, observers could detect the target just as fast when it was presented in an array of 39 items as when it was presented in an array of 3 (Treisman and Gelade, 1980). This observation is known as the 'pop out' effect. In addition, research using eye movement tracking has shown that objects with a high information content, i.e., more recognizable objects, tend to be fixated upon longer (Mackworth and Morandi, 1967). This observation holds also for objects that are unfamiliar in a certain situation (Loftus and Mackworth, 1978). Hence, it seems reasonable

---

[3] Note that at some point during the interaction, the salience of objects may change because of changes in the domain of conversation.

to conclude that objects that differ with respect to their environment tend to capture more attention and, as a result, can be identified more easily.

Salience of an object can also arise from changes in the features of the object. Alerting mechanisms direct attention to any gross change in the environment after it has been detected (Glass and Holyoak, 1986). This means that if a visually detectable feature of an object changes, such as contrast or location, the attention is directed towards this object.

How salience of an object in a certain environment may influence the production of the expression to refer to this object and the effort to identify it was shown by Clark, Schreuder and Buttrick. In an experiment they carried out, listeners were able to identify objects on the basis of ambiguous references by choosing the object that was perceptually most salient (Clark, Schreuder and Buttrick, 1983).

To conclude, a salient object is easier to refer to, since it suffices to use reduced information. A salient object is also easier for the listener to identify, since it differs from the environment. The following hypothesis, presented in the form of an instruction to the speaker, can be derived from the literature discussed above:

Hypothesis 1: *'If the target object is inherently salient within the domain of conversation, use reduced information.'*

Current Focus of Attention. When talking about focus of attention, a clear distinction has to be made between the focus of attention within the dialogue and the focus of attention within the domain of conversation. Research about the focus of attention within the dialogue has centered around the possibilities for using pronominal expressions to refer to an object that has been mentioned recently. Since we concentrate in this chapter on first reference to objects, we will mainly consider focus in the domain of conversation. However, the focus of attention within the dialogue often coexists with a focus of attention within the domain of conversation.

It can be argued that the current focus of attention within the dialogue consists of a collection of features of the entity that has been referred to recently (the explicit focus), possibly supplemented by some features of related entities (the implicit focus). If we look at focus like this, we can observe that the speaker is allowed to omit the features in the current referring expression that have already been mentioned in the previous expression. A clear example of this is the use of type information. If all of the objects being referred to have the same type (e.g., a block) it is not necessary to convey this information in every single referential expression that is used. Grammatically, these reductions are treated as cases of ellipsis. Links with objects mentioned previously can also be expressed explicitly, e.g., in expressions such as 'the same one'. The case of pronominal reference to objects that are referred to repeatedly can be seen as the extreme case, where all features of the two entities are identical and only a pronominal 'place-filler' is necessary.

Beside the inherent salience of objects that may attract attention, which was discussed in the previous subsection, there is also a more dynamic component of the focus of attention. This is the focus of attention that is continually established and changed during the course of the dialogue and the actions in the domain of conversation. This focus can be seen as a kind of spotlight that is controlled by the participants as the interaction unfolds. The counterpart in the domain of the explicit focus of attention in the dialogue is the object that has just been manipulated. In many cases, this object is also the last one mentioned in the dialogue. If such an object is referred to for the second time, pronominal reference is possible.

We will call the counterpart in the domain of the implicit focus of attention in the dialogue the *spatial focus of attention* (see Cremers, 1994). It can be argued that the objects that are located close to the one that has just been mentioned and/or manipulated are in the spatial focus of attention. Together with the object in explicit focus they form a focus area. If a speaker refers to an object that is located within the focus area, only the objects in the focus area have to be considered as alternative target objects. This usually means that the amount of information in the referential expression is reduced, which leads us to the following hypothesis:

Hypothesis 2: *'If the target object is located in the current focus area, use only information that distinguishes the object from other objects in the focus area.'*

3.3 Features in the Description

In the previous section we have described what the effect of reducing the focus space is on the number of features that have to be used in referential expressions. A conclusion from this is that the smaller the space that has to be taken into consideration, relatively the less features have to be used. In this section we will try to describe which features, given the focus space, speakers prefer to use to refer to a target object.

In general, a speaker's referential expression indicating some object in the environment is a function of what alternative objects there are in the context of reference (Olson, 1970). Speakers try to choose the descriptive content that distinguishes the target object from the surrounding ones most effectively. If there are two distinguishing features that are equally powerful, usually the speaker chooses the one that is most salient (Herrmann, 1983).

From our perspective salience is only one of the predominant criteria for choosing a particular feature. Speakers also have the choice to use either absolute or relative features to refer to a certain object. From the principle of minimal cooperative effort the prediction can be made that speakers have a preference for using absolute features, since to produce and understand those features no other objects than the target object have to be taken into account. This implies for the speaker that only one object has to be described instead of two or more, and for the addressee that only one object has to be identified. Hence, we would expect that both speaker and addressee need to expend less effort when reference by means of absolute features is used.

However, sometimes uttering absolute features may cause problems from both a generation and an interpretation point of view, because the features are inherently difficult or because too many features are needed to distinguish the target object from other objects. Compare, for instance, the following utterances: 'the block that is located at the coordinates 318, 248' and 'the block next to the large blue block'. In those cases it may be more efficient to (also) use relative features, since it may reduce the total amount of collaborative effort required to achieve the goal of the common knowledge that the target object has been identified. The point at which a speaker will shift from using absolute features to using relative features is a complicated matter which should be investigated empirically. These considerations lead us to the following hypothesis:

> Hypothesis 3: *'Use absolute features as much as possible and use relative features only if necessary.'*

If relative features are used, both speaker and addressee should be aware of the implicit or explicit relatum that should be chosen from the potential relata. From a language production point of view, it takes less effort to use an implicit relatum, since in that case the relatum does not have to be expressed. If there is no possibility for using an implicit relatum, an explicit relatum has to be chosen. This leads to a process of *recursion*: in order to refer to an object, some other object has to be referred to. If we apply the principle of minimal cooperative effort again, we can predict that the chosen relatum will be an object that is relatively easy to identify. The hypothesis related to this observation is:

> Hypothesis 4: *'If an explicit relatum is needed for referring to the target object, choose as relatum an object that is in the focus of attention.'*

Probably the object that can be identified most easily is the object that was mentioned most recently, in other words, the object in the current explicit focus of attention. If the object in explicit focus is used as a relatum, it can be referred to by means of a pronominal expression. This results in a reduction of the number of words in the referential expression. If the target object is located close to an inherently salient object, this object can be chosen as a relatum. However, in that case pronominal reference is not possible.

3.4   Reduced Information

In the results and the discussion below, we will express reduction of information in terms of ambiguity and redundancy of the referential act with respect to a competitive set of objects. We will say that a referential act is ambiguous if two or more objects fit the description of the act; the act is redundant if any part of the descriptive content can be left out without becoming ambiguous. A referential act that is neither redundant, nor ambiguous will be called optimal.

The notions of ambiguity and redundancy will be applied to the current focus area as well as the whole domain (see Figures 1 and 2). For example, in a domain with two yellow blocks and a blue block, of which one yellow block and the blue block are present in the current focus area, the expression 'the yellow one' is ambiguous with respect to the whole domain, but optimal with respect to the focus area. We also include the pointing act of the speaker in our definition; so, if the speaker in the previous example also would have pointed to the yellow block, the referential act would be redundant with respect to the focus area and the whole domain, but not ambiguous. Unambiguous pointing actions combined with descriptive features (e.g., 'the yellow one †') are always considered as redundant.

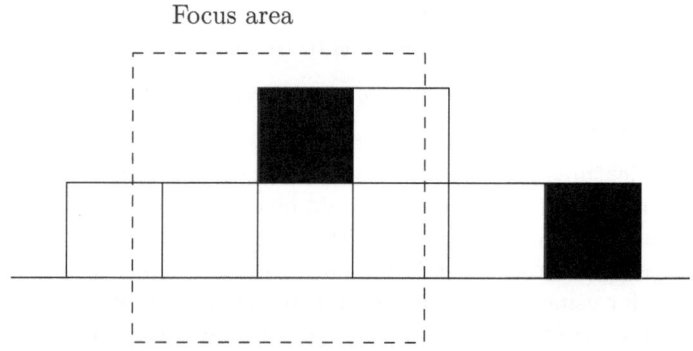

Fig. 1. The utterance 'the black one' is optimal with respect to the current focus area, but ambiguous in the domain.

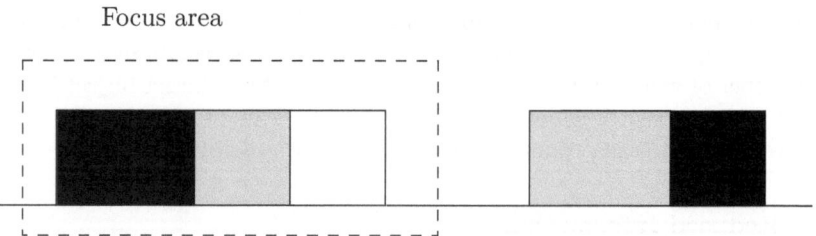

Fig. 2. The utterance 'the big black one' is redundant with respect to the current focus area, but optimal in the domain.

Notice that, if a focus area is present, ambiguity of the referential act within the focus area always implies ambiguity within the whole domain. Vice versa, redundancy within the domain always implies redundancy within the focus area. Also, the definition implies that the referential act can never be both ambiguous and redundant with respect to the whole domain.

4 Empirical Setup

In order to find evidence for the hypotheses that were formulated in the previous section, we carried out an empirical study during which two participants were asked to perform a specific task in a shared domain of conversation. The situation is depicted in Figure 3 and can be described as follows.

Two participants were seated side by side at a table, but were separated by a screen. To avoid other communication than by spoken language and gesturing, only their hands were visible to one another, and only when placed on top of the table. One of the participants (the instructor, I) was told to instruct the other (the builder, B) in rebuilding a block building on a green toy foundation plate, located on top of the table such that the building would become a replica of the example building visible only to the instructor. Both participants were allowed to observe the building domain, to talk about it, and to gesticulate in it, but only the builder was allowed to manipulate blocks.

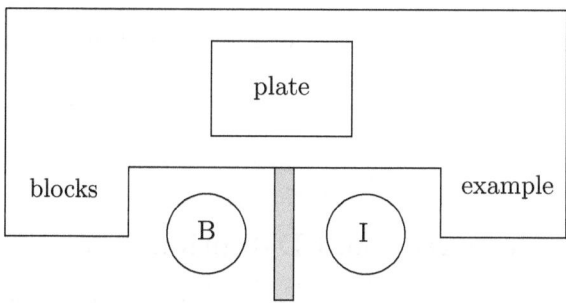

Fig. 3. Experimental Configuration (Top View), B=Builder, I=Instructor.

The building consisted of blocks of one of four different colors (red, green, blue and yellow), three sizes (small, medium, large) and four shapes (square, bar, convex, concave).[4] Schematic pictures of the 29 blocks that were involved in the building sessions are provided in Figure 4. These objects were chosen because we wanted objects that were simple and non-figurative, in order to avoid extensive reasoning on domain specific knowledge by the participants.

---

[4] In fact, the blocks were samples of the DUPLO-series of LEGO.

Ten pairs of Dutch subjects participated in the empirical study. Half of the subjects was male and half female, and their ages varied from 20 to 60 years. The 10 building sessions were recorded on video-tape and the spoken communication was transcribed (Cremers, 1993). The dialogues that occurred during the sessions were similar to Grosz's task dialogues (Grosz, 1977).

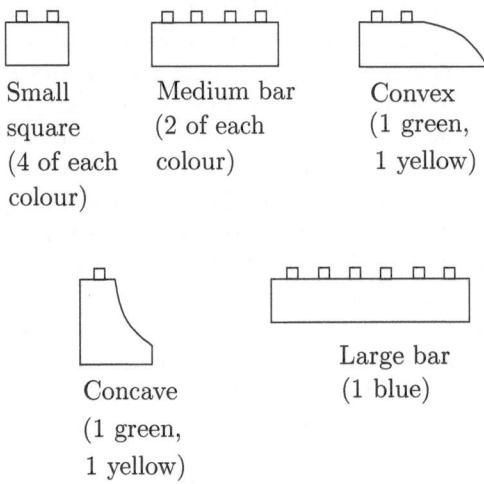

Fig. 4. Types, Numbers, and Colors of Blocks Used in the Experiment (Side View).

5   Domain Properties and Definitions

Before we discuss the results in terms of the model sketched in Section 3, we first have to convert the abstract notions such as 'salience', and 'focus' into concrete domain properties.

5.1   Inherent Salience

During the rebuilding task, blocks were removed and others were added. On the average, 24 blocks were present on the foundation plate, only two of them were convex or concave. So, due to their deviated form and their relative small number of occurrence, these two types were considered inherently salient with respect to the bar and square types.

Although it can be argued that, due to the perceptual properties of the eye, yellow objects are inherently more salient than other colored objects, we did not include this in our analysis. This was done because the color feature was randomly distributed over the objects and yellow appeared almost equally often as the other colors.

5.2   The Focus Area

In our domain the spatial focus of attention is the predominant type of focus, since the nature of the task calls for the instructor to spatially scan the domain to look for parts of the block building that should be altered. We have distinguished five indicators that determine if an object is located in the current focus area. Occurring indicators are either domain-related or linguistic criteria, or combinations of both types.[5]

Domain-related indicators for objects within the focus area

- the target object is located adjacent (or relatively close) to the previous target object
- the target object is part of a set of objects that has been indicated in a previous utterance and identified by the partner (e.g., 'the group of blocks on the left')

Linguistic indicators for objects within the focus area

- a relatum which is the previous target object is used in the referential expression
- a definite expression is used, which indicates that the object is easy to identify
- linguistic markers are used indicating to stay at the same location or that the (sub-)task has not yet been finished (e.g., 'here', 'we still have to...')

Example (4) illustrates the use of a referential expression to refer to an object within the focus area.[6] In this example a large and a small yellow block and a small blue block are all stacked on top of a red block that is mounted directly onto the foundation plate.

4. (Dialogue 10.21-22; Cremers, 1993)

    I: Dit (raakt grote en kleine gele, kleine blauwe aan) **moet er allemaal af**.

    B: (pakt grote en kleine gele, kleine blauwe vast)

---

[5] In the list of criteria no task-related indicators are added. The possibility exists that the addressee is aware that the (sub-)task at hand is not finished yet, and that therefore the referential act is probably used to refer to an object within the current focus area. In our type of task this effect did not seem to be very prevalent, because the specific details with respect to the performance of the task were not prescribed. Task-related effects on the choice of references have been treated in depth by Grosz (1977).

[6] Comments by the transcriber about actions that were carried out are added between brackets in all examples.

I: (1.9) `Blijft alleen die rode op de grond staan.`

B: `Ja ja.` (haalt grote kleine gele, kleine blauwe eraf)

I: *These* (touches large and small yellow one, small blue one) *should all be removed.*

B: (grips large and small yellow one, small blue one)

I: (1.9) *Only the red one stays on the ground.*

B: *Yes yes.* (removes large and small yellow ones, small blue one)

In this example, 'die rode op de grond' ('the red one ... on the ground') was located in the vicinity of the large and small yellow ones and the small blue one. The referring expression is ambiguous within the current domain, since at least one more red block was located at the foundation plate. Also, the definite expression 'die' ('the') is used. Furthermore, the uses of 'blijft' ('stays') and 'alleen' ('only') suggest that the total subtask has not been carried out yet, since they express a restriction to the number of blocks that have to be removed.

If the target object is not located in the current focus area, a focus transition has to take place. Speakers may signal this transition explicitly by indicating the next focus area (e.g., 'let's go to the upper right part now'). If it is clear that the addressee has understood the nature of the transition, the next target object can be considered to be in focus. However, if no explicit indication is given, the referring expression itself should include enough information to identify the target object. Criteria that indicate that the target object is located outside of the current focus area are listed below. The domain-related indicators are complementary to those formulated earlier for objects within the focus area. The linguistic indicators are only partly complementary.

Domain-related indicators for objects outside of the focus area

- the target object is located relatively far from the previous target object (and certainly not adjacent to it)
- the target object is not part of the set of objects that were mentioned last

Linguistic indicators for objects outside of the focus area

- a relatum is used in the referential expression that is not the previous target object, but an inherently salient object
- an indefinite expression is used
- linguistic markers are used that indicate to move to another location or that the previous task or subtask has already been finished (e.g., 'let's move to the right', 'that part is ready')

In example (5) a focus transition to a new focus area is illustrated.

5. (Dialogue 2.63-64; Cremers, 1993)

B: `Zo?` (plaatst kleine blauwe)

I: `Ja, ... (1.5) ja. ... (1.4) Nou, en -- Even kijken. Dan zie`
`je op zeker moment, een beetje aan de noordkant, zie je een`
`groen`
`blokje.`

B: *Like this?* (places small blue one)
I: *Yes, ... (1.5) yes. ... (1.4) Well, and – Let's see. Then at a certain*
moment you see, a bit to the north side, you see a green block.

In this example, the target object was located relatively far from the previous target object, and was not a part of some set of blocks introduced previously. Also, an indefinite referring expression is used: 'een' ('a'). Finally, a linguistic marker for a focus transition is given: 'een beetje aan de noordkant' ('a bit to the north side').

6   Results

6.1   General Observations

During the execution of the task that was explained in Section 4, the subjects used a total of 665 referential acts. Of these references, 145 were first references to objects located in the domain of conversation. Below we consider only these 145 first references.

Spatial Focus: Based on the criteria formulated in the previous section, we were able to identify 45 objects (31%) out of the spatial focus area as a result of a focus change and 100 objects (69%) in the focus area at the time of the utterance; these results were scored independently by the two authors. In only four cases we had initial disagreement, but we decided on the criterion of linguistic markers that were used to move to another location (2 cases) or that indicated that the previous task had been finished (2 cases).

Pointing: In 69 cases (48%) a pointing act was used. The total number of pointing acts is slightly biased though, because three subjects declared afterwards that they tried to carry out the task without pointing. (The subjects were only told that they were allowed to point, not that they had to.) Leaving out these three subjects, the percentage of pointing actions was 68%.

Ambiguity and Redundancy: Ambiguous references with respect to the whole domain occurred in 62 cases (43%); if a focus area was present, ambiguity with respect to the current focus area occurred in 12 cases (12%; 12 out of 100). In 44 cases (30%) the expression was redundant with respect to the whole domain; if a focus area was present, in 28 cases (28%; 28 out of 100) the expression was redundant with respect to the focus area. In 39 cases (27%) the reference was optimal.

Salience: In total, 13 references to salient objects were counted, such as 'the green slide' (concave type) or 'the half rounded one' (convex type). In 3 of these cases the referential act was redundant with respect to the whole domain, but it was never redundant in cases where the salient object was inside the focus area (3 times). Only 2 expressions were clearly ambiguous with respect to the whole domain.

Descriptive Features: Of the total amount of 145 first referential acts that occurred in the dialogues, 90 (62%) just included absolute features (colour and/or shape). In 2 (1%) of the cases only relative features were used. In 27 cases (19%) combinations of relative and absolute features were used. Beside relative and absolute features, demonstrative expressions accompanied by a pointing action were used in 26 cases (18%).

Explicit Relata: In only 19 cases (13%) an explicit relatum was used in the referential expression. In none of these cases a pointing action was used. Sometimes, the relatum referred to an object that was not a block (e.g., 'the floor', the participants), or was an abstract object (e.g., 'the second level'). In 4 cases one or two of the participants were mentioned as relatum, in 13 cases some object in the domain served as an explicit relatum, and in 2 cases both a participant and an object were explicit relata. If a domain object was used as a relatum (15 cases), in 10 cases this object was mentioned previously. In one case the relatum was located in the current focus area. In the 4 remaining cases the relatum was either inherently salient or a unique object within the domain.

6.2   The Influence of Changing the Focus Area

In Table 1 we have indicated a. the number of pointing actions, b. the salience of the target object, and c. the ambiguity and d. redundancy of the referential act with respect to the domain as a function of in or out focus of the target object. '+' indicates that these characteristics are present; '-' indicates that they were absent. For instance, in 10 cases where the referential act referred to a salient object, the object was out of focus; in 97 cases the object was in focus, but not salient.

Except for the pointing action, the differences between in or out focus results differed significantly (Pointing: $\chi^2_{df=1} = 2.34$, $p < 0.2$; Salient object: $\chi^2_{df=1} = 14.7$, $p < 0.001$; Domain ambiguity: $\chi^2_{df=1} = 10.6$, $p < 0.005$; Domain redundancy: $\chi^2_{df=1} = 13.28$, $p < 0.001$). In other words, redundancy of the referential expression appeared relatively more often when the target object was out of focus; vice versa, ambiguity appeared relatively more often when the object was in focus. Moreover, when a focus change appeared, relatively more reference was made to a salient object.

We did not find significant differences in the use of particular descriptive features (e.g., color, shape or the use of relata) as a function of being in or out focus of the target object.

Table 1. The number of pointing actions, the salience of the target object, and the ambiguity and redundancy of the referential act with respect to the domain as a function of in or out focus of the target object. '+' indicates that these characteristics are present; '-' indicates that they were absent.

	Pointing		Salient object		Dom. ambiguity		Dom. redundancy		Total
	+	-	+	-	+	-	+	-	
Out Focus	25	18	10	35	10	35	23	22	45
In Focus	44	58	3	97	52	48	21	79	100
Total	69	76	13	132	62	83	44	101	145

7   Discussion

We will now discuss the outcome of the empirical study in more detail and relate the results to the hypotheses discussed in Section 3.

7.1   Salience

Our first hypothesis was that *if the object is inherently salient within the domain of conversation, the speaker uses reduced information.*

In other words, we would expect most of the referential acts to the concave and convex objects ambiguous with respect to the whole domain. As we can read from the results, however, only two of the 13 references were ambiguous, and even less expected, 3 cases were redundant. These numbers are relatively low, so we should be careful to draw too many conclusions from this.

But let us go a little more deeply in these redundant cases. In two cases, redundancy was caused by the combination of a pointing act and a descriptive feature in the referential act; in one case, the redundancy was caused by the appearance of two descriptive features 'green' and 'slide', instead of 'slide' only. So the redundancy is at least minimal, caused by only one extra descriptive feature.

Also, in all three cases the redundancy appeared when the target object was not in the current focus area. Important here are the results of the redundancy of descriptions in general. As we can see in Table 1, in general descriptions of objects out of focus contain significantly more redundancy than descriptions of objects in focus. But the descriptions of salient objects out of focus contain redundancy in only 33% of the cases (3 out of 10), while descriptions of non-salient objects out of focus contain redundancy in 57% of the cases (20 out of 35). Due to the low total number of salient object descriptions the difference is not significant ($\chi^2_{df=1} = 1.87$, $0.1 < p < 0.2$), but there is at least a strong tendency for reduction of descriptive features when the object is salient.

So, the result is in line with the hypothesis and we would expect a strong tendency for ambiguity if more salient objects would be in focus. Testing this in a natural dialogue situation will often be difficult, though, since salient objects are always limited in number and are often picked out as a marker for establishing a new focus area (see Table 1). An important conclusion is that reduction of information cannot simply be explained in terms of ambiguity or redundancy with respect to the whole domain, but that at least a distinction has to be made between objects in focus and objects out of focus.

7.2   Redundancy of Information

From the second hypothesis, i.e., *'if the target object is located in the current focus area, use only information that distinguishes the object from other objects in the focus area'*, we would expect that most of the references are ambiguous with respect to the domain or at least not redundant with respect to the focus area. This was indeed supported by the results. In 28%, however, we still noticed redundancy in the act, but this redundancy was always caused by an extra pointing act, not by the addition of extra descriptive features.

In only three of the 52 cases the ambiguity caused an identification problem for the hearer, so both speaker and hearer not only used a focus area to reduce the information, but must have been mutually aware about each others focus area.

From the third hypothesis, i.e., *'use only information that distinguishes the target object from other objects that would also be suitable for use in carrying out the current action'*, we would expect that some of the references are ambiguous within the focus area and can be resolved by means of functional information. Apart from one case where the ambiguity could not be resolved without extra dialogue acts, in all other cases (11) the resolution process was supported by functional information. The functional information that was made use of was related to the four basic operations that the participants were expected to carry out, namely, to remove an object from the domain, to move it within the domain, to leave it laying at the same location or to use it as a relatum.

Although these results strongly support the hypotheses on redundancy of information, again we have to be careful to draw too many conclusions here. First, sometimes the unequivocal determination of a specific focus area is difficult and it may be the case that sometimes specific objects were in the focus area without being classified as such and vice versa. Therefore, to determine the focus area, we only included those objects where the objects were adjacent to the target object.[7] Second, in some cases spatial and functional information cannot easily be distinguished, since objects in the neighborhood are often both functionally relevant and in the focus area.

An important finding is that references to objects outside the focus area are significantly more redundant than references inside the focus area. A reason for this redundancy is probably that the speaker is simply unable to overview the whole domain in short time and, therefore, cannot decide which and how many of the possible features to use in order to minimize the contribution (see also Pechmann, 1984). Probably speakers deliberately give more information to help their hearers to find the target object; in our words, they place a relatively

---

[7] Note that in these cases we did not have linguistic information at our disposal.

larger part of the cooperative effort at their own side of the scale. This can be explained by realizing that speakers probably give more information to avoid an explanatory sub-dialogue in case the hearer has not understood the initial expression. So, the principle of minimality is still maintained, but not on the level of descriptive features, but on the level of identification and speech act turns.

7.3   Descriptive Features

The third hypothesis, *'use absolute features as much as possible and use relative features only if necessary'* is strongly supported by the data. Only 20% of the references contained relative features. But again we should be careful in our conclusions, since these numbers may highly depend on the domain, its properties, the task and the communicative situation. It may well be that in other situations, for instance, where pointing is impossible, or where objects are significantly different and absolute features play just a minor role (e.g., 'Look at the man with the funny hat'), the data on referential acts may not support the hypothesis in such a convincing way.

Finally, the fourth hypothesis, *'if an explicit relatum is needed for referring to the target object, choose as relatum an object that is in the focus of attention'*, is also strongly supported by the data. Either participants or other objects or both were used as explicit relata. Participants are always in the focus of attention, because their perspective always has to be taken into account by the speaker while formulating the referential expression. This means that in the 4 cases where a participant was used as a relatum, the relatum was in the focus of attention.

Domain objects can be considered to be in the focus of attention if they have been mentioned previously (explicit focus of attention), are located in the current focus area (spatial focus of attention), are inherently salient or a unique object. The functional focus of attention does not apply here, because a relatum that is needed for referring to a target object is never involved in the action that should be carried out. As can be seen in the results, in all cases the relata fulfilled these requirements.

7.4   Focus and the Principle of Connectivity

The distribution of first references referring to objects within the focus area as opposed to objects out of the focus area turned out not to be balanced (69% in focus, 31% out of focus). In terms of the principle of minimal cooperative effort there are two possible reasons for this imbalance.

In the first place, people may have a preference for referring to objects in focus, because the referential expression that is needed will generally be shorter, and the chance that only absolute features are needed will be larger.

The second reason is that there may be a preference for staying in the same focus area or even choosing the object that is directly connected to (i.e., touching) to the one mentioned previously. This preference is the result of a higher level general strategy to solve problems. When people are trying to solve a complicated problem, they tend to decompose this problem and first solve the parts before solving the whole (Thomas, 1974). In terms of the block-building task this would mean that participants first finish a part of the building (which is probably also the current focus area), and then choose a new part until the whole building has been completed. This strategy takes less effort than the alternative strategy which suggests to move to another focus area after every referential act. The problem of having to return to a previous focus area because a part of it has not been revised yet is also avoided.

Following the general problem solving strategy, participants prefer to choose an object within the current focus area. Exactly which object is chosen as the next target object is probably related the principle of connectivity, which predicts that "a speaker will go over a pattern as much as possible "without lifting the pencil", the mental pencil's point being the speaker's focus of attention" (Levelt, 1982: p.140). In Levelt's case, subjects applied this principle when asked to describe spatial-grid-like networks. They chose as the next node to be described, wherever possible, one that had a direct connection to the current node. Levelt states that the principle of connectivity is a general ordering principle in perception and memory. However, he does not explain why this is the case. This process probably works in the same way as the problem solving strategy. Speakers probably choose the object closest to the previous one, in order to use less effort than would be needed to 'switch' to some object located further away (but still within the focus area). They also try to keep track of what they have been doing in order not to forget an object, since in that case they would have to return to it later, probably even after already having left the current focus area.

By applying the problem solving strategy of using subgoals and the principle of connectivity, coherence in the discourse may arise. If a focus transition marker is used, it may be relative with respect to the previous focus area (e.g., 'move further to the right'), and in this way connect the new discourse segment (and also the new focus area) to the previous one. Within a focus area, explicit connections can be expressed by using the previous target object as a relatum for the current one (e.g., 'the yellow block to the right of it'). However, participants may experience a sense of coherence even if coherence in the discourse is not created explicitly by expressing the relation between the previous and the current target object, because of the visual feedback they receive from the domain of conversation. For example, if no explicit relatum is used, participants can still see that the current target object is located close to the previous one, and may feel that the choice of the current target object is a coherent move in the interaction.

By using the term 'focus' for all types of focus that have been discussed in this chapter, we can state that, in our domain, focus of attention is the main cause of coherence. We should however be careful not to extrapolate these findings to other domains of conversation too easily. On the one hand, in order to communicate about the present domain not much world knowledge was needed, so top-down coherence-establishing devices such as scripts and frames (see Brown and Yule, 1983) were not used. On the other hand, it may turn out that scripts and frames can be interpreted as devices that highlight certain entities in a particular context, hereby bringing these entities into 'focus'.

7.5 Limitations

The present study is limited in a number of ways. In the first place, we have focused on the descriptive content of the referential act, because this is the main part where information is localized that helps the addressee to identify the referent object. However, beside the descriptive content, determiners and gestures may also form part of the referential act.

Important information is expressed in the determiner that helps to carry out the identification; the information about the accessibility of the referent (Ariel, 1990) is especially useful here. For instance, based on the same Dutch data, it has been shown in Piwek, Beun and Cremers (1995) that proximate demonstratives are used in cases were the speaker wants to signal to the addressee a need for extra effort to find the intended referent, while distals are used in cases where the referent is more 'given' with regard to the addressee's consciousness.

Of course, important information can also be expressed by means of gestures. Not only can gestures help to identify a location, but they can also indicate, for example, shapes and sizes of objects (Knapp and Hall, 1992). In the referential acts we studied only pointing gestures were used in order to support the verbal information.

Also, we did not take into account the process of cooperatively building up to the agreement that a certain object is indeed the referent object. We assumed that just one referential act would suffice to achieve this. In reality this was not true, and sometimes more turns were needed, mainly at places where misunderstandings occurred. Main causes for miscommunication can be erroneous specificity, improper focus, wrong context or a bad analogy with another object (Goodman, 1986). In our data, 6 occurrences of confusions and/or miscommunications occurred (in 4% of the first references to objects in the domain). In one case the misunderstanding took place because the instructor provided wrong information. In all other (5) cases misunderstandings were in some way related to the focus of attention. In two cases the instructor probably assumed that the focus was still directed at a certain focus area and accordingly used reduced reference, which the builder failed to understand immediately. In two cases misunderstandings occurred at focus transitions, probably because it was not clear to the builder what the new focus area was going to be. One misunderstanding was the result of a focus clash that has already been discussed in the previous subsection and illustrated in example (9).

A final important limitation of this study is that we have only analyzed referential behavior in a blocks domain during a building task. In other types of domains and/or tasks the focus mechanisms and the choice of the types of features could turn out to be different from what we found. For example, in another type of task the functional focus may be more prevalent than was the case here. However, we claim that by choosing simple nonfigurative objects and a simple task, we were able to find basic characteristics underlying object reference.

8 Conclusions

In this chapter, we have tried to describe the basic principles underlying the choice of a particular type of referential act to refer to an object in a shared domain of conversation in which a task is carried out cooperatively. We have done so in line with Clark and Wilkes-Gibbs' principle of minimal cooperative effort and payed especially attention to the amalgam of the processes of object identification and object reference. From the principle we were able to formulate two consequences of this principle: first, speakers limit the number of potential alternative target objects by making use of the assumed focus of attention of their addressees, second, speakers try to include as few objects as possible in the referential expression itself, either explicitly or implicitly. These two devices help, on the one hand, to keep the referential expression as short as possible, and, on the other hand, to limit the number of objects that have to be considered in order to find the target object. Thus, the principle of minimal cooperative effort cuts both ways here; it takes less effort both for the speaker to utter the expression and for the addressee to identify the target object.

By means of an empirical study, we were able to show that focus is not only a discourse-related phenomenon, but also a result of particular properties of the domain of conversation combined with the perceptual abilities of the dialogue partners. In both cases, if an object is in the current focus of attention, reduced information to refer to this object can be used. We found that speakers used reduced information in more than half of the cases where the target object was located in the focus area to refer to an object for the first time. Speakers also tried to avoid using explicit relative features. They only used these features if this was really necessary in order to avoid ambiguities. The relata that were used were always either objects in the current focus of attention or salient objects.

An important finding from the experimental study was that references to objects outside the focus area are significantly more redundant than references inside the focus area. This showed that the notion of reduction of information is a complex matter that cannot simply be explained in terms of redundancy or ambiguity of information with respect to the whole domain. With respect to the type of descriptive features, we did not find significant differences between in or out focus references.

Limitations of the present study are mainly due to the type of referential acts that were studied (first references with the emphasis on the descriptive content), and to the choice of domain and the task that was carried out. Future research should be broadened to include non-initial referential acts, other tasks and domains, and other modalities of communication. Since the concepts introduced in this chapter are basic properties of almost every human communication situation, we expect, however, the results to be relevant for a broad field of applications.

Acknowledgments

This research was funded by the Universities of Brabant Joint Research Organization (SOBU). We would like to thank Kees van Deemter and Paul Piwek for extensive and useful comments on earlier drafts of this chapter.

References

Ariel, M. (1990) *Accessing noun-phrase antecedents*. London: Routledge.

Bennis, H. and Hoekstra, T. (1983) *De syntaxis van het Nederlands: een inleiding in de regeer- en bindtheorie*. Dordrecht: Foris.

Brown, G. and Yule, G. (1983) *Discourse analysis*. Cambridge: Cambridge University Press.

Clark, H.H., Schreuder, R., and Buttrick, S. (1983) Common ground and the understanding of demonstrative reference. *Journal of Verbal Learning and Verbal Behavior* 22:245–258.

Clark, H.H. and Wilkes-Gibbs, D. (1986) Referring as a collaborative process. *Cognition* 22:1–39.

Cremers, A.H.M. (1993) *Transcripties dialogen blokken-experiment (Transcriptions dialogues blocks-experiment)*. IPO Report no. 889. Eindhoven: Institute for Perception Research.

Cremers, A.H.M. (1994) Referring in a shared workspace. In M.D. Brouwer-Janse and T.L. Harrington (eds), *Human-machine communication for educational systems design (NATO ASI Series, Subseries F, Computer and Systems Design 129)*. Heidelberg: Springer Verlag, 71–78.

Glass, A.L. and Holyoak, K.J. (1986) *Cognition*. New York: Random House.

Goodman, B.A. (1986) Reference identification and reference identification failures. *Computational Linguistics* 12(4):273–305.

Grosz, B.J. (1977) *The representation and use of focus in dialogue understanding*. *Technical Note 151*. Menlo Park: SRI International.

Grosz, B.J. and Sidner, C.L. (1986) Attention, intentions and the structure of discourse. *Computational Linguistics* 12(3):175–204.

Herrmann, Th. (1983) *Speech and situation: a psychological conception of situated speaking*. Berlin: Springer Verlag.

Knapp, M.L. and Hall, J.A. (1992) *Nonverbal communication in human interaction*. Harcourt Brace Jovanovich College Publ.

Levelt, W.J.M. (1982) Linearization in describing spatial networks. In S. Peters and E. Saarinen (eds) *Processes, beliefs, and questions*. Dordrecht: Reidel.

Levelt, W.J.M. (1989) *Speaking: from intention to articulation*. Cambridge and London: The MIT Press.

Lewis, D. (1979) Scorekeeping in a language game. In Bäuerle et al. (eds) *Semantics from different points of view*. Berlin: Springer.

Loftus, G.R. and Mackworth, N.H. (1978) Cognitive determinants of fixation location during picture viewing. *Journal of Experimental Psychology: Human Perception and Performance* 4:565–572.

Mackworth, N.H. and Morandi, A.J. (1967) The gaze selects informative details within pictures. *Perception and psychophysics* 2:547–552.

Olson, D.R. (1970) Language and thought: aspects of a cognitive theory of semantics. *Psychological Review* 77:257–273.

Pechmann, Th. (1984) *Überspezifizierung und Betonung in referentieller Kommunikation*. (Dissertation). Mannheim.

Piwek, P.L.A., Beun, R.-J., and Cremers, A.H.M. (1995) Deictic use of Dutch demonstratives. *IPO Annual Progress Report, 30.* Eindhoven: Institute for Perception Research.

Quirk, R., Greenbaum, S., Leech, G., and Svartvik, J. (1972) *A grammar of contemporary English.* London: Longman.

Sperber, D. and Wilson, D. (1986) *Relevance: communication and cognition.* Cambridge: Harvard University Press.

Thomas, J.C. (1974) An analysis of behavior in the hobbits-orcs problem. *Cognitive Psychology* 6:257–269.

Treisman, A.M. and Gelade, G. (1980) A feature-integration theory of perception. *Cognitive Psychology* 12:97–136.

Part 2:

Multimodal Cooperation

Augmenting and Executing SharedPlans for Multimodal Communication

Oliviero Stock, Carlo Strapparava, and Massimo Zancanaro

Istituto per la Ricerca Scientifica e Tecnologica
I-38050 Povo, Trento, Italy
{stock,strappa,zancana}@irst.itc.it

Abstract. The adoption of SharedPlans as a basis for multimodal dialogues is discussed. An extension to the model of plan augmentation for discourse is proposed so that it applies for multimodal interaction. The proposed process exploits SharedPlans and Adjacency Pairs in conjunction to account for global and local collaboration. Finally, multimedia coordination is taken into account. An example is followed throughout the chapter to make the consequences of the proposal more concrete.

1 Collaborating on the Interface

Intelligent interactive systems can be considered as agents provided with the ability (to various degrees) of getting involved in an interaction with a human being. According to the BDI (Beliefs, Desires, Intentions) model of agency (see for example, Cohen and Levesque 1990), representations and processors must be developed so that an autonomous, artificial mind maintains a structured representation of its beliefs, develops concrete intentions from unconstrained desires, and in conclusion develops plans for actions, evaluates them and executes them, updating coherently its internal representations. In the case of multiple agents the situation also requires the representation of nested beliefs so that one can represent in the agent also the beliefs it maintains about the other agent's beliefs (and intentions) including the ascribed other agent's beliefs about the subject and so on. This subjectiveness is essential also at the level of plans for achieving the intended goals. The basis for collaborating lies in the sharing of these plans and in developing a structured set of intentions that converge, leading to a more detailed plan and contributing toward the overall result.

Sometimes the adjective 'multimodal' is applied to an intelligent interactive system to mean that it is able to understand and use different communicative modalities (i.e. spoken/typed natural language, direct manipulation, graphics, etc.) In these cases, the system's front-end to the user is designed to support the use of the different modalities and possibly different media are exploited. Usually, the front-end of a system is also the only channel it has with 'the rest of the world'.

A key point that motivates the discussion in this chapter, is that the multimodal interface is really a peculiar place where actions occur that may be

H. Bunt and R.-J. Beun (Eds.): CMC'98, LNAI 2155, pp. 89–112, 2001.
© Springer-Verlag Berlin Heidelberg 2001

considered as domain actions and communicative (linguistic and nonlinguistic) actions. This is true both for user actions and for system actions: when the system holds the initiative it performs some domain actions, some communicative actions, or actions of both kinds.

The interface is at the same time: (i) the sensorial organ of the system; (ii) the medium (or media) through which communication is realized, and (iii) a place where domain actions are performed by both the user and the system. In the old *teletype approach* this ambiguity was not present, as the very simple interface constituted only 'the ears and the mouth' of the system, that was otherwise blind and inert. Take for instance the following classical example (Grosz and Sidner, 1986):

Ex.1:
*1. **A**: How do I remove the flywheel?*
*2. **E**: First, loosen the two allen head setscrews ...*
*3. **A**: OK*

In the follow up (Ex. 2), in the multimodal case, the expert could have used a pointing act to express what he is saying in words.

Ex.2:
*1. **A**: I can only find one screw. Where's the other one?*
*2. **E**: On the hub of the flywheel.*

The developing of a coherent interaction between user and system, with the delicate aspects that this involves, is at the basis of developments of HCI. Talking about multimodal and multimedia systems, we must also consider the more complex aspect that one communication act can assume, as the medium or the modality are consequences of a choice and are not 'neutral', and as various more elementary acts across different media can contribute to the same communicative act.

What is the most convenient framework for studying coherent unfolding of multimodal interaction? Certainly the scientific community that has developed the most elaborate concepts useful for moving in this direction is the Natural Language Processing one. Dialogue processing is a complex area and most approaches have necessarily tried to focus on only some of the intricacies of the topic.

The types of discourse most widely studied in the NLP community are task-oriented ones, because the existence of a well-defined domain task that guides the communication simplifies the overall modeling. In general we can say that, following the theories of philosophers of language, it is widely recognized that communication is a purpose-oriented activity. Task-oriented dialogues are those types of dialogues for which this property is most evident.

Dialogue is most often modeled through planning and plan recognition processes. Different approaches have been proposed to this end (including efforts for representing the mental status of the involved agents in the various phases of the process and for establishing the rational basis of their behavior). Some of the most notable are Cohen (1978), Allen (1983), Litman (1985), Cohen and Levesque (1990) and Perrault (1990).

A recent proposal emphasizes the collaborative aspect of communication, by means of a peculiar kind of plans called SharedPlans. The theory of SharedPlans (Grosz and Kraus, 1993) is based on the notion of 'plans as complex mental attitudes' (Pollack, 1990) in which emphasis is put on the difference between the plans that an agent 'knows' (i.e. recipes for actions) and the plans an agent adopts (i.e. a structured collection of beliefs and intentions). The SharedPlan theory is intended to model interaction as a joint activity in which the participants try to build a plan (in the second way above) together: the plan is shared in the sense that both participants have a compatible set of beliefs and intentions. In this framework, communication is seen as the way in which agents agree on the various stages of the plan construction.

The difficulties of applying the SharedPlan theory to multimodal interaction arise from the double nature of the interface: some actions (especially the linguistic ones) are intended to augment the current SharedPlan while others are primarily intended to execute the related recipe, but at the same time, if these actions take place on the interface, in some way they contribute to the augmentation of the plan too. For example, if an agent is committed to do an action it must perform it and then inform the other agent of its execution: but if the effects of the action are apparent on the interface neither the explicit commitment nor the informing are actually necessary. In the above Ex.1, utterance 3 counts as a commitment to do the action, but the actual performance of the action could make that unnecessary. And, in relation to Ex.2, not every nonlinguistic action actually executes (part of) the recipe related to the current SharedPlan.

With the present work we discuss the adoption of such an approach. We try to introduce some elaborations necessary for the view of the interface pointed out above. Also, the original proposal of SharedPlans was concerned with what was called the *intentional* state of communication (Grosz and Sidner, 1990) treated at quite an abstract level. So one question is how to ground the approach in real exchanges, at least restricting the ambiguities, and without taking the complexity of the apparatus too far. This point becomes even more critical in a multimodal setting, where elementary acts can have widely different meanings, if considered out of local context.

In this chapter, we propose an extension to the model of plan augmentation for discourse by Grosz and Sidner (1990) and Lochbaum (1994) so that it applies to multimodal interaction: SharedPlans are meant not only to be augmented but actually executed. In certain cases, execution of domain actions counts as an augmentation as well.

2   Grosz and Sidner's Theory of Discourse Structure

The theory proposed by Grosz and Sidner (1986) considers discourse structure as composed of three distinct but interacting components: the linguistic structure (a structure of the sequence of utterances), the intentional structure (a structure of the discourse purposes) and the attentional state (the state of the focus of attention).

- The *linguistic structure* consists of the sequence of utterances, the segments in which they naturally aggregate and the embedding relations between segments.
- The *intentional structure* consists of the discourse segment purposes and relations that specify how segments contribute to the achieving of the overall discourse purpose and the relations among them. The authors suppose that these relations are of only two types: *dominance* and *satisfaction-precedence*. The former holds when a purpose is intended to provide part of the satisfaction of another one. The latter holds whenever the order of satisfaction of two segment purposes is significant.
- The *attentional state* models the focus of attention of the discourse participants. It contains all the objects, relations and segment purposes relevant at a particular stage of the discourse.

Although the three components are strongly connected (i.e. segmentation, change of segment purpose and change of focus space are mutually dependent), in this chapter we concentrate only on the intentional structure.

Discourses are examples of collaborative behavior: participants work together to satisfy both individual and joint goals. Discourses require collaboration on two levels: on the domain of discourse and on the discourse itself. The latter level includes turn coordination, appropriate use of referring expressions and collaboration with respect to the discourse purposes.

The theory of SharedPlans (Grosz and Sidner, 1990; Lochbaum *et al.*, 1990; Lochbaum, 1991, 1994) has been proposed for modeling collaboration with respect to discourse purposes.

2.1   The SharedPlan Theory

The SharedPlan theory, as developed in Grosz and Sidner (1990), Grosz and Kraus (1993) and Lochbaum (1994) extends Pollack's mental state model of plans (Pollack, 1990) to deal with the situation in which two agents jointly have to plan to perform an action.

The theory uses a first order logic augmented with several modal operators. The foremost of these are the Bel$(G, prop)$ operator for the belief of an agent G of the proposition *prop*, and the MB$(G_1, G_2, prop)$ operator for the mutual belief of agents G_1 and G_2 of a proposition *prop*.[1] Four types of intention operator are used:

---

[1] MB$(G_1, G_2, prop)$ is defined as Bel$(G_1, prop) \land$ MB$(G_2, G_1, prop)$.

- *Int. To*: is action-directed and commits an agent to means-ends reasoning;
- *Int. Th*: is proposition-directed and does not directly engender means-ends reasoning but constrains an agent to avoid adopting conflicting intentions;
- the corresponding potential intentions *Pot.Int. To*, *Pot.Int. Th* which are used to account for an agent's need to weigh different possible courses of action.

A family of ability operators, which encode requirements on an agent's ability to perform an action, are also defined: CBA (Can Bring About), BCBA (Believes Can Bring About), and the respective group operators CBAG (Can Bring About Group), MBCBAG (Mutually Believes Can Bring About Group). They cope with the fact that an agent's (or group of agents') ability to perform an act depends upon its ability to satisfy the constraints of the recipe for that act (see Lochbaum (1994)).

The notion of Full Individual Plan and Full SharedPlan are then defined as follows (for a more formal definition see Grosz and Kraus, 1993, 1996):

Full Individual Plan (FIP) Definition: *An agent G has a full individual plan at time T_p to perform act α at time T_α using recipe R_α in context C_α:*

$$\text{FIP}(G, \alpha, T_p, T_\alpha, R_\alpha, C_\alpha) \Longleftrightarrow$$

1. G has a recipe for α
2. For each constituent act β_i of the recipe
   (a) G intends to perform β_i
   (b) There is a recipe R_{β_i} such that
      i. G believes that it can perform β_i according to the recipe
      ii. G has a full plan for β_i using the recipe.

Full SharedPlan (FSP) Definition: *A group of agents GR has a full shared plan at time T_p to perform act α at time T_α using recipe R_α in context C_α:*

$$\text{FSP}(GR, \alpha, T_p, T_\alpha, R_\alpha, C_\alpha) \Longleftrightarrow$$

1. GR has a recipe for α
2. For each single-agent constituent act of the recipe, there is an agent $G_{\beta_i} \in GR$ such that
   (a) G_{β_i} intends to perform β_i
   (b) There is a recipe R_{β_i} for β_i such that
      i. G_{β_i} believes that it can perform β_i according to the recipe
      ii. G_{β_i} has a full individual plan for β_i using the recipe
   (c) The group GR mutually believes 2a and 2b
   (d) The group GR is committed to G_{β_i}'s success
3. For each multi-agent constituent act of the recipe, there is a subgroup of agents $GR_{\beta_i} \subseteq GR$ such that
   (a) There is a recipe R_{β_i} for β_i such that

      i. GR_{β_i} mutually believes that they can perform β_i according to the recipe

      ii. GR_{β_i} has a full SharedPlan for β_i using the recipe

  (b) The group GR mutually believes 3a

  (c) The group GR is committed to G_{β_i}'s success.

The notions of Partial Individual Plan (PIP) and Partial Shared Plan (PSP) follow from the above definitions when the agent (or the group of agents in the shared case) has not yet assumed all the intentions and beliefs required.

The notion of a SharedPlan for α can thus be recursively defined as the case in which a group of agents has either a Full SharedPlan for α or a Partial SharedPlan for α with a SharedPlan to achieve the Full SharedPlan for α.

In what follows, temporal elements in contextual arguments are often omitted for readability.

2.2   Modeling the Intentional Structure

The SharedPlan theory models the intentional structure in the following way. Let us assume that G_1 and G_2 are communicating about $PSP(\{G_1, G_2\}, \alpha)$ then *the purpose of the current segment DS_c is*

$$DSP_c = \text{Int.Th}(\text{ICP}, \text{FSP}(\{G_1, G_2\}, \alpha))$$

where ICP (which stands for Initiating Conversation Participant) is the agent who holds the initiative during the current turn. DSPs of this form can be recognized using the conversational default rule CDR_A:

Definition: Conversational Default Rule CDR_A

1. (a) Bel(G_1, [communicates(G_2, G_1, Desires(G_2, occurs(β), T)) $\wedge$
   (b)   Bel(G_2, ($\exists R_\beta$) CBAG($\{G_1, G_2\}$, β, R_β), T)], T) $\longrightarrow$
2. Bel(G_1, Int.Th(G_2, FSP($\{ G_1, G_2 \}$, β)), T)

The major limitation of this rule is that it requires an ICP to communicate the act that it desires to collaborate on at the outset of a segment (Lochbaum, 1994).

Finally, relationships between segments are established on the basis of relationships between SharedPlans:

– DSP_1 *dominates* DSP_2 if SP_2 subsidiary SP_1
– DSP_1 *satisfaction-precedes* DSP_2 if SP_1 temporal-precedes SP_2

Two augmentation processes are defined in Figure 1 (see Lochbaum, 1994).

Algorithm 1: Interpretation
Assume:
$PSP(\{G_1, G_2\}, \alpha)$
G_1 is the agent being modeled.
G_1 is the hearer and must interpret G_2's utterance. Let *Prop* be the proposition communicated by G_2's utterance.

1. As a result of communication, G_1 assumes
$$MB(\{G_1, G_2\}, BEL(G_2, Prop))$$
2. G_1 must determine the relationship of *Prop* to the current SharedPlan context:
   (a) if G_1 believes that *Prop* indicates the initiation of a subsidiary SharedPlan for an act β, then G_1 will
      i. ascribe $IntTh(G_1, FSP(G_2, \beta))$
      ii. determine if he is also willing to adopt such an intention
   (b) if G_1 believes that *Prop* indicates the completion of the current SharedPlan, then G_1 will
      i. ascribe $BEL(G_2, FSP(G_2, \alpha))$
      ii. determine if he also believes the agent's current SharedPlan to be complete
   (c) otherwise, G_1 will
      i. ascribe to G_2 a belief that *Prop* is relevant to the agents' current SharedPlan
      ii. determine if he also believes that to be the case (rgraph construction algorithm)
3. (a) if step 2 is successful, then G_1 will signal his agreement and assume mutual belief of the inferred relationship as appropriate
   (b) otherwise, G_1 will query G_2 and/or communicate his dissent.

Algorithm 2: Generation
Assume:
$PSP(\{G_1, G_2\}, \alpha)$
G_1 is the agent being modeled.
G_1 is the speaker and must decide what to communicate.

1. G_1 inspects his beliefs about the state of the agents' PSP to determine what beliefs and intentions the agent must establish to complete it (this set is called G_1's Agenda).
2. (a) if the Agenda is empty, then G_1 believes that the PSP is complete and so communicates that belief to G_2;
   (b) otherwise, G_1
      i. chooses an item from the Agenda to establish,
      ii. decides upon a means of establishing it,
      iii. communicates his intent to G_2;
3. unless G_2 disagrees, G_1 assumes mutual belief of what he communicated and updates his beliefs about the state of the PSP accordingly.

Fig. 1. Algorithms for the Augmentation Processes.

3 Augmenting and Executing a SharedPlan

Lochbaum (1994) discusses the augmentation process with reference to some examples; one of them is Ex.3. As we can see, it is notified that NM performs a domain action (to reboot saturn); yet in the augmentation algorithm such a decision is not expressed.

Ex.3:
1. **U**: *We have a connectivity problem between mars and saturn that we need to fix.*
2. **NM**: *Okay.*
3. **U**: *Please, determine the connection type for me.*
4. **NM**: *It's an intrasegment connection; they're both in Segment1.*
5. **U**: *Good.*

    Let's repair it then.
    Do a remote ping from mars to saturn.
6. **NM**: *I can't. Saturn seems to be down.*
    I'll take care of that first.
    <NM reboots the machine>
    OK, saturn's back up and the remote ping was successful.
7. **U**: *Good.*
    Verify mars' IP address for saturn for me.
8. **NM**: *The entry for saturn was wrong, but I corrected it.*
9. **U**: *Okay good. We're done then.*

As a matter of fact, NM performs a lot of domain actions besides the above one as it is made apparent by Ex.4.

Ex.4:
1. **U**: *We have a connectivity problem between mars and saturn that we need to fix.*
2. **NM**: *Okay.*
3. **U**: *Please, determine the connection type for me.*
4. **NM**: *<NM checks the type of connection between mars and saturn>*
    It's an intrasegment connection; they're both in Segment1.
5. **U**: *Good.*
    Let's repair it then.
    Do a remote ping from mars to saturn.
6. **NM**: *<NM does a remote ping from mars to saturn>*
    I can't. Saturn seems to be down.
    I'll take care of that first.
    <NM reboots the machine>
    <NM does a remote ping from mars to saturn>
    OK, saturn's back up and the remote ping was successful.
7. **U**: *Good.*
    Verify mars' IP address for saturn for me.
8. **NM**: *< NM verifies mars' IP address for saturn>*
    < NM corrects mars' IP address for saturn>
    The entry for saturn was wrong, but I corrected it.
9. **U**: *Okay good. We're done then.*

In order to better explain our ideas, we slightly modified the scenario above. We will presume the following situation: NM is a *super-user* while user is a *normal network user*, that is some actions are only executable by NM, for example to reboot a machine and to modify and IP address, while other are executable by both, for example to ping a machine or to determine the connection type. We suppose that natural language utterances are realized by speech, while actions are typed in as unix-like commands. Of course, this is only one possible scenario: we will not deal here neither with specific aspects of speech nor with the plausibility of the actions in a real environment.

In this scenario, the interaction above could reasonably become that of Ex.5. We shall suppose that NM is female and the user male. By the first utterance the user declares his intention to build a SharedPlan together with NM, the *Okay* of NM in 2 counts as an acknowledgment. Then, in 3, the user actually performs an action and its performance counts also as an implicit declaration of the particular recipe that he intends to use. We can note that, if NM had not believed that the determination of the connection is part of a recipe to fix a connectivity, she would have disagreed explicitly. Since she also believes it, she does not need to explicitly agree (except for 2 and the final turns there are no explicit acknowledgments in the interaction.) The same happens in the subsequent utterance (*Let's repair it then.*) which declares a subsidiary SharedPlan and the following action and utterances which begin to execute (and augment) it. In 4, NM executes the action the user asked her for, and as the action is performed immediately, she does not need to express her commitment linguistically. And because the user can see the action performed by NM, she does not need to inform him of the successful execution. Also, she knows (from the SharedPlan) that the action was part of a more general recipe, so she goes on and performs the remote ping herself.

The following Ex.5 will be analyzed in some more detail.

Ex.5:
1. **U:** *We need to fix a connectivity problem between mars and saturn.*
2. **NM:** *Okay.*
3. **U:**
3.1. > `type-conn mars saturn`
   `intrasegment`
3.2. *Let's repair it then.*
3.3. > `remote-ping saturn -from mars`
   `not responding`
3.4. *Saturn seems to be down.*
3.5. *Can you reboot the machine?*

4. **NM:**
4.1. > `reboot saturn`
4.2. > `remote-ping saturn -from mars`
   `saturn is alive`
5. **U:** *Verify mars' IP address for saturn for me.*
6. **NM:**
6.1. > `ip-address mars -from saturn`
   `123345`
6.2. > `address mars`

```
      334512
```
6.3. The entry for saturn is wrong.

6.4. > `set-ip-address mars 123345 -from saturn`
```
      123345
```
7. **U**:

7.1. Okay good.

7.2. We're done then.

In order to account for Ex.5 we need a way to formalize the notion of expectation: at a given stage in the dialogue only some particular contributions are reasonably expected. Furthermore we consider only felicitous contributions, while misconceptions and communication failures are not considered.

The intentional structure is meant to model discourse-level intentions and relationships among them (Grosz and Sidner, 1986); the treatment of utterance-level intentions and relationships among them is not expressed in the theory.

So we need rules that specify an expected range of responses to every kind of action performed, to guide both the system's interpretation of the user's actions and the system's performance of actions. Defeasibility is a required property in order to deal with occasional discrepancies between expectations and non-conventional communication. The kind of rules developed in Conversation Analysis (CA, for short) seems an appropriate choice, as we will see later.

4   Adopting a Modified Adjacency Pairs Model

Conversation can be seen as divided in *turns* where dialogue participants alternate at performing the role of speaker.

The primary unit of conversation (at the level of description considered by CA, that is local management) is the *adjacency pair* (AP, for short). APs are pairs of utterances that are (Levinson, 1983):

1. adjacent;
2. produced by different speakers;
3. ordered into a *first part* and a *second part*;
4. typed so that a particular first part requires a particular range of second parts.

The turn-taking process is modeled by a rule governing the use of adjacency pairs (Levinson, 1983):

> *Having produced the first part of some pair, the current speaker must stop speaking, and the next speaker must produce at that point a second part to the same pair.*

	Request	Offer/Invite	Assessment	Question	Blame
Preferred	acceptance	acceptance	agreement	expected answer	denial
Dispreferred	refusal	refusal	disagreement	unexpected or non-answer	admission

The simple model of conversation sketched above is too strict for many reasons (this has already been noted by many authors, see e.g. Levinson, 1983.) Before presenting some improvements, it may be useful to represent Ex.5 from the point of view of CA.

Utterance 1 is a request, that we can consider a request to build a SharedPlan: utterance 2 is its acceptance.

Utterance 3.2 is another request to build a SharedPlan (subsidiary to the first one); the user does not stop (he is not behaving according to the rule). If NM did not accept to build the plan she would have communicated her refusal; as long as she accepts it her acceptance is left implicit (i.e. as a rule of thumb, preferred second turns can be left implicit while dispreferred ones can not). The same goes for 3.4.

Utterance 3.5 is a request to perform an action, the performance of which in 4.1 counts as an acceptance.

In 4.2, NM begins a new AP, the decision to do so is derived from the necessity to execute the SharedPlan. In this case the first part is a domain action.

In 5 things are more complex, 5 actually is not a command (i.e. an utterance with a request illocutionary force) but a request-if. By that, despite its surface form, the user asks NM to check the truth value of a proposition of the kind: "Mars' IP address is correct". We are not dealing here with the problem of correctly inferring the illocutionary force of utterances but we suppose that some machinery does the job.

Thus, 6.1 cannot be the second part of utterance 5 because it is not the performance of a verification, and because otherwise 6.2 should be a first part of a new contribution. Instead, the second part of 5 is 6.3, while 6.1 and 6.2 together with their implicit acknowledgment are two APs inserted in the Request-if/Inform-if AP.

By 6.4 the NM opens a new AP (following the SharedPlan) which is then closed by 7.1.

Finally, 7.2 opens an AP the content of which is to establish mutual belief of the fact that the SharedPlan has been successfully built and executed. Again, the acceptance can be left implicit.

For our purposes, the CA model presented above can be modified in the following way:

1. the rule should be restated in order to consider also implicit (i.e. not expressed) second parts (in particular acceptances);
2. condition 1 should be relaxed to account for *insertion* between first and second parts;
3. in some cases, domain actions should count as contributions (either as first or second part of an AP):

(a) not only performance of actions but also execution of entire recipes can count as contributions;

(b) the range of domain actions or recipes that can count as contributions is constrained by the SharedPlan;

In the rest of this section an extension of the AP model is proposed based on illocutionary forces. In Section 5 an augmentation-execution process will then be outlined in which both the conditions outlined above and the need to relate the local coherence established by means of AP and the global coherence induced by the SharedPlan are met. Some restrictions on the kind of dialogues dealt with must be put forward:

− there are only two participants and the processes and data described are internal to one of them;

− the first utterance of each segment 'declares' the SharedPlan;

− an action can be executed immediately after the request.

We also assume the (too restrictive) hypothesis that both executions of actions and their results are always apparent to both participants. We will extend the discussion on this topic in Section 6.

Let us begin with the following Adjacency Pairs:

	Request	Inform	Ack	d-action
Preferred	Commissive action or Ack	Ack		Ack
Dispreferred	Inform		Inform	Inform

A Request has two possible preferred second parts, depending on the fact that it is a request to establish a SharedPlan (i.e. *desire* in Lochbaum, 1994) or a request to execute an Individual Plan (i.e. *communicate* in Lochbaum, 1994). Acknowledgements do not have second parts; we are aware that this is an over-simplification (see Traum, 1994)) but we shall not deal with this point here. When a domain action *d-action* realizes a first part an acknowledgement is intended as the preferred second part whereas an Inform has to be realized as a dispreferred second part.

We also propose two rules:

1. the hearer does not interrupt the speaker to realize a preferred second part
2. for some AP, if the agent whose the turn it is has more than one action to perform and one of these actions is the realization of a preferred second part, this can be left implicit.

The first rule accounts for the case 3 in which the user does not release the turn, and for utterances 4, 5. The second rule accounts for all NM's turns but his first one. Not all the second parts can be left implicit, in particular second parts for Request-If (and possibly for Request-Ref) should be always explicit.

5   The Augmentation-Execution Process

In this section we shall describe the main overall interaction process. Our proposal is meant to provide a basis for dealing with multimedia exchanges, as will become clear when, in the following section, we introduce a specific multimedia coordination component and discuss the revisited example.

We shall model complex interaction by means of an augmentation-execution process similar to the one outlined in Lochbaum (1994). The process makes use of various sources of knowledge; here we shall make particular reference to adjacency pairs. From now on, moving toward the multimodal setting, we shall speak of *message producer* and *message recipient* instead of speaker and hearer.

We propose to use APs to model local collaboration whereas the SharedPlan models global collaboration. The two levels are linked together by means of augmentation-execution processes. Following Lochbaum (1994) we consider two different processes, one for the interpretation phase in which the modeled agent is the message recipient and one for the generation phase in which the modeled agent is the message producer. Unlike Lochbaum (1994) we consider speech acts as input to the process (as far as linguistic contributions are considered). There are two reasons for this:

1. there is a substantial amount of experience in computational linguistics for dealing with speech act generation and interpretation;
2. with this view, all the input to the dialogue manager consists of actions, either linguistic or other.

We assume a default logic to deal with beliefs: beliefs are ascribed to both agents in the absence of evidence for the contrary. Besides, our process is intended to model a cooperative and felicitous interaction between two sincere agents. Some kind of truth maintainer is postulated to deal with the misconceptions arising when the beliefs of two agents do not agree.

In the specification of the augmentation-execution process we make use of the formalization proposed in Grosz and Kraus (1996) and in Lochbaum (1994).

We also assume the presence of an agenda where the intentions adopted by the system during the interaction are put and from where they are selected for planning actions. This agenda is similar to the one proposed in Lochbaum (1994) with the difference that it is organized in terms of contexts (in our example the reboot action in 4.1 is in the context of the preceding action of remote ping in 3.3).

5.1   The Augmentation-Execution Process I: Interpretation

The interpretation part of the augmentation-execution process is further divided into two parts: one dealing with first parts of APs, the other with the complex case of expected second parts.

The possibility of leaving the second part of some AP implicit is modeled by closing the AP and not enforcing a G_1 turn unless the closure is a dispreferred second part. This accounts for the fact that if G_2 releases the turn, G_1 must have the possibility to realize the closure explicitly or not, but if G_2 does not release the turn, G_1 should not interrupt him.

We shall first specify the process and then briefly comment on it. Assume that $PSP(\{G_1, G_2\}, \alpha)$; G_1 is the agent being modeled; G_1 is the message recipient and must interpret G_2's message. Let Act be the action (linguistic or not) performed by G_2.

A First Part Is Expected:

- REQUEST-CASE: $Act = \text{Request}(G_2, G_1, \beta)$
  1. if $\neg\text{cooperative}(G_1, G_2, \beta)$ then
     (a) close AP with DisPref
     (b) enforce G_1 turn
  2. else if $\text{FIP}(G_1, \beta)$ then
     (a) assume $\text{Bel}(G_2, \text{contributes}(\beta, \text{PSP}))$
     (b) if $\text{Bel}(G_1, \text{contributes}(\beta, \text{PSP}))$ then
         • $\text{MB}(G_1, G_2, \text{Int.To}(G_1, \beta))$
         • close AP with Pref
     (c) else
         • close AP with DisPref
         • enforce G_1 turn
  3. else *(the SharedPlan case)*
     (a) assume $\text{Bel}(G_2, \text{subsidiary}(\beta, \text{PSP}))$
     (b) if $\text{Bel}(G_1, \text{subsidiary}(\beta, \text{PSP}))$ then
         • $\text{MB}(G_1, G_2, \text{subsidiary}(\beta, \text{PSP}))$
         • $\text{MB}(G_1, G_2, \text{FSP}(\{G_1, G_2\}, \beta))$
         • close AP with Pref
     (c) else
         • close AP with DisPref
         • enforce G_1 turn
- INFORM-CASE: $Act = \text{Inform}(G_2, G_1, prop)$
  1. assume $\text{Bel}(G_2, prop)$
  2. if not holds that $\text{Bel}(G_1, \neg prop)$ then
     • assume $\text{MB}(G_1, G_2, prop)$
     • close AP with Pref
  3. else
     • close AP with DisPref
     • enforce G_1 turn
- REQUEST-IF-CASE: $Act = \text{Request-if}(G_2, G_1, prop)$
  1. assume $\text{Bel}(G_2, \text{Know-If}(G_1, prop))$
  2. if G_1 can assume $\text{Int.To}(G_1, \text{Test}(prop))$ then
     • assume $\text{Int.To}(G_1, \text{Test}(prop))$
     • assume $\text{MB}(G_1, G_2, \text{Int.To}(G_1, \text{Test}(prop)))$
     • close AP with Pref

   3. else
- close AP with DisPref
- enforce G_1 turn

- D-ACTION-CASE: *Act* is a domain action δ performed by G_2
  1. assume $\text{Bel}(G_2, \text{contributes}(\delta, \text{PSP}))$
  2. if $\text{Bel}(G_1, \text{contributes}(\delta, \text{PSP}))$ then
     - (a) assume $\text{MB}(G_1, G_2, \text{contributes}(\delta, \text{PSP}))$
     - (b) if successful(δ) then
       - if done(δ) realizes done(*Act*) for the act *Act* actually in focus then
         * drop the context of that act from the agenda
       - close AP with Pref
     - (c) else
       - assume $\text{Int.Th}(G_2, \text{achieve}(\text{done}(\delta)))$
       - close AP with Pref
  3. else
     - close AP with DisPref
     - enforce G_1.

As far as REQUEST-CASE is concerned, we are not using the Conversational Default Rules of Grosz and Sidner (1990); instead we model the difference between the request to begin a new SharedPlan and the request to perform an action exploiting the distinction between Partial SharedPlan and Full Individual Plan.

We can see that whenever G_2 makes a request for an act β (be it either a FIP or a PSP), G_1 assumes that G_2 believes β is useful for the current PSP (that is either β contributes to it or β is subsidiary to it). If G_1· thinks he can assume the same belief he also assumes the corresponding mutual beliefs.

The INFORM-CASE is similar: if G_1 does not assume the belief that *prop* does not hold he assumes the mutual belief of *prop*.

The D-ACTION-CASE is more complex. First of all, G_1 assumes that G_2 believes that the action δ contributes to the current PSP. If G_1 can not assume the same belief, he closes the AP with DisPref and takes the turn to explicitly express his disagreement. Otherwise, after having assumed the mutual belief of the contribution, G_1 reasons about the performance of δ. If he is not successful, G_1 ascribes to G_2 the intention to achieve the successful performance of the action (this accounts for cases such as 4.2 in our example, where NM performs an action already performed unsuccessfully by the user). Even if the action is successful, it could be the case that G_2 is performing not a single action, requested by G_1, but executing a recipe to execute the act; only when the act is completely realized it is dropped from the agenda.

A Second Part Is Expected:

- the first part was a REQUEST(G_1, G_2, β):
    1. the action requested was single-agent:
        (a) INFORM-CASE: $Act = $ Inform(G_2, G_1, $prop$)
            i. the current AP is closed with DisPref
            ii. assume Bel(G_2, $prop$)
            iii. if Bel(G_1, $prop$) then
                • MB(G_1, G_2, $prop$)
            iv. enforce G_1 turn
        (b) COMMISSIVE-CASE: $Act = $ Commissive(G_2, G_1, β)
            i. the current AP is closed with Pref
            ii. MB(G_1, G_2,Int.To(G_2, β))
        (c) otherwise,
            i. the current AP is closed with Pref
            ii. MB(G_1, G_2,Int.To(G_2, β))
            iii. start the augmentation-execution process again with Act
    2. the action requested was multi-agent:
        (a) INFORM-CASE: $Act = $ Inform(G_2, G_1, $prop$)
            i. the current AP is closed with DisPref
            ii. assume Bel(G_2, $prop$)
            iii. if Bel(G_1, $prop$) then
                • MB(G_1, G_2, $prop$)
            iv. enforce G_1 turn
        (b) ACK-CASE: $Act = $ Ack(G_2, G_1)
            i. the current AP is closed with Pref
            ii. MB(G_1, G_2, subsidiary(β, PSP))
            iii. MB(G_1, G_2, FSP($\{G_1, G_2\}$, β))
        (c) otherwise,
            i. the current AP is closed with Pref
            ii. MB(G_1, G_2, subsidiary(β, PSP))
            iii. MB(G_1, G_2, FSP($\{G_1, G_2\}$, β))
            iv. start the augmentation-execution process again with Act
- the first part was an INFORM(G_1, G_2, $prop$):
    1. INFORM-CASE: $Act = $ Inform(G_2, G_1, $prop$)
        (a) the current AP is closed with DisPref
        (b) assume Bel(G_2, $prop$)
        (c) enforce G_1 turn
    2. ACK-CASE: $Act = $ Ack(G_2, G_1)
        (a) the current AP is closed with Pref
        (b) assume MB(G_1, G_2, $prop$)
    3. otherwise,
        (a) the current AP is closed with Pref
        (b) assume MB(G_1, G_2, $prop$)
        (c) start the augmentation-execution process again with Act

- the first part was a REQUEST-IF(G_1, G_2, *prop*):
  1. INFORM-CASE: *Act* = Inform(G_2, G_1, *prop*)
     (a) the current AP is closed with DisPref
     (b) assume Bel(G_2, *prop*)
     (c) enforce G_1 turn
  2. INFORM-IF-CASE: *Act* = Inform-If(G_2, G_1, *prop*$^+$)[2]
     (a) assume Bel(G_2, *prop*$^+$)
     (b) if not Bel(G_1, ¬*prop*$^+$) then
         • assume MB(G_1, G_2, *prop*$^+$)
         • remove from the agenda the related intentions
         • the current AP is closed with Pref
     (c) else
         • the current AP is closed with DisPref
         • enforce G_1 turn
  3. otherwise,
     (a) start the augmentation-execution process again with *Act*
- the first part was a D-ACTION δ performed by G_1:
  1. INFORM-CASE: *Act* = Inform(G_2, G_1, *prop*)
     (a) the current AP is closed with DisPref
     (b) assume Bel(G_2, *prop*)
     (c) if Bel(G_1, *prop*) then
         • MB(G_1, G_2, *prop*)
     (d) enforce G_1 turn
  2. ACK-CASE: *Act* = Ack(G_2, G_1)
     (a) the current AP is closed with Pref
     (b) assume MB(G_1, G_2, contributes(δ, PSP))
     (c) if successful(δ) then
         i. MB(G_1, G_2,done(δ))
         ii. if done(δ) realizes done(*Act*) for the act *Act* actually in focus
             then
             • drop the context of that act from the agenda
  3. otherwise,
     (a) the current AP is closed with Pref
     (b) assume MB(G_1, G_2, contributes(δ, PSP))
     (c) if successful(δ) then
         i. MB(G_1, G_2,done(δ))
         ii. if done(δ) realizes done(*Act*) for the act *Act* actually in focus
             then
             • drop the context of that act from the agenda
     (d) start the augmentation-execution process again with *Act*.

The most difficult aspect in dealing with expected second parts is that G_2 can actually perform a first part implicitly while performing a second one. To deal with this phenomenon we suppose that whenever a contribution is neither an expected preferred second part nor a dispreferred one, the process continues

---

[2] *prop*$^+$ is the proposition that expresses the truth value of *prop*.

just as with a preferred second part and then it is started again on the same *Act*. The only exception to this is with the REQUEST-IF as first part: in this case the second part cannot be left implicit. The process is started again but the AP is not closed allowing for insertion of one or more other AP (see 6.1 and 6.2 in the example).

5.2   The Augmentation-Execution Process II: Generation

The generation part of the augmentation-execution process models the situations in which the system must produce its contribution. It is divided in two parts: the system has the initiative and it has to produce the first part of an AP, and the system has to close (i.e. to produce a second part of) an AP opened by the user.

Assume that $PSP(\{G_1, G_2\}, \alpha)$; G_1 is the agent being modeled. G_1 is the message producer.

A First Part Is Required:

1. If the current context on the agenda is empty, release the turn
2. else
   (a) if $Int.To(G_1, \beta)$ then
       - a new AP is opened
       - perform β
   (b) if $Int.Th(G_1, Int.To(G_2, \beta))$ then
       - a new AP is opened
       - perform a $Request(G_1, G_2, \beta)$
   (c) if $Int.Th(G_1, Bel(G_2, prop))$ then
       - a new AP is opened
       - perform an $Inform(G_1, G_2, prop)$
   (d) ...

This part of the process is only sketched here because it depends heavily on the agenda. The main idea is that for every intention assumed in the current context the system performs a communicative action, a domain action or a combination of the two types of actions (see also section 6).

A Second Part Is Required:

1. remove all open APs but the last one;
2. if the last AP should be closed with a DisPref, perform the required speech act(s);
3. if there are some tasks in the agenda and the last AP should be closed with a Pref, then execute the tasks and close the AP implicitly (i.e. do not perform the closure speech acts).

There are two problems with generating second parts. The first one is that more than one of the APs may have been closed implicitly during the interpretation part of the process. Thus in 1 the system implicitly removes all APs but the last one (of course all open APs but possibly the last one must have been closed with Pref). The second problem is to decide whether to express the second part explicitly. If it is a dispreferred act (see 2) it must be expressed explicitly, but if it is a preferred act (see 3) the decision depends on whether some other action should be performed in that context (see 2 in the example).

6   The Multimedia Case

In a multimodal environment, the dialogue participants can engage in complex nonlinguistic exchanges, for example starting with a clicking act on a button or menu. Domain actions and possibly non-linguistic communicative actions can be mixed. Although we do not want to address the problem of nonlinguistic communicative act recognition here (see Stock *et al.*, 1995 for a preliminary discussion), we contend that the augmentation-execution process shown in Section 5 is general enough to cope with multimodal communication in a uniform way.

Any intelligent multimedia system requires a component that exploits the dialogue context to make presentation decisions (media selection, coordination, allocation, etc...) or to interpret multi-channel input Maybury (1993a). We call this component the multimedia coordinator.

In particular, given information that needs to be displayed to the user, the multimedia coordinator builds a coherent and coordinated presentation using a combination of available media. For some proposed advanced multimodal presentation systems see Andre and Rist (1994), Han and Zukerman (1998), Maybury (1993b), Wahlster *et al.* (1992), Wahlster *et al.* (1993). As far as input is concerned the multimedia coordinator's task is to provide the appropriate media substrates and to integrate the various user actions.

Following Arens, Hovy and Vosser (1993) any complex multimedia coordinator needs to be built around a collection of models: a model of virtual devices, a model of the characteristics of information to be displayed, a model of the discourse and the communicative context, a model of the dialogue participants' beliefs, goals, attitudes, capabilities and interests. Input and output processes interact with the dialogue manager that maintains the discourse structure and ensures a coherent interaction between the participants.

An important point is whether action execution is observable (and in principle interpretable as desired) by the other agent on the interface. This depends on the ability of the multimedia coordinator to plan a meaningful presentation with the available media. The multimedia coordinator is instructed by the dialogue manager as to the communicative intentions and returns the planned presentation to the dialogue manager. The dialogue manager in turn evaluates the expected effects on the other agent, and whether the case requires further planning. For instance, in case the presentation is not perspicuous enough, the dialogue manager may decide to plan a further communicative action (for example an inform action).

We now revisit Ex. 5 and consider two different possible realizations in a multimedia environment, made possible by the apparatus described in the preceding sections combined with the multimedia coordinator.

First case: The interface is able to express graphically the fact that the system saturn is down. The domain action of rebooting saturn is perspicuous enough on the interface and there is no need for a further Inform communicative action.

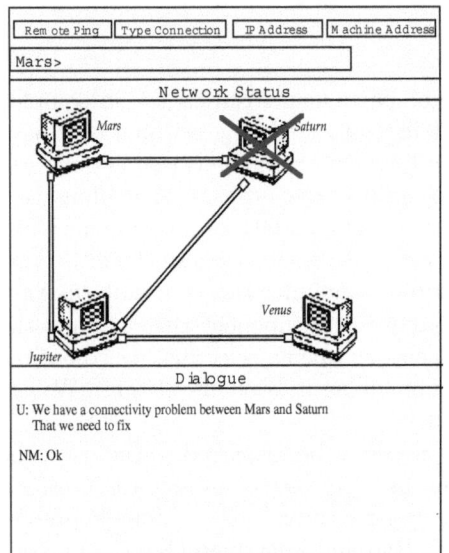
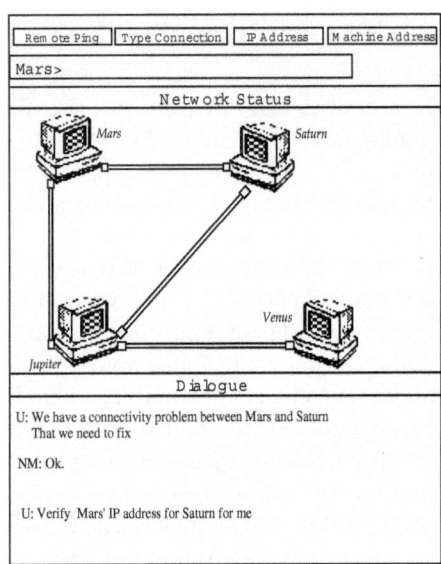

Fig. 2   **Fig. 3**

The user is working on mars. By the first utterance the user declares his intention to build a SharedPlan together with NM; the *Okay* of NM counts as an acknowledgment (Figure 2). By looking at the interface the user becomes aware that saturn is down. Immediately after (Figure 3) the user can see that saturn has been rebooted by the NM successfully and the NM does not need to inform the user any further.

Second case: The interface is not able to show the act of rebooting saturn, so the network manager has to communicate the result of the action linguistically.

The user is working on mars. The user's utterance (*Let's repair it then.*) declares a subsidiary SharedPlan. After selecting saturn on the interface (it now appears shaded), he chooses a remote ping action from the top menu. This action is the beginning of the SharedPlan execution (and augmentation) (see Figure 4). Saturn is not responding; the user asks NM to reboot the machine. NM reboots saturn, makes a remote ping on it (it knows from the SharedPlan that the action was part of a more general recipe) and communicates the success of its actions to the user (Figure 5).

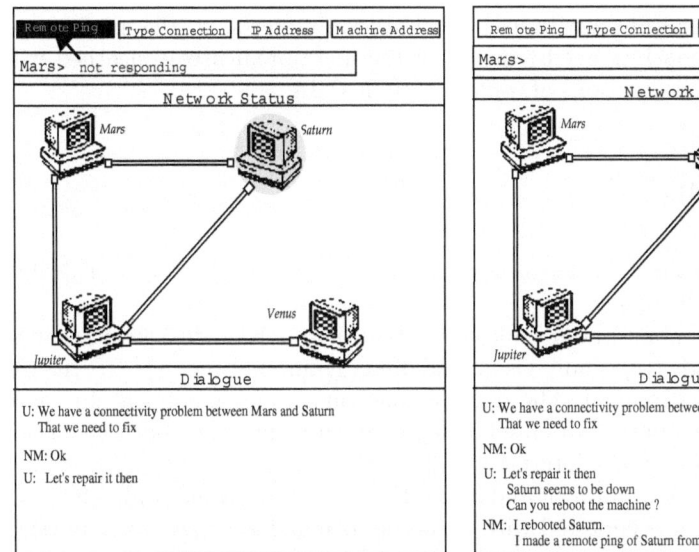

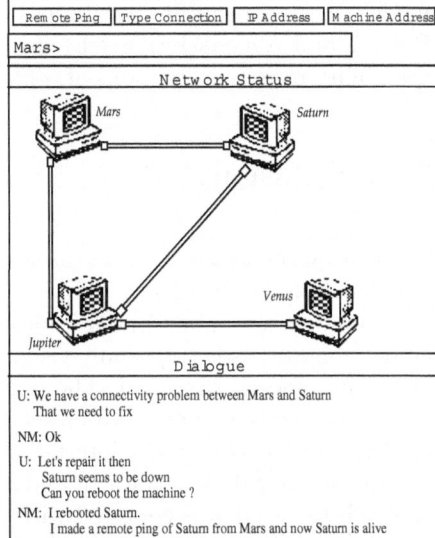

Fig. 4   **Fig.** 5

We conclude this section with the schematic representation of the architecture underlying the process discussed here.

The architecture is sketched in Figure 6. The core of the system is the Augmentation-Execution process, interacting with the Agenda via the intention operators (*Int.To*, *Int.That*, *Pot.Int.to*, etc...) and with the Recipes by means of the *contributes* and *subsidiary* relations and of meta-predicates such as FIP and PIP. The Augmentation-Execution process has access to the domain and user models via the belief modal operators (Bel, MB). It interacts with the multimedia coordinator, as seen before. The multimedia coordinator has access to the various media and related processors, to the characteristics of objects in the domain as conceived by the system, and to some global aspects of the user

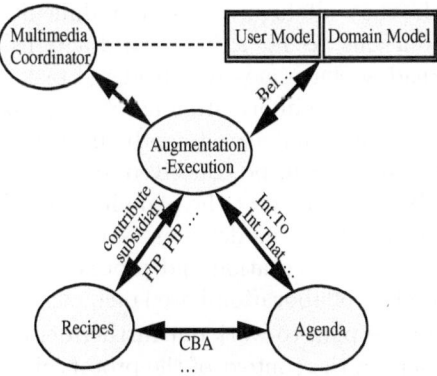

Fig. 6 Architecture.

model, in particular his attitudes, capabilities, interests, media preferences. Recipes and Agenda interact by means of the meta-predicates concerned with the ability to perform actions of a plan, such as CBA.

7   Conclusions

In this chapter we have discussed how to make SharedPlans a basis for dealing with multimodal dialogues.

A fundamental point of our approach is that in a multimedia setting that includes non-linguistic (especially visual and direct manipulation) aspects, the role of the interface is extended. The domain space and the communication space, traditional elements in task-oriented dialogue research, may well both be considered to be expressed on the interface. A clear illustration and recognition of this for the interface design can be found in the DENK system (Bunt et al., 1998). Of course if the system is endowed with actuators it may intervene in the physical world; similarly the user may act in the external world, but communication itself has a different meaning and extension with a multimedia interface than with a purely linguistic one. We have proposed a specific augmentation and execution process for SharedPlans that can accommodate our view. Two basic elements needed to also find their place: a) a 'local coherence' technique that could be combined with the higher level coherence of the SharedPlan approach that views communication as a collaborative activity, and b) multimedia coordination. For the first point, the adaptation of SharedPlans and its integration with elements of Conversation Analysis puts forward a promising direction of work. It permits also the integration of a multimedia coordinator, leaving to the overall dialogue manager the responsibility of evaluating the effects that all actions in the interface (explicitly communicative as well as noncommunicative) have on the user. We have tried to show incrementally how effective interaction can take place by extending the initial linguistic example to include multimodality.

In most of our previous work on multimodality we have dealt with explorative, information access dialogues (Stock *et al.*, 1993, Zancanaro *et al.*, 1994, Stock *et al.*, 1995). In these dialogues it is more difficult for the system to recognize the user's intentions, as far as real world actions are concerned. In the present chapter instead we have mostly considered task-oriented dialogues. We believe that in the explorative information access case the attentional aspect is more relevant; yet the intentional aspect can be fruitfully inserted as well. General strategies of exploration can be conceived, even if not every action on the part of the user can be interpreted at the planning level. Besides, some dialogue fragments certainly can only be modeled as task-oriented. A flexible combination of a more 'localist' representation and processing, such as the ones based on adjacency pairs and a collaboration-based one, can be appropriate also here.

In the near future, we plan to work out further details and experiment with the ideas described here in the context of the prototypical systems we are developing.

References

Arens, Y. E. Hovy, and M. Vosser (1993) On the knowledge underlying multimedia presentations. In M.T. Maybury (ed.) *Intelligent Multimodal Interfaces.* Cambridge MA: MIT Press.

Allen, J. (1983) Recognizing intentions from natural language utterances. In M. Brady and R. Berwick (eds.) *Computational Models of Discourse*, Cambridge, MA: MIT Press, 1982, 107–166.

Andre, E. and T. Rist (1994) Supporting passive and active viewing of multimedia presentations. In P. Johnson, S. Feiner, J. Marks, M. Maybury, and J. Moore (eds.) *AAAI Spring Symposium Series: Intelligent Multimedia Multimodal System*, Stanford University, March 1994.

Brady, M. and R. Berwick (1983) *Computational Models of Discourse.* Cambridge, MA: MIT Press.

Bunt, H., R. Ahn, R.J. Beun, T. Borghuis and K. van Overveld (1998) *Multimodal Cooperation with the* DeNK *system.* In H. Bunt, R.J. Beun and T. Borghuis (eds) *Multimodal Human-Computer Communication.* Berlin: Springer Verlag, 39–67.

Cohen, P.R. and H.J. Levesque (1990) Rational interaction as the basis for communication. In P.R. Cohen, J. Morgan, and M. Pollack (eds.) *Intentions in Communication.* Cambridge, MA: MIT Press, 221–256.

Cohen, P.R., J. Morgan, and M. Pollack (eds.) (1990) *Intentions in Communication.* Cambridge, MA: MIT Press.

Cohen, P.R. (1978) *On Knowing what to Say: Planning Speech Acts.* PhD thesis, University of Toronto.

Grosz, B. and S. Kraus (1993) Collaborative plans for group activities. In *Proceedings of 13th International Joint Conference on Artificial Intelligence*, Chambéry.

Grosz, B. and S. Kraus (1996) Collaborative plans for complex group action. *Artificial Intelligenc*, 86(2).

Grosz, B. and S. Kraus (1999) The evolution of sharedplans. In A. Rao and M. Wooldridge (eds.) *Foundations and Theories of Rational Agencies*, 227–262.

Grosz, B. and C. Sidner (1986) Attention, intention and the structure of discourse. *Computational Linguistics*, 12(3):175–204.

Grosz, B. and C. Sidner (1990) Plans for discourse. In P.R. Cohen, J. Morgan, and M. Pollack (eds.) *Intentions in Communication.* Cambridge, MA: MIT Press, 417–444.

Han, Y. and I. Zukerman (1998) Using Cooperative Agents to Plan Multimodal Presentations. In H. Bunt, R.J. Beun, and T. Borghuis (eds.) *Multimodal Human-Computer Communication; Systems, Techniques and Experiments*, Berlin: Springer, 122–157.

Levinson, S. (1983) *Pragmatics.* Cambridge University Press.

Lochbaum, K., B. Grosz, and C. Sidner (1990) Models of plans to support communication: an initial report. In *Proceedings of AAAI-90*, Boston.

Litman, D. (1985) *Plan Recognition and Discourse Analysis: an Integrated Approach for Understanding Dialogues.* PhD thesis, University of Rochester, 1985.

Lochbaum, K. (1991) An algorithm for plan recognition in collaborative discourse. In *Proceedings of ACL-91*, Berkeley.

Lochbaum, K. (1994) *Using Collaborative Plans to Model the Intentional Structure of Discourse.* PhD thesis, Harvard University, Cambridge, MA.

Maybury (1993a) *Intelligent Multimedia Interfaces.* Menlo Park CA/Cambridge MA: AAAI Press/MIT Press.

Maybury (1993b) Planning multimedia explanation using communicative acts. In M.T. Maybury (ed.) *Intelligent Multimedia Interfaces*. Cambridge MA: MIT Press.

Perrault, C.R. (1990) An application of default logic to speech act theory. In P.R. Cohen, J. Morgan, and M. Pollack (eds.) *Intentions in Communication*, Cambridge, MA: MIT Press, 161–186.

Pollack, M. (1990) Plans as complex mental attitudes. In P.R. Cohen, J. Morgan, and M. Pollack (eds.) *Intentions in Communication*, Cambridge, MA: MIT Press, 77–104.

Stock, O., C. Strapparava, and M. Zancanaro (1995) Explorations in a natural language multimodal information access environment. In M. Maybury (ed.) *IJCAI-95 Workshop on Intelligent Multimedia Information Retrieval*, Montréal, August 1995.

Stock, O. and The ALFRESCO Project Team. ALFRESCO: Enjoying the combination of NLP and hypermedia for information exploration. In M.T. Maybury (ed.) *Intelligent Multimodal Interfaces*. Cambridge MA: MIT Press.

Traum, D. (1994) *A Computational Theory of Grounding in Natural Language Conversation*. PhD thesis, University of Rochester, 1994.

Wahlster, W., E. Andre, S. Bandyopadyay, W. Graf, and T. Rist (1992) WIP: The coordinated generation of multimodal presentations from a common representation. In A. Ortony, J. Slack, and O. Stock (eds.) *Communication from Artificial Intelligence Perspective: Theoretical and Applied Issues*. Berlin: Springer Verlag.

Wahlster, W., E. André, W. Finkler, H.J. Profitlich, and T. Rist. Plan-based integration of natural language and graphics generation. *Artificial Intelligence*, 63:387–427.

Zancanaro, M., O. Stock, and C. Strapparava (1994) To the rescue of the lost explorer: Steps toward overcoming the problems in information access dialogues. In P. Johnson, S. Feiner, J. Marks, M. Maybury, and J. Moore, (eds.) *AAAI Spring Symposium Series: Intelligent Multimedia Multimodal System*, Stanford University, March 1994.

Cooperation and Flexibility in Multimodal Communication

Jens Allwood

Department of Linguistics, Göteborg University
Göteborg, Sweden
jens@ling.gu.se

Abstract. This chapter discusses cooperation in communication, with a view to future cooperative human-computer interfaces. First, cooperation and multimodal communication are defined and characterized. It is then proposed that cooperation can be extended into a notion of 'mutual flexibility' and this notion is subsequently characterized. In a following section, an empirical study of how verbal and nonverbal gestural means are used to achieve flexibility are presented. Finally, some possible implications for the design of future interactive systems are mentioned.

1 Introduction

The design of cooperative dialogue systems, new human-computer interfaces (Schomacher et al., 1995) and avatars in various types of virtual environments can all be improved by better knowledge of features of real human-human multimodal communication. In this chapter I discuss the nature of cooperation in dialogue. I will also discuss what might be called features of flexibility and conflict prevention and how they are related to cooperation. I will illustrate the features of flexibility and conflict prevention by examples drawing on video-recorded and transcribed human-human dialogue. The main focus will be on nonverbal gestural means, since verbal means are somewhat better known. The chapter is intended to illustrate how new ideas about the design of dialogue systems (Pandzic et al., 1996, 1997) will also lead to an interest in aspects of human-human communication that have received less attention so far.

2 Cooperation in Communication

The notion of cooperation may be defined as follows (Allwood, 1976 and Grice, 1975): Two or more agents may be said to cooperate to the extent that they

1. Consider each other cognitively in interaction
2. Have a joint purpose
3. Consider each other ethically in interaction
4. Trust each other to act according to 1–3.

H. Bunt and R.-J. Beun (Eds.): CMC'98, LNAI 2155, pp. 113–124, 2001.
© Springer-Verlag Berlin Heidelberg 2001

If all four requirements are met, we have ideal cooperation. Normally, only some of the requirements are met, and we may therefore speak of degrees of cooperativeness. Cooperation is not an 'all or nothing' phenomenon but a matter of degree. In dialogue, participants can be cooperative to a greater or lesser extent, rather than just cooperative or not cooperative.

In dialogue, participants cooperate through the contributions they make. These contributions in direct spoken interaction are multimodal, i.e., a *yes* can be replaced or accompanied by a nod, a *no* by a shake of the head, etc.

Let me now exemplify the four requirements mentioned above. The first requirement for cooperation – 'cognitive consideration' – means that A in interacting should attempt to perceive and understand what B is doing. This is a kind of base requirement for there to be any cooperation and communication at all.

The second requirement of having a 'joint purpose' means that both global and local purposes are jointly pursued. For example, A and B can cooperatively pursue the activity of teaching if they restrict their behaviour in accordance with the roles of 'teacher' and 'student'. On a local level it means that evocative intentions of preceding contributions are evaluated and responded to. So if A asks B a question, B should, if he/she is cooperative, evaluate whether he/she can answer the question and, if he/she can, do so.

The third requirement – 'ethical consideration' – means that A should consider and try to make it possible for B to continue interaction as a rational motivated agent, i.e., he/she should have correct information, not be given unnecessary pain, and be allowed to act as freely as possible.

The fourth requirement for ideal cooperation – 'trust' – means that A not only tries to pursue joint purposes while ethically and cognitively considering B, but also believes B to do the same, i.e., trust that B is acting in A's best interests.

Some Characteristics of Cooperation in Dialogue

Some of the main ways in which participants contribute to cooperation in dialogue are therefore the following:

1. Cognitive consideration: Contributions are based on cognitive consideration if they are relevant to what other interlocutors have said or done.
2. Joint purpose: Contributions are also cooperative if they further a joint purpose. This could be a global purpose of the activity or a more local purpose. Global purposes like negotiating, card playing or planning are sometimes but not always tied to specific topics, the pursuit of which furthers the joint purpose. Global structuring of an activity can often be indicated by various sequence markers, like *O.K.* or *right*.
3. Ethical consideration: Contributions show ethical consideration if they take other interlocutors' interests into account. One of the main ways in which this can be done is through supportive feedback signals of various types.
4. Trust: Contributions show trust if they rely on the good will and ethical consideration of other participants. This can, for example, be done by admitting fault or weakness, trusting in the good will of others.

3   Multimodal Communication

Normal face-to-face communication is multimodal (Duncan, 1974 and Heritage, 1984), employing several modalities of production and perception in order to share information.

The two primary modes of production are speech and various types of bodily gestures, perhaps primarily facial gestures, head movements and manual gestures. The two primary modes of perception are, accordingly, hearing and vision.

In this case, the spoken message will normally predominate, while bodily gestures provide additional information. The gestures are often, in turn, reinforced by prosody, resulting in a situation where utterances through words and grammatical constructions are given supplementary support by gestures and prosody.

Several different relations can hold between the messages produced in the different modalities (Cassell, 1995). One possibility is that they are more or less identical – one mode of expression adding redundancy and reinforcement to the other. Another possibility is that they are partially or totally different – one mode of expression adding information to the other. A third possibility is that one modality changes the message given by another modality.

If information is added, three of the possible supplementary relations between modalities in talk are the following:

(i) Adding emotions and attitudes to verbal messages by prosody and gesture. In this way, factual and affective information may be activated simultaneously, which is crucial to interpersonal cooperation. Another effect is that information about the identity of the speaker is given simultaneously with the message.
(ii) Adding illustrations to verbal message by iconic or conventional gestures. In this way, communication can become livelier and more engaging. Such gestures can also be used to specify or make the verbal message more precise, thereby increasing mutual comprehension of shared information.
(iii) Adding information pertaining to interactive communication management, i.e., giving information about who the intended addressee is, the length of one's utterance, a wish to speak etc.

When it comes to change, multimodal communication also adds to the possibilities of adapting or changing the content of what is communicated flexibly on-line. For example, it adds gesture to the means whereby a self-correction or other type of change can be made clear to an interlocutor (Allwood, Nivre and Ahlsén, 1990). There are also other ways of changing the verbal content through gestural modification; a message which, on a verbal level, looks like a straightforward statement can, through gestural modification, become something very different, like a joke or an instance of sarcasm.

4   Cooperation and Mutual Flexibility

If the analysis of cooperation given above is accepted, one of the consequences is that dialogue and communication can exhibit varying degrees of cooperativeness and be cooperative in several different ways. Two concepts which are closely related to several features of cooperation are what might be called 'flexibility' and 'conflict prevention'. They both involve cognitive and ethical consideration as well as trust. They encompass a range of phenomena in the service of the goals of keeping options open and preventing conflict or disharmony. They are therefore often a kind of prerequisite for more constructive and substantial cooperation in the pursuit of some joint activity purpose. Some of the means whereby flexibility and conflict prevention are achieved are verbal, other are nonverbal. Before discussing the various means in more detail, I will, however, briefly try to characterize the phenomena I have in mind.

Means of mutual flexibility and conflict prevention are communicative means which are used by participants to maintain one or several of the following goals.

1. Mutual friendliness
2. Lack of tension (tension release)
3. Lack of need to defend a position
4. Admitting weakness or uncertainty
5. Lack of attempts to overtly impose opinions on others
6. Coordination of attention and movements
7. Giving and eliciting feedback expressing mutual support and agreement
8. Showing consideration and interest
9. Invoking mutual awareness and beliefs

The properties in the list are not mutually exclusive but can be related to each other in various ways. Indeed, they often condition or support each other. I will now discuss the properties one by one and relate the notion of cooperativeness to them.

1. Mutual friendliness: Friendliness is related to cognitive and ethical consideration as well as to trust. Mostly, you don't hurt your friends, you trust them and you try to attend to their needs. Friendliness is, thus, a holistic attitude which promotes good feeling and a wish for continued interaction which is a good basis for cooperation. Even though friendliness is perhaps not a necessary feature of cooperation, cooperation is much easier if it is present and much harder if it is absent.
2. Lack of tension: Persons who intend to cooperate can often feel some tension, especially if they are not familiar with each other. If this tension can be diminished or released, interaction can proceed with increased flexibility and smoothness. Recognizing the need for, or at least allowing for, participating in tension release can thus be related to ethical consideration and trust.
3. Lack of need to defend a position: If we analyze the expressive and evocative functions of a statement (see Allwood, 1992), we find that statements, when used seriously in the most typical manner, serve, on the one hand, to express beliefs and, on the other, to evoke similar beliefs in interlocutors. If we add to this an analysis of obligations, we find that statements when used seriously impose a requirement on the speaker of sincerity, grounding and consideration of the interlocutor. Sincerity implies stating only what is believed to be true, grounding implies stating only what one has some grounds or evidence for, and consideration of the interlocutor means that one takes

the interlocutor's level of understanding and interests into account.

Although all these features of statements are desirable in some contexts, they do not necessarily allow for flexibility. Speakers have therefore adopted a number of strategies which allow statements to be used in a more flexible way. One of the ways is to make what is claimed by the statement so vague that it almost has to be true. This can be achieved by so-called hedges or other qualifiers that make statements vaguer. Two examples in English are *sort of* and *kind of*.

(1)   It is sort of ugly
(2)   It is kind of ugly

Use of these expressions has the effect of making a statement both more like a platitude and easier for an interlocutor to accept. It also keeps your options open for a flexible specification if you were to be challenged. Another way to weaken a statement is to remove or soften its truth claim. This can be done by indicating that it is not serious, or at least might not be serious.

Both the move of making statements vaguer and the move of making them less serious have the effect of diminishing their clarity and weakening their truth claims. In the case of a pure joke, the truth claim completely disappears. The effect of this, in turn, reduces the need to defend the statements, since it is not clear whether anything specific really has been claimed, which, in turn, removes or weakens the obligations of sincerity and grounding. Both moves, thus, represent ethically acceptable ways of lifting ethical restrictions which, if broken, might otherwise lead to rigidity and disharmony.

4. Admitting own weakness or uncertainty: Another way to increase flexibility is to admit weakness and uncertainty. This makes any statement or opinion expressed open to revision and removes the need to defend. If not exaggerated, this type of move can, by showing trust, help to create further trust.

5. Lack of attempts to overtly impose opinions on others: If we return to the analysis of the communicative functions of a statement mentioned above, we see that its evocative function is that the listener shares the belief expressed in the statement; i.e. an attempt to influence the listener. If the listener is cooperative, he/she has to evaluate whether he/she is willing and able to share the belief and in some way indicate the result of this evaluation to the speaker. If beliefs are expressed which the listener either does not want to share or is unable to share, this means that there is a risk of overt non-mutuality of beliefs. Since this is not desirable in discourse which is supposed to be smooth and flexible, there will be attempts to reduce the evocative force of the statements which are made. This can be achieved by the means just discussed, i.e. making statements vague, uncertain or non-serious.

An alternative strategy is not to reduce the evocative force of the statement but to accompany it by clear indications of friendliness, in this way dampening the potential irritation that might result from nonagreement.

6. Coordination of attention and movements: Flexibility and cooperation are also aided by coordination of attention and movements among speakers.

Means of this are perhaps primarily nonverbal, such as attending to speakers by gazing at them, or moving in synchrony with other interlocutors. Coordination of attention and movements is closely related to cognitive consideration, where coordination of movement might even be on a more basic level than cognitive consideration.

7. Giving and eliciting mutual support and agreement: An important ingredient in creating an atmosphere of flexibility, trust and consideration can be achieved by giving positive and supportive feedback to other speakers. This promotes activity and reduces insecurity and inhibitions. Some interlocutors use this strategy even when they do not in fact share the beliefs expressed. From a short-term flexibility point of view, this can be effective but, from a long-term perspective, it may of course raise ethical problems.

One of the most important ways of giving support and signalling agreement is through linguistic and more generally communicative feedback (Allwood, Nivre and Ahlsén, 1992 and Heritage, 1984). Feedback signals are one of the main ways in which cooperation is pursued in dialogue. Through communicative feedback, interlocutors can inform each other whether and in what way the following basic requirements of communication, but also of cooperation, are met:

(i)   continuation of contact
(ii) perception
(iii) understanding
(iv) evaluation and response to evocative intentions

Feedback signals can be related to all requirements of cooperation. Basically, they indicate cognitive and ethical consideration of a speaker's attempt to bring about shared understanding by directly signalling information as to whether this is successful. Their use is therefore a prerequisite for trust and the pursuit of further goals which require shared understanding.

Feedback signals giving these kinds of information in direct face-to-face communication are multimodal. They involve prosodic, lexical and syntactic features of spoken utterances as well as bodily gestures. However, feedback is not only given, it is also actively elicited in dialogue. By use of verbal means such as *right*, or tag questions, and nonverbal means such as raising a hand or an eyebrow, speakers actively seek feedback from other interlocutors in order to ascertain whether communication continues to be coordinated and cooperative.

8. Showing consideration and interest: Consideration and interest can be shown by attending to other speakers. It can also be shown by reacting clearly and by sympathetically showing, for example, surprise or pleasure at what others say. Finally, it is indicated through an interest in the reactions of others, something which can be overtly expressed by attempting to elicit feedback. Show of consideration and interest is, thus, a fairly direct manifestation of the cognitive and ethical consideration mentioned above as two of the features of cooperation.

9. Invoking mutual awareness and belief: Another function which is related to the ones already discussed is that of invoking rather than expressing

consensus. In English, this can, for example, be achieved by use of the phrase *you know* which when added to a statement (Aijmer, 1996) indicates that what is stated is already shared by the interlocutor, thus obviating any need for controversy.

5 Means of Achieving Mutual Flexibility and Preventing Conflict

Let me now turn to a discussion of some of the means of achieving mutual flexibility and preventing conflict. As we have already noted, the means can be both verbal and nonverbal. My focus will mainly be on nonverbal gestural means.

5.1 Verbal Means

Verbal means of expressing friendliness include various ways of showing liking and appreciation of other interlocutors, as well as refraining from showing dislike or non-appreciation.

As we have seen, verbal means also include use of humor, e.g. jokes, and making claims and evocative functions vaguer. They include expressions of uncertainty like *I don't know* and all the various means of giving and eliciting linguistic feedback by phrases such as *m, yes, yeah, sure, great, precisely, eh* and tag questions (Allwood, Nivre and Ahlsén, 1992). Finally, they include means of invoking consensus such as *you know*.

5.2 Nonverbal Gestural Means

The nonverbal gestural means of achieving mutual flexibility are perhaps even richer than the verbal ones (Mehrabian, 1971). Perhaps they are also more basic, since interlocutors often believe or feel that nonverbal communicative expressions are more directly causally linked to the true feelings and attitudes of a speaker and thus more genuine. A classification of nonverbal means of communication can be very detailed, which is what is needed, for example, for an analysis of deaf sign language.

However, since my main purpose at present is to capture some of the main nonverbal means of mutual flexibility and conflict prevention, I will here use a simpler scheme of classification, including only the following gestural articulators:

1. Head – head/movements e.g. nods, shakes, tilts
2.   facial gestures (other than smiles)
3.   gazing
4.   smiles
5. Laughter
6. Body posture
7. Movements of arms and hands

For each of these gestural articulators, I will now mention some of their main functions, indicating by the use of 'bullet signs' which of these serve as a means of achieving mutual flexibility or preventing conflict. In the tables below, the terms *indicate, express* and *show* are used more or less synonymously to refer to the manifestation of inner states through gestures. The list is based on an analysis of videorecorded and transcribed human-human conversations and is meant to be illustrative rather than exhaustive.

Gesture	Function
Head Movements	
Shaking the head	- rejection, denial both as a proper turn and as overlapping with another person's turn
	• agreement with negated statement both as a proper turn and as overlapping support of another person's statement
	- support of own negated statement
	• indicating bewilderment over content in own or other person's statement
	• non-insistence on point made
Nodding (the head)	• agreement both as supportive overlap and as own turn
	- reinforcing own turn
	- rejection of negative statement
Tilting head to one side	• accompanying own objection to soften it
	• eliciting feedback
	• indicating insecurity, shyness
Rocking head	• indicating lack of knowledge,
	• indicating humor
	• indicating bewilderment
Jerking head backwards	• "what do I know"
Raising head	• indicating surprise
Forward rocking	• eliciting feedback
Pushing head forward	• indicating surprise
	• indicating that someone else's statement is noteworthy
Facial Gestures	
Wrinkling eyebrows	• indicating lack of understanding of facts related
	• indicating something unpleasant in own utterance
	• indicating difficulty of finding the right word
	• indicating surprise at other's utterance
Raising eyebrows	• indicating surprise at other's utterance

Gaze

Gazing around at other interlocutors	• to elicit confirmation - to announce new information • observing reactions of other
Gazing at own hands gesturing	- directing attention
Gazing down	• breaking contact when silence occurs, avoiding confrontation - indicating insecurity
Gazing at handling of artefacts	• allowing for break and decrease of concentration
Gazing at speaker	• attending to speaker
Seeking eye contact	• elicitation of feedback

Smiles

Smiles	• indicating insecurity, uncertainty • giving confirmation • indicating friendliness • eliciting confirmation • removing seriousness • removing effects of own statement • apologizing • indicating self-irony • removing danger • indicating humour • indicating that something is daring or controversial • weakening opposition • indicating that something is unpleasant

Laughter

Laughter	• releasing tension, collective and individual • showing agreement, consensus, collective and individual • expressing surprise
Laughter + smile	• expressing uncertainty • indicating that something is a joke • indicating insecurity • giving confirmation • eliciting confirmation

Body Posture

Leaning forward	• showing interest
Body contracted	• indicating insecurity
Moving shoulders	• indicating that something is to be taken as a rough estimate

Movements of Arms and Hands

Fidgeting with clothes, hair	• expressing insecurity
	• tension release
Striking out	• tension release
Iconic illustrations	- supplementing content
Baton gesture	- emphasizing
Arms crossed	- indicating negative attitude
Moving artifacts	- obviating need for talk
Moving finger	- indicating waiting, expectation
Pointing	- symbolic or concrete deixis

If we try to summarize the observations on gestures in relation to the various ways to achieve flexibility and non-conflict mentioned above, we can see the following.

1. Mutual friendliness: Friendliness is above all expressed through smiles.
2. Lack of tension: Lack of tension is primarily achieved through laughter and hand movements, but also probably by downward gazing allowing for breaks of concentration.
3. Lack of need to defend a position: This is above all achieved by smiles softening the content, removing seriousness and apologizing, as well as by head movements indicating non-insistence and non-seriousness. There are also shoulder shrugs indicating vagueness.
4. Admitting weakness or uncertainty: This is achieved by head movements expressing lack of knowledge, lack of understanding, uncertainty, insecurity, bewilderment.
5. Lack of attempts to overtly impose opinions on others: The means mentioned in (3) and (4) above also serve to diminish the evocative force of the statements made.
6. Coordination of attention and movements: This is primarily indicated through coordinated hand movements and body postures.
7. Giving and eliciting mutual support and agreement: Support and agreement are primarily given through head nods, head shakes and smiles. Elicitation of feedback is done through gaze, head raising and smiles.
8. Showing consideration and interest: This can be seen in a gaze directed at the speaker or gazing around to see the reactions of other interlocutors. It can also be seen in clear, overt, friendly bodily reactions to other speakers.
9. Invoking mutual awareness and beliefs: Perhaps this is chiefly done by attempting to create an atmosphere of mutual non-seriousness.

The most important of the bodily means used seem to be head movements, gazing, smiles and laughter, and the most important functions of flexibility and conflict prevention seem to be giving support, showing friendliness, releasing tension, indicating non-seriousness and admission of one's own weakness or uncertainty. All of the means and functions are frequent in normal face-to-face communication. In interchanges that are characterized by cooperation, flexibility and conflict prevention, one or other of the means seems to accompany almost every utterance. This implies that multimodality is a crucial means of achieving these goals in normal human-human dialogue.

We have also seen that all three of the relations between verbal and nonverbal communciation discussed above – support, supplementary information and change – occur. Gestures can be used to support both your own contributions and those of others in different respects. They can be used for supplementary purposes, to give iconic or indexical illustrations, as well as for attitudinal information or tension release, or to change the message, for example, by weakening the expressive and evocative functions of different communicative acts.

6   Concluding Remarks

This chapter has explored some of the ways cooperativeness is multimodally manifested in dialogue. Claiming that cooperativeness is a matter of degree, it is suggested that it can therefore be related to phenomena like coordination, flexibility and conflict prevention. An attempt to analyze this relation is made by relating cooperativeness to nine subgoals for flexibility and conflict prevention. A further attempt to clarify the role of flexibility and conflict prevention is made by examining some of the nonverbal (and verbal) means to achieve these goals. Hopefully, the types of communicative flexibility and conflict prevention that have been discussed are of a fairly generic nature, even though they are, in fact, based on particular empirical data from Swedish face-to-face conversation.

Hopefully, they can therefore serve both to throw light on human dialogue and as an addition to knowledge about communicative functions which could be incorporated in the design of human-computer interfaces, cooperative dialogue systems, or avatars in virtual environments. We might, for example, pose questions such as the following: Should systems be friendly? Should they allow for release of tension? Should they sometimes be non-serious or vague? Should they be non-imposing? Should they be coordinated with the user? Should they give and elicit supportive or other types of feedback? Should they show consideration and interest, and should they be able to invoke mutual awareness and belief?

If the answer to any of these questions is yes, and there are already a number of systems which have some of these features, the next question is, of course, what means to use. With the advent of multimodal cooperative systems, it is more than likely that a lasting source of inspiration will be the way cooperation, flexibility and conflict prevention is achieved multimodally in human-human dialogue.

References

Aijmer, K. (1996) *Conversational Routines in English – Convention and Creativity.* London: Longman.

Allwood, J. (1976) *Linguistic Communication as Action and Cooperation,* Gothenburg Monographs in Linguistics 2, University of Göteborg, Department of Linguistics.

Allwood, J. (1995) An Activity Based Approach to Pragmatics. In H. Bunt and W. Black (eds.) *Abduction, Belief and Context in Dialogue; Studies in Computational Pragmatics.* Amsterdam: John Benjamins, 47–80.

Allwood, J., Nivre, J., and Ahlsén, E. (1990) Speech Management – On the nonwritten Life of Speech. *Nordic Journal of Linguistics* 13, 3–48.

Allwood, J., Nivre, J., and Ahlsén, E. (1992) On the Semantics and Pragmatics of Linguistic Feedback. *Journal of Semantics*, (1992, also in *Gothenburg Papers in Theoretical Linguistics*, 64, University of Göteborg, Department of Linguistics.

Cassell, J. (1995) Speech, Action and Gestures as Context for Ongoing Task-oriented Talk. *In AAAI Fall Symposium Working Notes: Embodied Language.*

Duncan, S. (1974) Some Signals and Rules for Taking Speaker Turns in Conversations. in Weitz, S. (ed.) *Nonverbal Communication.* New York: Oxford University Press.

Grice, H.P. (1975) Logic and Conversation. In Cole, P. and Morgan, J.L. (eds.) *Syntax and Semantics* Vol 3: Speech acts. New York: Seminar Press, 41–58.

Heritage, J. (1984) A Change of State Roken and Aspects of its Sequential Placement. In Atkinson, M. and Heritage, J. *Structures of Social Action: Studies in Conversation Analysis.* Cambridge: Cambridge University Press.

Mehrabian, A. (1971) *Silent Messages.* Belmont, CA: Wadsworth Publishing Company.

Pandzic, I., Capin, T., Thalmann, N. and Thalmann, D. (1996) Towards Natural Communication in Networked Collaborative Virtual Environments. http://miralabwww.unige.ch/ARTICLES/five96B.html.

Pandzic, I., Capin, T., Lee, E., Magnenat, N., and Thalmann, D. (1997) A Flexible Architecture for Virtual Humans in Networked Collaborative Virtual Environments. http://miralabwww.unige.ch/ARTICLES/eurographics97B.html.

Schomacher, L, Nijtmans, J., Camurri, A., Lavagetto, F., Morasso, P., Benoit, C., Guiard-Marigny, T, Le Goff, B., Robert-Ribes, J., Adjoudani, A., Defée, E., Münch, S., Hartung, K., and Blauert, J. (1995) A taxonomy of Multimodal Interaction in the Human Information System. *A Report of Esprit project 8579*, WP1.

Communication and Manipulation Acts in a Collaborative Dialogue Model

Martine Hurault-Plantet and Cecile Balkanski

LIMSI-CNRS, Orsay, France
{mhp,cecile}@limsi.fr

Abstract. We present in this chapter a dialogue model and an under-lying theory of action that we have developed and tested through an application that simulates a telephone switchboard. The main features of this model are that it rests on a theory of collaborative discourse, and that it allows for the treatment of both communication and ma-nipulation acts. The model thus allows for cooperative human-machine communication in a multimodal context where natural language (in our context typed rather than spoken) is used in combination with direct manipulation.

1 Introduction

We present in this chapter a dialogue model and an underlying theory of action, that we have developed and that we are currently testing through an applica-tion that simulates a telephone switchboard. The main features of this model are that it rests on a theory of collaborative discourse, and that it allows for the treatment of both communication and manipulation acts. The model thus allows for cooperative human-machine communication in a multimodal context where natural language (in our context typed rather than spoken) is used in combination with direct manipulation.

Our data is drawn from a set of human-human dialogues, selected and tran-scribed from a day-long recording of a telephone switchboard in an industrial setting (Castaing, 1993). The full recording consists of about 500 dialogues, vary-ing in length from a minimum of three exchanges (two by the operator and one by the caller) to almost thirty. In these dialogues, the switchboard operator has to establish a communication link, via the telephone, between the calling person and the person with whom this caller wants to talk, a task which may lead to many unexpected (and interesting) difficulties.

The sample dialogue in Fig. 1 illustrates the type of discourse provided in this corpus[1]. It provides an insightful example of the cooperation which is needed in such a task. It shows, in particular, how the cooperative behaviour of the speakers (C, the caller, R, the receptionist) is translated into actions, as well as the knowledge that is implied by this behaviour.

---

[1] Words between '//' indicate an overlap between the two speakers' utterances.

H. Bunt and R.-J. Beun (Eds.): CMC'98, LNAI 2155, pp. 125–139, 2001.
© Springer-Verlag Berlin Heidelberg 2001

(1)	C:	\<appel\>	C: \<telephone call\>
(2)	R:	CNRS	R: CNRS
(3)	C:	bonjour Mme euh je voudrais le	C: hello miss hm I'd like the
		– Mr. A svp	– Mr. A please
(4)	R:	Mr. A. //oui// quel est son poste	R: Mr. A //yes// what's his position
(5)	C:	c'est euh il travaille avec	C: it's hm he works with
		Mme Muzeu	Mrs. Muzeu
(6)	R:	Mme	R: Mrs.
(7)	C:	MUZEU	C: MUZEU
(8)	R:	j'connais pas Muzeu a m'dit	R: I don't have a Muzeu I don't know
		vous savez ou elle se trouve	do you know where she is
		dans quel...	in which
(9)	C:	hou la la la la c'est au LEI mais	C: oh well it's at the LEI but
		//ah oui effectivement//	//oh yes indeed//
(10)	R:	22-26 j'vous la passe hein	R: 22-26 I'll transfer you over to her

Fig. 1. Example Dialogue with Telephone Switchboard.

In this example, the caller wants to speak to Mr. A. The task begins with two actions, given in lines (1) and (2), that are part of a plan which allows the caller to establish communication with the receptionist. The first action is a manipulation action (dialing a phone number), while the second is a communication action uttered in response to the caller's action. The caller then states his goal (3), which the receptionist has trouble understanding. Her reply (4) is thus a request for confirmation of the name of the person that the caller would like to talk to. The caller confirms the information, but the receptionist apparently cannot find that person in her database. If she were not cooperative, she could have then just answered *I don't know Mr. A.*, suggesting an end to the conversation. However, as illustrated in our corpus, even if this type of response is uttered, it is always followed by a cooperative request for information. These requests take different forms: asking for a phone number, for the department where the person works, or for the name of an intermediary person. In our corpus, these alternatives are typically tried in the same order, apparently linked to the increasing complexity of the underlying plan. The caller's response in (5),*he works with Mrs. Muzeu*, shows that he is aware of the cooperative strategies of the receptionist and that he uses this knowledge in a cooperative manner. Although he does not provide the information explicitly requested (a telephone number), he does provide alternative information that will help the receptionist.

Thus, we may say that the caller and the receptionist have a 'shared plan' (Grosz and Sidner, 1986), namely one of allowing the user and Mr. A to communicate, and that they are both trying to achieve it together. The study of our corpus showed that, when a problem arises, receptionists use systematic cooperative strategies to allow the shared plan to be successful. The corpus also provides information concerning knowledge that is implicitly shared between the speakers. Indeed, callers often have knowledge (often correct) on the way receptionists achieve their task and they both assume this shared knowledge as long as one of them does not give indication of the contrary.

It is, among other things, this cooperative behaviour, and the knowledge it implies, that we wanted to model in our system and which we will present in this chapter. We will show that the system's cooperative behaviour is driven both by its knowledge (knowing a certain number of actions, and how to perform them) and by its reasoning capabilities (knowing when to perform these actions, and how to instantiate them). It is important to note that although the example described above contains only one manipulation action on the part of the user, the model is built in such a way that other manipulation acts could be treated without requiring additional components or knowledge (in addition to the representation of the action itself of course). Communicative and non-communicative actions are represented with the same structures, and they are reasoned about according to the same rules.

In the next section we describe our dialogue model. We begin by presenting its underlying theoretical basis – namely the theory of collaborative discourse developed by Grosz and Sidner (1986; 1990), and further extended by Lochbaum (1994; 1995), and then describe the architecture of our model, showing how our model extends that of Lochbaum's. In the subsequent section we describe the cooperative aspects of our model, first through the knowledge of the system, then through its reasoning capabilities.

2   Dialogue Model

2.1   Underlying Theory

Our model is based on the theory of collaborative discourse developed by Grosz and Sidner (1986; 1990), and further extended by Lochbaum (1994; 1995; see also Stock et al. in this volume). This work rests on the claim that discourses, like many other non-linguistic activities, involve collaborative behaviour. Grosz and Sidner (1990) used the example in Fig. 2 to illustrate the fact that collaborative behaviour cannot be explained solely in terms of the private plans of individual agents. The two agents in this situation have some sort of joint plan that includes actions by each of them.

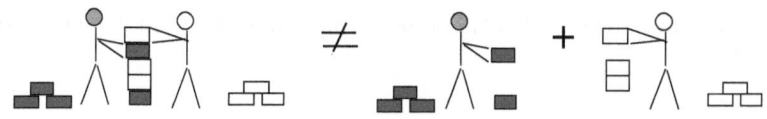

Fig. 2. A Collaborative Block-Building Example (Grosz and Sidner, 1990).

To provide a foundation for theories of collaboration, they introduced the notion of a SharedPlan. A SharedPlan is a construct used to model the set of beliefs and intentions that agents must hold for their collaboration to be successful, thereby allowing for an integrated treatment of the mental states of the agents involved. A high-level overview formalization centered around Shared-Plans is given in Fig. 3, which lists key components of the mental states of agents when they have a collaborative plan to do a group action.

To have a collaborative plan for an action, a group of agents must have :

1. mutual belief of a (partial) recipe
2a. individual intentions that the action be done
2b. individual intentions that collaborators succeed in doing the (identified) constituent subactions
3. individual or collaborative plans for the subactions

Fig. 3. Key Components of the Mental States of Collaborative Agents (Grosz and Kraus, 1996).

Items given in (2a) et (2b) reflect the commitments that agents must have to the actions of the group as a whole and to those of other agents. These commitments, which engender the cooperative behaviour of the agents, are formalized in Grosz and Kraus' definition of a SharedPlan definition with the Int.Th operator (*intend-that* as opposed to *intend-to*). Figure 4 provides two axioms centered around this operator, which represent the adoption of helpful, and thus cooperative, behaviour (Grosz and Kraus, 1996).

Axiom (A5)

G Int.Th some *prop* which G does not believe is true
and G believes it can do something (α) that will bring about *prop*'s holding
$\Rightarrow$ G will consider doing α.

Axiom (A6)

G Int.Th some *prop* which G does not believe is true
and G believes it can do something (α) that will enable another agent to do something else (β) that will bring about *prop*'s holding
$\Rightarrow$ G will consider doing α.

Fig. 4. Simplified English Description of Axioms A5 and A6 for Int.Th (Grosz and Kraus 1996).

The first axiom, A5, provides for direct help, while the second, A6, provides for more indirect help. According to A5, if an agent intends that a proposition *prop* holds, while not believing that *prop* holds, and believes that his performing an action α would lead to *prop* becoming true, then that agent will consider doing α^2. This situation is reflected in the dialogue given in the Introduction, when the caller realizes that the receptionist will not be able to transfer him over to Mr. A since she does not have his phone number. The caller thus performs the communicative action of informing her about the name of a person with whom Mr. A works, an action that will allow the receptionist to subsequently execute the required transfer action.

The second axiom, A6, applies in situations where an agent believes that his performing an action α would allow another agent to perform another action β that would lead to *prop* becoming true. Both these axioms assume that each agent has beliefs concerning actions and recipes known by the other agents, as well as beliefs concerning actions that it could perform to help them.

The need for SharedPlans does not mean that agents must necessarily have a full SharedPlan from the outset of the conversation (or of any other kind of collaborative activity). Instead, agents typically start out with a partial Shared-Plan, and gradually complete it with additional beliefs and intentions, acquired as the dialogue proceeds. For example, an agent G1 suggesting to perform action A, and the other agent G2 replying *OK* and then suggesting to perform B, shows that G1 and G2 mutually believe that G1 intends to perform A and that he is capable to do so (if it were not the case, G2 would not have answered OK^3). Utterances are thus understood (and produced) in terms of their contribution to the agents' partial SharedPlan.

Lochbaum (1994) subsequently proposed a computational model, based on the SharedPlan formalism, for recognizing intentional structure and utilizing that structure in discourse processing[4]. She introduced in particular a structure, named a Recipe Graph, or Rgraph, which we will be referring to in this chapter, and which she uses in her algorithm modelling the reasoning process by which an agent determines the relevance of an utterance to the agents' current partial SharedPlan. Rgraphs represent the beliefs of the agent being modelled as to how all of the acts underlying the agents' discourse are related at a given point in the dialogue, and that will therefore have to be performed by the collaborating agents to accomplish their individual and shared objectives.

---

[2] In the formal definition of this axiom, the agent is said to adopt a *potential intention to do* α, where potential intentions are used to represent an agent's mental state when it is considering adopting an intention but has not yet deliberated about the interaction of that intention with the others it currently holds (Grosz and Kraus, 1996).

[3] The *OK* is not even necessary for inferring the mutual belief. G2 simply not interrupting G1 is an indication of G2's implicit assent, and therefore of the adopting of a mutual belief.

[4] The intentional structure of discourse consists of the intentions underlying discourse segments (called discourse segment purposes) and of the relationships between them (Grosz and Sidner, 1986).

2.2   Architecture of the System

A schematic representation of our model is given in Fig. 5. In the telephone switchboard domain, we model two agents: the User, who assumes the role of the caller, and the System, which assumes the role of the receptionist. The User agent includes few elements: we do not know anything about his knowledge, but this agent will serve, in the future, to build a user model. The System agent, in contrast, has knowledge both about the task and about the dialogue; some of this is static and some is dynamic. Its static knowledge consists of a knowledge base of actions (basic or complex, communicative or manipulative), recipes (a set of constituent acts, with associated constraints, necessary for the performance of complex actions), and entities (objects, persons, which can be discussed and which appear as parameters of the actions).

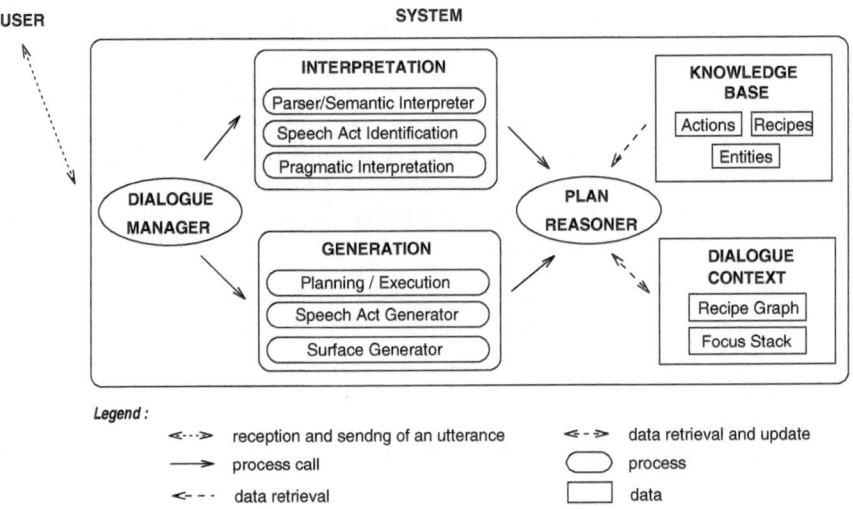

Fig. 5. Schematic Diagram of the Model.

Recipes represent what agents know when they know a way of doing something. They are represented by one-level trees, each node being an action, basic or complex. A sample recipe is given below in Fig. 6. The square boxes represent actions, the oval box gives the name of the recipe. This recipe reflects the fact that for a caller G1 to speak to a callee G2, he must first establish communication with G2, and then speak. Recipes include constraints which allow the system to maintain coherence between the parameters (agents, time, entities) of the actions in the recipe (and, after inclusion of the recipe in the Rgraph, between actions in the Rgraph), as well as temporal constraints on action execution and, when necessary, other contextual constraints. For presentation purposes, we represent graphically equality constraints between agents by using the same variable names, and temporal constraints by presenting the actions of the recipes in their temporal order. The agent of an action is always its first parameter.

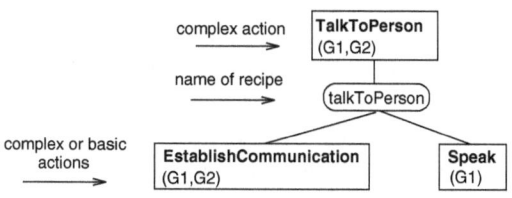

Fig. 6. The talkToPerson Recipe.

The system's dynamic knowledge consists of knowledge about the discourse context. It is updated as the dialogue progresses, and consists of an Rgraph and a focus stack, both of which are structures borrowed from Grosz and Sidner's work (1986), as well as that of Lochbaum's (1994). In this chapter, we focus on the Rgraph. Its role in modelling an agent's reasoning concerning another agent's utterances was presented in the preceding section. Below we describe the Rgraph representation and how this structure is used and updated by the reasoning process in our model.

An Rgraph is a dynamic representation, resulting from instantiating and composing recipes. It includes more information than just a concatenation of existing recipes. In particular it contains more specialized information by including instantiations of parameters, agents, and times. It also includes status information, indicating, for each action in the graph, its state in the agent's underlying plan. Finally, it also contains actions added to the Rgraph not because they are part of recipes, but because they are needed to allow the subsequent performance of other actions included in the Rgraph. Examples will be provided in the next section.

The system's reasoning capabilities are built into four main components, a Dialogue Manager, an Interpretation module, a Generation module and a Plan Reasoner, as shown in Fig. 5. The Dialogue Manager receives the input, a natural language utterance, sends it to the Interpretation module, then calls the Generation module to produce its response. The Interpretation and Generation modules call the Plan Reasoner when the reasoning required involves retrieving information from the knowledge base, and/or manipulating the discourse context. An utterance is thus viewed as an action which modifies the mental states of the agents involved.

When called by the Interpretation module, the Plan Reasoner's role is to perform the pragmatic interpretation of the utterance, updating the discourse context so as to reflect the contribution of the current utterance to the dialogue. It does so by using the Rgraph to determine if, and if so how, the performance of the act A underlying the current utterance is relevant given the system's beliefs about recipes and the current discourse context. An act will be relevant if a link can be found between that act and the act currently in focus. If a link can be found, the act A is added to the Rgraph. Building the Rgraph therefore means adding and then instantiating actions and/or recipes to the Rgraph, reflecting the system's reasoning process as it makes progress on the task.

When called by the Generation Module, the Plan Reasoner's role is to make as much progress as possible in the task underlying the dialogue and then to generate the system's response. The reasoning processes required are modelled by an algorithm which we call the Task Advancement algorithm. The goal of this algorithm is to determine which actions the system can perform, and in which order, so as to allow the overall task to progress. It also determines when to plan further actions, when to replan an action that failed, or when to produce an utterance and what it should contain. It does so by manipulating the Rgraph, making choices by assigning to the various options priorities guided toward action execution. The overall structure of the Task Advancement algorithm is a loop. Its initialization consists in determining the current action in the Rgraph (namely the first action to be performed in the temporal order of the actions in the Rgraph, or, if all actions have been performed, the last action performed); its stopping condition is verified when the system needs to produce a speech act, and its body consists in applying a number of rules to allow the task to progress. The choice of the rule to apply depends of the status of the action in the Rgraph. Status information evolves as the dialogue proceeds, and indicates, for each action in the Rgraph, the belief of the agent being modeled about its state in the agent's underlying plan, e.g., if it is only intended on the part of the agent, or has also been planned for, or has already been executed.

The main component of the discourse context, namely the Rgraph, was borrowed from Lochbaum (1994). Our work differs from hers in allowing the system to process dialogue openings, interleave execution and planning, and handle generation. Our model further substantially extends Lochbaum's model by providing an interpretation algorithm that allows for a more extensive search through the Rgraph than her Rgraph Augmentation algorithm and by developing a Task Advancement algorithm that gives the system planning and generation capabilities that her system lacks. Our interpretation algorithm, indeed, constructs the Rgraph in an upward or downward manner, and the search for a link between actions may lead to the addition of more than one recipe. Our Task Advancement algorithm is able to determine what to do next, whereas the implementation of the generation module of her system makes use of an 'oracle' (i.e., the user) for selecting a task (e.g., execute an action or instantiate a parameter) among all tasks that are possible at a given point in the dialogue. The Task Advancement algorithm is further detailed in previous work of the authors (Balkanski and Hurault-Plantet, 1997).

3   Cooperation

The cooperative behaviour of the system is made possible both through its knowledge of specific actions and recipes to perform in situations where a problem needs to be solved (because of incomplete or erroneous knowledge on the part of one of the agents for instance) and through the mechanism of task advancement, embodied in the Plan Reasoner, which allows the system to use this knowledge appropriately.

3.1 Cooperative Recipes

As briefly mentioned in the preceding section, the performance of a complex action, as opposed to that of a basic action, requires the performance of each action in its recipe, under certain conditions. Actions may have several recipes, that is, several ways of being performed. Most recipes in our application inherently involve cooperation between agents in that some of the constituent acts are to be performed by the user while others are to be performed by the system. The cooperative behaviour of agents also manifests itself through communicative actions, which allow agents to provide information when the other agent makes a request, or to keep the other agent informed of the result of manipulation actions that have been performed, thereby providing information on the status of the underlying task.

When a plan initially adopted fails, because of an action that cannot be performed, or because some information is lacking, then the agents have to make use of a different type of cooperation: they have to try alternative solutions, while exchanging information on the additional information that may be involved. This cooperative behaviour rests on specific knowledge that is the basis of a number of recipes which we call 'cooperative recipes'. For example, returning to the sample dialogue given in introduction, the receptionist used systematic cooperative requests when she had difficulties reaching her goal. These requests involved more complex plans than simple information retrieval, as initially planned for. As we will show, our cooperative recipes model these different cooperative strategies. Thus the system and user not only try to achieve a task together, sharing a common goal, they also know, and use, recipes to help each other reach that goal.

Figure 7 shows the Rgraph constructed by the Plan Reasoner during the planning phase following the interpretation of a simplified version utterance (3), *I would like to speak to Mr. A.*. This graph includes the status information associated with each action, referred to earlier, and indicates the state of each action with respect to the underlying plan. These statuses are given in Table 1. Thus, at this point in the dialogue, the EstablishCommunication(user,system) action has been performed.

As indicated in the Rgraph in Fig. 7, the system believes that to talk to Mr. A, the user first has to establish communication with Mr. A [5]. For the user to establish communication with Mr. A, he must first establish communication

---

[5] Complex actions with status 4 rest on the assumption that the system believes that the user also agrees with this particular recipe, or else it would have to ask for confirmation each time it selects a recipe, which would be an unrealistic burden on the dialogue.

134   Martine Hurault-Plantet and Cecile Balkanski

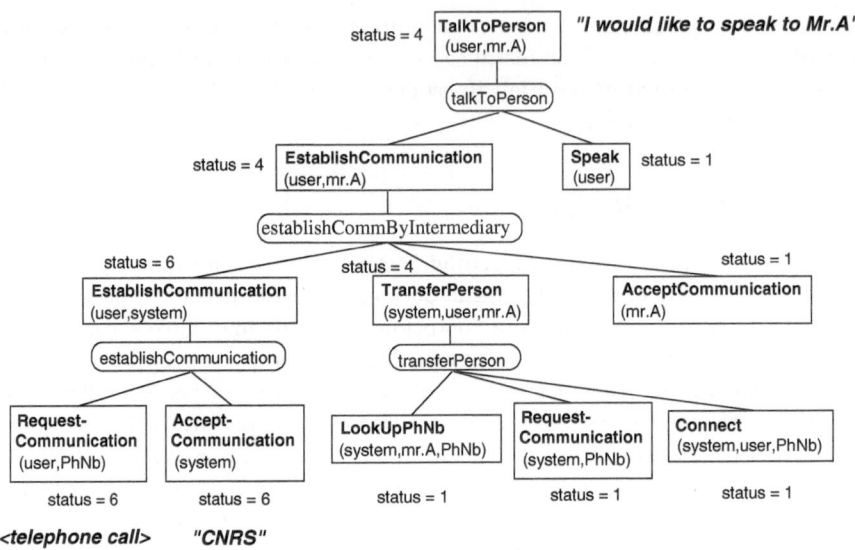

Fig. 7. Recipe Graph after Utterance (3).

Table 1. Action Statuses and their Corresponding Meanings.

1	the agent being modeled believes that the act will be part of the agents' joint plan
2	the agent being modeled believes that the agents agree that the act is an element of their joint plan
3	the act is basic and the agent being modeled believes that the agents agree to its performance
4	the act is complex and the agent being modeled believes that the agents agree to a particular recipe for the act
5	the act cannot be performed (repair is required)
6	the act has been performed, with or without success (if failure, no more repair of this act is possible)

with the receptionist (the system), then the receptionist has to transfer the call over to Mr. A and finally Mr. A has to accept the communication. For the receptionist to transfer the call over to Mr. A, he has to look up Mr. A's phone number (in his data base of entities), then request a communication with Mr. A.

The plan underlying this Rgraph may fail for a number of reasons: the receptionist may be temporarily unavailable (failure of the AcceptCommunication(system) action), Mr. A. may be away from his office (failure of the AcceptCommunication(Mr. A) action), or the receptionist may lack necessary knowledge (failure of the LookUpPhNb action). It is this last situation which occurs in our sample dialogue: for the receptionist to look up Mr. A's phone number, Mr. A has to be in his database, which's phone number, Mr. A has to be in its database, which is not the case. After an initial (and failed) attempt at resolving this problem by asking for the value of the person requested and his phone number ((4) *Mr. A //yes// what's his number*), the receptionist tries, on the user's initiative, a strategy consisting in looking for an intermediary person, whom both the receptionist and the user know, and who knows Mr. A. We model this strategy by using the transferPersonByIntermediary cooperative recipe, given in Fig. 8, and already instantiated with respect to the current discourse context. This recipe will replace the transferPerson recipe already included in the Rgraph.

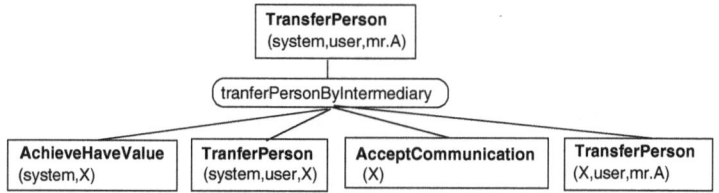

Fig. 8. Instantiated transferPersonByIntermediary Recipe.

The AchieveHaveValue action appearing in this recipe is a complex communicative action. Our knowledge base currently contains three recipes for this action, given in Fig. 9. The first, achieveValueByRequest, is used when G1 does not yet have a value for the parameter P, and leads to the generation of a wh-question. The second, achieveValueByConfirm, is used when G1 does already have a value for the parameter, and leads to the generation of a yes/no question. The v1 value indicated for the parameter P in the CheckValue action is the value that G1 is seeking to verify. The v2 value indicated for the parameter P in the ConfirmValue action will be the same as v1 if G2 answers positively; otherwise, v2 is the new value provided by G2. The v value indicated for the parameter P in the AchieveHaveValue action will then be equal to v1 or v2 depending on G2's answer. The ConfirmValue action is therefore a complex action, with several possible recipes, to model, among others things, the fact that a speaker may or may not provide an alternative value in the case of a negative answer (see Bunt (1989) for a possible formalization of different sorts of answer functions). The third, achieveValueByInform, is used when G1 is provided with the missing information without having previously asked for it explicitly. In our example, since the user provides the information identifying this intermediary person without being asked for this information by the system, this last recipe is the one which is used.

The selection of particular recipes, in this example, illustrates how the two intention axioms presented earlier in the chapter (see Fig. 4) are at play in situations where agents seek to assist each other. The user's utterance in (5), *He works with Mrs. Muzeu.*, is an example of a situation corresponding to Axiom 5. The agent G referred to in this axiom, here the user, intends that the system

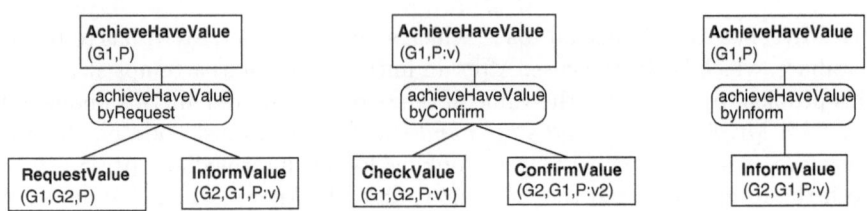

Fig. 9. Different achieveHaveValue Recipes.

transfers him over to Mr. A, but does not believe that the system will be able
to do so (since the system does not know the number of Mr. A). However, the
user, who does not know the number of Mr. A. either, believes he can make
this transfer possible by using an intermediary person, namely Mrs. Muzeu. He
therefore provides the necessary information to the system.

The use of Axiom 6 would correspond to a situation in which the system
would produce the following utterance, instead of utterance (4) given in the
initial dialogue.

(4) R: Mr. A //yes// I don't have a Mr. A.
      Would you know with whom he works?

In this situation, the agent G referred to in the axiom corresponds to the
system. It believes that it will not be able to transfer the user over to Mr. A, but
does believe that he could perform another act, namely asking the user for the
name of a co-worker of Mr. A, that will enable the user to do an action, namely
providing the missing information, that will allow the subsequent transfer action.

3.2   Generating the System's Utterances

The second way in which cooperation is embodied in our model is through the
use of cooperatives recipes, such as those described in the previous section, as
well as of communicative action, by the Task Advancement algorithm during the
planning phase of the generation module.

Actions in a Rgraph may be communicative, in which case the Task Advancement
algorithm sends them to the Generation module where they get
translated into utterances by the Speech Act and Surface Generator modules, or
non-communicative, and both may lead to cooperative behaviour. Communication
actions allow agents to come to share knowledge necessary to the success of
the shared goal. This was illustrated in the example of the Introduction, where
cooperation between the caller and the receptionist required that these agents
share a certain amount of knowledge. This shared, or mutual, knowledge may
exist before the initiation of the dialogue, or may be acquired during the dialogue
by information exchange between the agents. The acquisition of shared
knowledge is indeed a critical aspect of cooperation (Grosz and Sidner, 1990;
Bunt et al., 1995; Novick and Hansen, 1995)

Communicative actions are necessary on the part of the system either *as part of* the execution of the task, or *about* the execution of the task. The first type involves exchanges of information concerning additional knowledge that agents must share to be able to execute certain actions in the Rgraph, for instance, utterances concerning the entities manipulated by these actions. The achieve-HaveValue recipes, given earlier in Fig. 9, show the different ways in which agents may come to share information. They include the communicative actions of requesting, informing, checking, confirming, all relating to information concerning the value of an entity, that entity being used as a parameter of an action to be executed at some point during the dialogue.

For example, these communicative actions serve to model the initial, and failed, attempt at resolving the problem of finding the right instantiations for parameters in the transferPerson recipe, referred to during the discussion of the transferPersonByIntermediary cooperative recipe in Sect. 3.1. Figure 10 provides a partial representation of the Rgraph built by the system right after the generation of utterance (4).

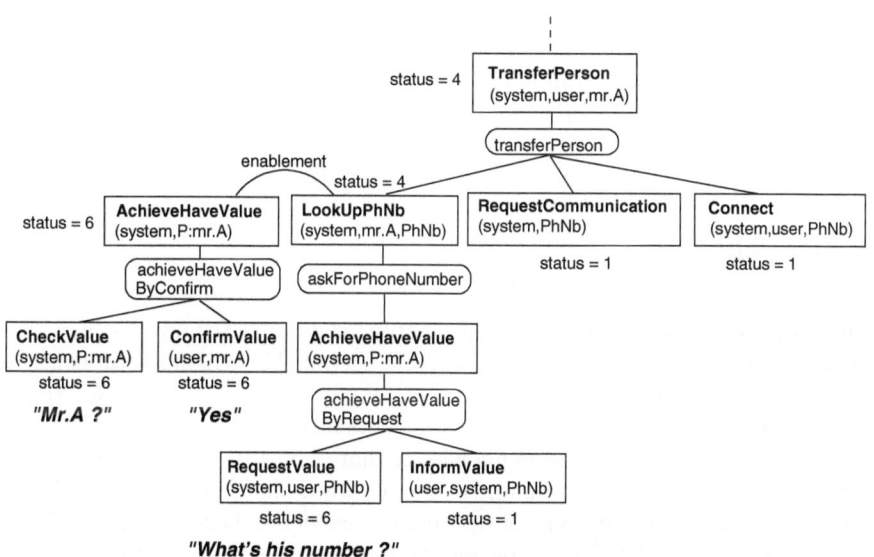

Fig. 10. Partial Rgraph after the System's Utterance (4).

As indicated in this graph, the system began by asking for confirmation of the Mr. A parameter value. This attempt is modelled by the addition of the AchieveHaveValue action to the graph, connected to the LookUpPhNb action by an enablement link (the goal of this action is to satisfy a knowledge precondition of the LookUpPhNb action (Lochbaum, 1995), thereby allowing, if successful, the subsequent performance of that action). Since the value of this parameter is confirmed, the LookUpPhNb action fails. The cooperative recipe askForPhoneNumber is then added to the graph. This recipe leads to the system performing the communicative action of requesting the phone number value to the user.

The second type of communicative actions, those involving information about task execution, consists of actions performed by the system to inform the user of the success or failure of an action, or of the necessity for the user to perform an action. These actions are also necessary for successful cooperation. They concern the status of the task, rather than the task itself, and are therefore at a level of meta-communication with respect to the task. Since the task is reflected in the Rgraph, these actions are not part of the graph, and are therefore not generated in the same way as the actions which are part of the graph. They are generated, for instance, when the Plan Reasoner has to execute a non-communicative task, but cannot do so and cannot find a cooperative recipe that will allow this action to succeed in this case; it then sends a failure signal back to the Generation module. This signal will be translated into an utterance in which the system communicates to the user that it cannot perform a given act, necessary at that point during the dialogue. Other examples of communicative actions that are not part of the Rgraph occur when the system decides that the next action to be performed is an action of which the user is the agent – in this case it sends back to the Generation module the result of the last action executed – or when it realizes that there are no more actions to perform – in which case it signals the end of the task.

4   Conclusion

The dialogue model presented in this chapter rests on a theory of collaborative discourse based on the mental states of the agents. This theory establishes necessary conditions regarding the beliefs and intentions of the agents for them to be able to cooperate. We showed how our model, resting on this theory, includes means of representing and using knowledge that allows an agent, namely the system, to act in a cooperative manner. Cooperation among agents in a dialogue, even when induced by the type of task being considered, is nonetheless a decision that has to be translated into specific strategies, i.e., actions and recipes.

Our model is currently being implemented in Smalltalk. We have a general interface, allowing the user to 'call' the system and to inspect its knowledge base. Our knowledge base contains information about the entities that were revealed by our corpus analysis, that is, actions, recipes, entities, as well as information about these entities. For our syntactic/semantic front-end, we use a parser based on an LFG grammar (Bresnan and Kaplan, 1981) and a semantic interpreter based on conceptual graphs (Sowa, 1984) that have been developed by members of our research group (Briffault et al., 1997). The component that has been completely implemented is the Plan Reasoner, with the associated Interpretation and Task Advancement algorithms. Future extensions to our implemented system include a wider coverage of the syntactic and semantic interpreter, as well as additional recipes to be able to test our model in situations where the knowledge base is larger.

References

Balkanski, C. and Hurault-Plantet, M. (1997) Communicative Actions in a Dialogue Model for Cooperative Discourse: an initial report. In: *Proceedings of AAAI Fall 1997 Symposium on communicative action in humans and machines*. Cambridge, MA.

Bresnan, J. and Kaplan, R. (1981) Lexical functional grammar: a formal system for grammatical representation. In: Bresnan, J. (ed.) *The mental representation of grammatical relations*. MIT Press, Cambridge, MA.

Briffault, X., Chibout, K., Sabah, G., and Vapillon, J. (1997) An object-oriented linguistic engineering environment using Lexical Functional Grammar and Conceptual Graphs. In: *Proceedings of The Lexical Functional Grammar Conference*. University of California, San Diego, CA.

Bunt, H.C. (1989) Information dialogues as communicative action in relation to partner modelling and information processing. In: M.M. Taylor, F. Néel, and D.G. Bouwhuis (eds.) *The structure of multimodal dialogue*. North-Holland, Amsterdam, 47–73.

Bunt, H.C., Ahn, R., Beun, R.J., Borghuis, T., and van Overveld, K. (1995) Multimodal Cooperation with the DenK System. In: H.C.Bunt, R.J.Beun, and T.Borghuis (eds.) *Multimodal Human-Computer Communication*. Springer Verlag, Berlin, 39–67.

Castaing, M.F. (1993) *Corpus de dialogues enregistrés dans un standard téléphonique*. Notes et documents LIMSI 93-9, LIMSI/CNRS, Orsay.

Grosz, B.J.and Sidner, C.L. 1986. Attention, intentions, and the structure of discourse. *Computational Linguistics* 12(3):175–204.

Grosz, B.J. and Sidner, C.L. (1990) Plans for discourse. Intentions and Communication. In: Cohen, P.R., Morgan, J.L., and Pollack, M.E. (eds.). *Intentions in Communication*. MIT Press, Cambridge, MA, 417–444.

Grosz, B.J. and Kraus, S. (1996) Collaborative plans for complex group action. *Artificial Intelligence 86(2)*.

Lochbaum, K.E. (1994) *Using collaborative plans to model the intentional structure of discourse* TR-25-94, Harvard University, Ph.D. dissertation, Cambridge, MA.

Lochbaum, K.E. (1995) The use of knowledge preconditions in language processing. In: *Proceedings of IJCAI'95*, 1260–1266.

Novick, D.G. and Hansen, B. (1995) Mutuality Strategies for Reference in Task-Oriented Dialogue. In: *Proceedings of the Ninth Twente Workshop on Language Technology on Corpus-based Approaches to Dialogue Modelling*. University of Twente, Enschede, The Netherlands.

Sowa, J. (1984) *Conceptual Structures: Information Processing in Man and Machine*. Addison-Wesley, Reading, MA.

Stock, O., Strapparava, C., and Zancanaro, M. (2001) Augmenting and Executing SharedPlans for Multimodal Communication. *This volume, pp. 89–112*.

Relating Imperatives to Action

Paul Piwek

ITRI, University of Brighton, Brighton, UK
Paul.Piwek@itri.bton.ac.uk

Abstract. The aim of this chapter is to provide an analysis of the use of logically complex imperatives, in particular, imperatives of the form *Do A_1 or A_2* and *Do A, if B*. We argue for an analysis of imperatives in terms of classical logic which takes into account the influence of background information on imperatives. We show that by doing so one can avoid some counter-intuitive results which have been associated with analyses of imperatives in terms of classical logic. In particular, I address Hamblin's observations concerning rule-like imperatives and Ross' Paradox. The analysis is carried out within an agent-based logical framework. This analysis explicates what it means for an agent to have a successful policy for action with respect to satisfying his or her commitments, where some of these commitments have been introduced as a result of imperative language use.

1   Introduction

Imperatives[1] are typically used to get an addressee to do something. As a result, a key notion in the analysis of imperatives is the notion of the *satisfaction of an imperative* (by its addressee). Understanding the meaning of an imperative involves knowing under which circumstances it has been satisfied. Various authors, notably Stenius (1967) and Searle (1969), have proposed that we analyse this notion of *satisfaction* by assuming that an imperative conveys both a proposition and the instruction to make this proposition true. For instance, the imperative *Get off the table* conveys the proposition *that the addressee gets off the table* and the instruction that *the addressee makes it true that s/he gets off the table*. Whether or not an imperative has been satisfied can now be understood in terms of whether its propositional content has been made true. Although this account of imperatives sounds plausible, it has been shown to give rise to some apparently counter-intuitive results once it is formalised by means of classical (predicate) logic. In this chapter, we discuss a number of these results and demonstrate how they can be avoided by embedding the aforementioned type

---

[1] We will use the word 'imperative' as a short-hand for 'the utterance of an imperative clause'. Imperative clauses are traditionally characterised by the lack of a subject, the use of a base form of the verb, and the absence of modals as well as tense and aspect markers. Examples of naturally occurring imperatives are: *Get off the table, Don't forget about the deposit* and *Hold on, are we late?*. This definition and the examples are taken from Biber et al. (1999:219).

H. Bunt and R.-J. Beun (Eds.): CMC'98, LNAI 2155, pp. 140–155, 2001.
© Springer-Verlag Berlin Heidelberg 2001

of analysis in an agent-based model which takes into account the influence of background information on the use of imperatives.

2   The Puzzle of Logically Complex Imperatives

Let me indicate how a formalisation of the aforementioned analysis of imperatives appears to give rise to counter-intuitive results. In such a formalisation, the propositional content of imperatives is represented by means of predicate logical sentences. More precisely, there is a function f_C which maps an imperative clause, given some utterance context C, to a predicate logical representation of its propositional content. In particular, the natural language connective *or* is rendered by means of the logical disjunction '$\vee$' and the natural language construction '..., if ...' is represented by means of the material conditional '$\rightarrow$':

(1) $f_C(A_1 \ or \ A_2) = f_C(A_1) \vee f_C(A_2)$.

(2) $f_C(A, \ if \ B) = f_C(B) \rightarrow f_C(A)$.

The notion of the satisfaction of an imperative is defined in terms of the truth of the propositional content of the imperative in a model M of the actual world:

(3)   SATISFACTION
       Imperative **I**, uttered in context C to addressee A, has been *satisfied* in
       a world represented by model M, if and only if A makes it the case that
       $f_C(\mathbf{I})$ is true in the world represented by M.

In words, an imperative has been satisfied if and only if its addressee made its content true. A first possible objection to this definition is that the mere fact that the addressee made the content true is too weak, especially if we read 'satisfied' as 'complied with': consider a situation in which a person is told to get off a table and subsequently accidentally stumbles and falls off that table. In that situation, the propositional content of the imperative has been made true. Nevertheless, one would not want to claim that the person really complied with the imperative: his or her action was not influenced in the *appropriate way* by the utterance of the imperative clause.[2] The problem can be resolved by making a clear distinction between the notion of *satisfaction* of an imperative, and the notion of an addressee *complying with* an imperative. For the moment, let us assume that we are studying the former and look at another problem which casts a shadow over definition (3). Take a rule-like imperative such as:

---

[2] Suppose that the addressee of the imperative was a person named 'John' and the issuer a person named 'Mary'. In that situation, the following discourse would be, if not an infelicitous, certainly a misleading description of what took place: *Mary told John to get of the table and he complied.* Note that in the aforementioned situation *Mary told John to get of the table. He did not comply.* seems equally infelicitous/misleading, which suggests that 'A complied with imperative **I**' presupposes (rather than that it asserts) that A's action was influenced in the *appropriate way* by the utterance of **I**.

(4)   Make a cross, if you encounter a vampire.

In line with (2), the propositional content of this imperative is rendered by the following predicate logical sentence[3], assuming that the addressee's name is John:

(5) $encounter\_vampire(john) \rightarrow make\_cross(john)$

In words, if the addressee encounters a vampire, then he makes a cross. In classical logic the formulae of the form $p \rightarrow q$ and $\neg p \vee q$ (i.e., it is not the case that p or it is the case that q) express the same proposition: whenever one of them is true/false, the other one is as well. Thus, the propositional content of our imperative can also be expressed by the formula in (6).

(6) $\neg encounter\_vampire(john) \vee make\_cross(john)$

By combining this with the definition (3) we obtain: the imperative in (4) has been satisfied by John if and only if John makes at least one of the following two formulae true:

(7)   a. $\neg encounter\_vampire(john)$
        b. $make\_cross(john)$

According to this analysis, one possible way of satisfying the imperative would be for the addressee to simply avoid encountering a vampire (cf. Hamblin, 1987:84). In some sense, it is correct that in that case the imperative is satisfied (and even complied with), as predicted by definition (3). Still, we are left with the feeling (and hopefully the reader too) that the definition provides a very incomplete and potentially misleading analysis of the relation between imperatives and the actions which they give rise to. Imagine that the addressee of the imperative is interviewed and asked why he was avoiding vampires. What could the addressee reply to this question? Would it, for instance, be appropriate for him to say: *I avoided vampires because I was told that if I see one, I should make a cross?* To me, this answer sounds odd if it is uttered out of the blue. It is however, not difficult to imagine a situation in which this answer makes sense. A hearer who assumes that the addressee for some reason or other wants to avoid making a cross will have no difficulty interpreting the answer: if the addressee of (4) was already committed to not making a cross, then he would indeed need to avoid vampires in order to comply with the imperative.

Generally speaking, one may conclude that in order to understand how imperatives influence the behaviour of their addressees the background information which also influences the actions of an addressee needs to be taken into account. In particular, one needs to take into consideration further propositions to which the addressee is committed. This means that although definition (3) provides us with some idea of the meaning of imperatives (in terms of their conditions of satisfaction), it fails to give us a full picture of how imperatives are *used* and (are expected to) *affect* the behaviour of their addressees.

---

[3] For the moment, we are omitting an explicit representation of temporal reference.

3   Imperatives in Context: An Agent-Based Analysis

In order to examine the influence of background information on the relation between imperatives and the actions which they give rise to, I am going to describe a class of models for communicating agents and their environment. The influence of background information can then be formalised in terms of constraints on the behaviour of the agents in such a model. These constraints will be normative in nature: they describe how the agents are *expected* to behave when they have agreed to comply with an imperative. Additionally, we will describe a concrete policy for action which allows an agent to fulfil these expectations.

At the basis of a Communicating Agents Model – a formally more explicit, but in some respects different account from the one advocated here[4], can be found in Piwek (2000) – lies a time line. This line consists of discrete instants of time and is infinite in both directions. In addition to the domain of instants of time (D_t) which underlies the time line, the model includes domains containing events (D_e), states (D_s) and individuals (D_i). The set of agents is a subdomain of the domain of individuals. The set of actions constitutes a subdomain of the domain of events. An event is an action if and only if it involves on or more agents who play the actor/agent role of the event (cf. Parsons, 1990).

Each of the members of the domains of events and states are event/state *tokens*. They can, respectively, *occur between* or *hold at* instants of time. we assume that if an event token occurs between two instants t_x and t_y (where x is precedes y), then it also occurs between all the instants t_a and t_b (where a precedes b) such that t_x precedes t_a and t_b precedes t_y. For instance, if somebody is cooking a meal between three and six 'o clock, then s/he is also cooking a meal between four and five 'o clock. Furthermore, we assume that for each event token there is a unique *maximal* pair of instants of time $\langle t_x, t_y \rangle$, i.e., interval, between which it occurs: any other pair between which the event occurs is covered by this maximal interval.

In this chapter, we focus on a particular subclass of the subdomain of actions: the so-called *basic actions*. In AI planning theories these are usually conceived of as the leaves of hierarchical plans. They are the actions which an agent is supposed to directly execute: they do not permit decomposition into further constituent actions. In terms of the logical model which is proposed here, a basic action is an action whose occurrence cannot be entailed by the occurrence of another set of actions. Composite actions, on the other hand, are those actions whose occurrence is entailed by other actions. They do not exist independently of the actions by which they are entailed. An agent executes a composite action only indirectly by executing a number of basic actions which entail the occurrence of the composite action. Despite this elusive status of composite actions, agents can have propositional attitudes towards them: e.g., they can intend composite actions and devise plans to execute such actions. Usually such a plan consists of a sequence of (preferably basic) actions which entail the composite action. In the

---

[4] In particular, the interpretation of the predicate *occur* is different.

model-theoretic approach, which is adopted in this chapter, the relation between basic and composite actions has to be formalized through axioms. These axioms stipulate which composite actions are entailed by combinations of basic actions.

We have seen that events occur between instants of time. We have also seen that for any event there is a maximal interval at which it occurs. In the context of this chapter, it is helpful to have two-place relation $occur(e, t_x)$ which is interpreted as: event e starts to occur at the instant of time t_x. In other words, t_x is the beginning point of the maximal interval at which e takes place.

A state always holds *at* one or more instants of time. We write $hold(s, t)$ to say that state s holds at the instant of time t. For example, consider a situation in which an agent switches off the light in a room between the instants of time t_0 and t_1. This means that an event token e of the type *switch* took place at the transition from t_0 to t_1. Similar to Parsons (1990), we assume that an event can involve a number of objects: in this case, its actor (the agent who switches off the light) and its patient (the light which is switched off). Furthermore, there are two states s_0 and s_1: one in which the light is on and one in which the light is off. s_0 holds at $\ldots, t_{-2}, t_{-1}$ and t_0 whereas s_1 holds at $t_1, t_2, \ldots$ In general states are assumed to span a connected series of instants of time. In other words, if a particular state holds at two different instants of time t_x and t_y, then it also holds at all the instants between t_x and t_y. Additionally, a state (token) has the same type and involves the same objects at all the instants at which it occurs).

Agents are modelled as a subdomain of the domain of individuals. They are distinguished from other objects by their ability to carry (propositional) information and use that information to guide their actions. The role of information in the (dialogue) behaviour of agents has been studied extensively. See, for instance, Beun, (1992), Bunt and van Katwijk (1979), Bunt (1989), the collection of papers in Bunt and Black (2000), Lewis (1979) and Power (1979). A number of notions, such as desire, belief, intention, plan, goal and commitment, have become central to such studies (see, also, Cohen et al., 1990; Grosz and Kraus, 1996 and Lochbaum, 1994).

In this chapter, we assume that imperatives give rise to commitments and focus on how the commitments of an agent determine which actions s/he carries out. In order to clarify the notion of commitment, it is useful to relate it to (my interpretation of) some of the other aforementioned notions.

Let us start with the notion of desire. Desires lie at the basis of an agent's behaviour. They are not necessarily rational: an agent can desire something which s/he believes to be impossible or have mutually contradictory desires. Goals are situations which an agent (1) dubs desirable, (2) believes to be possible, i.e., the situation is not inconsistent with his or her beliefs *and* other goals, and last but not least (3) has decided to realize. If a particular situation S_g is a goal for an agent, we also say that s/he intends that S_g. The relation between a desire and a goal can be fairly indirect, e.g., an agent A might adopt a particular goal because another agent proposed that goal and A has a desire to *cooperate* with that agent.

In order for an agent to realize his or her goals, s/he has to translate these goals into a set of basic actions which s/he can carry out and which lead to the goal situation. Such a set (usually a partially or totally ordered one) of basic actions is known as a *plan*. From a logical point of view, finding a plan can be seen as finding a description of a set of basic actions such that the description together with the agent's beliefs entails his or her goals:

(8)   PLAN
       Given an agent A, a set of beliefs B and a set of goals G of A, a plan P
       is description of a set of basic actions by A such that $B \cup P \models G$.

Here we want to suggest a natural generalization of this notion of a plan which my formulation of the notion of a plan in logical terms invites. Let us relax the constraint that a plan is a description of set of basic actions. We still assume that a plan needs to entail the goals of the agent. The plan itself is, however, defined as a description of the agent's (controlable) behaviour: it can describe basic actions by the agent, but also the disposition to abstain from certain actions or to carry out or abstain from certain actions in particular circumstances.

We propose to provide a formal definition of the notion of a generalized plan through a negative characterization. Basically, the idea is that a generalized plan should not entail any information to the effect that some state or event –except for a basic action– holds at/occurs between some instants of time or does not, *or* holds at/occurs between some instants of time or does not provided that certain conditions hold.[5]

(9)   GENERALIZED PLAN
       Given an agent A, a set of beliefs B and a set of goals G of A, a generalized
       plan is a description P such that $B \cup P \models G$ and there is no formula F
       of the form $p \rightarrow q$ or of the form q such that (1) $P \models F$, (2) F is not a
       tautology and (3) q describes that an event or state which is not a basic
       action by A holds/occurs or does not at or between some instants of time.

Let me explain why this generalization is useful by means of an example. Suppose an agent has the goal not to be bitten by a vampire. Furthermore, suppose that the agent believes that he will be bitten by a vampire if and only if he encounters a vampire and the vampire is not deterred. Finally, our agent knows that a vampire can be deterred by making a cross. A perfectly valid plan for this agent would be the plan to make a cross if he encounters a vampire. Such a plan is, however, not captured by the traditional notion of a plan as paraphrased in (8). The proposition *that the agent makes a cross if he encounters a vampire* does not describe a basic action. Rather, it describes a disposition.

---

[5] The notion of a generalized plan is different from the notion of a *partial plan*, which is common in AI planning theories. A partial plan is a traditional hierarchical plan which has at least one leaf which is not a basic action. Partial plans, as opposed to generalized plans, do do not contain logically complex propositions.

Dispositions are covered by definition (9). The disposition *that the agent
makes a cross if he encounters a vampire* together with the agent's beliefs entails
that the agent will not be bitten, i.e., the first condition of (9). The definition
contains further conditions to prevent agents from adopting plans which they
cannot execute. For instance, an agent is not allowed to simply include in his
or her plan that some event or state (which is not a basic action) will or will
not occur/hold. Note that the condition also excludes as part of a plan formulae
which say that: If state *s* holds then event *e* will occur, where *e* is not a basic
action of the agent.

The notion of commitment and more specifically that of a commitment state
of an agent still needs to be defined. In this chapter the term commitment state
is used to refer to the union of an agent's plans and his or her beliefs. This is
the information which s/he is committed to.[6] The commitment state of an agent
puts constraints on the behaviour of the agent. When we look at the model from
the outside, we can speak of the satisfaction conditions of the commitment state.
We assume that (as an external observer) we have access to a function *Int* which
maps commitment states (of individual agents) onto predicate logical sentences.
The conditions of satisfaction of a commitment state correspond to the truth-
conditions of the corresponding predicate logical sentences in the model (which
includes the agent and its commitment state).[7]

The reader might feel somewhat uncomfortable with the assumption that an
observer has a function which returns the conditions of satisfactions of an agent's
commitment state. It seems that we can only guess at such a function based on
the behaviour of the agent, assuming that an agent strives for the satisfaction
of his or her commitments. This is certainly correct when we consider human
agents. However, the nice thing about building models is that we can simply
define such a function for the agents with which we populate the model and
then compare different policies for action with respect to this function. Thus
we can determine how successful different policies are with respect to satisfying
the agents' commitments. It will turn out that this perspective is very helpful
for understanding the role of imperatives. Now that a model is in place, let
us examine how we can use it to analyse the use of an imperative. Take the
imperative (4), here repeated as (10).

(10)   Make a cross, if you encounter a vampire.

---

[6] This definition of commitment deviates from the one given in Hamblin (1971). Hamblin is concerned with situations where an agent becomes publically committed to
some piece of information. It is beyond the scope of this chapter to delve into the
relation between the private commitments which are discussed here, and Hamblin's
public commitments.

[7] Technical details with respect to *Int* can be found in Piwek (2000). There, a par-
tialized truth-conditional semantics is employed to avoid paradoxes such as 'The
Liar'.

The utterance event u of this imperative is modelled as occurring between two instants of time, say t_0 and t_1.[8] This utterance event has certain physical properties and some of these properties will be perceived and processed by the addressee of the utterance. In other words, in parallel with the utterance event, i.e., also between t_0 and t_1, there will be an observation event (by the addressee) of the utterance event. This observation event causes a change to the commitment state of the addressee. It is beyond the scope of this chapter to provide a detailed analysis of how the perception affects the information state of the addressee (but see, for instance, Beun, 1994; Ahn, 2000).

Let us assume that the addressee perceives and understands the imperative and believes that the utterance was felicitous (e.g., the speaker was sincere; see Austin, 1962). The commitment state of the addressee at t_1 will then contain the information of the addressee's commitment state at t_0 extended with the belief that it is the goal of the speaker that the addressee makes a cross if s/he encounters a vampire.[9] It is up to the addressee to signal whether s/he is committed to satisfying the speaker's goal. In other words, if the addressee signals compliance with the imperative, then s/he signals to have adopted the goal and also to have a plan for realizing it. The latter becomes a commitment of the addressee.

Thus, we assume that signalling compliance is stronger than merely adopting a goal, it also encompasses being committed to having a plan for that goal. Consideration of certain dialogue fragments seems to provide some support for this hypothesis. Consider:

(11)   A: Finish the paper before tomorrow.
        B: Ok, but I might fail to do it.

Here, B's utterance appears to be incoherent. B cannot first signal compliance with the imperative and then suggest that s/he might fail to comply. Consider substituting *I intend to* for *ok* and then reconsider the dialogue fragment:

(12)   A: Finish the paper before tomorrow.
        B: (Well) I intend to, but I might fail.

There seems to be nothing wrong with B's reply. This suggests that the meaning of *ok* cannot be identical to *I intend to* and that a better paraphrase migth be *I will*. In other words, the agent believes that s/he will satisfy the goal which

---

[8] For the sake of the argument we assume that an utterance event consists of just one single transition between adjacent instants of time. In a more sophisticated analysis we would model an utterance as consisting of a composite event.

[9] In case the imperative is intended as advice, the speaker will have expressed the proposition that it is beneficial to the addressee to adhere to the propositional content of the imperative. This in contrast with a command where the speaker expresses his own goal or that of somebody different from both speaker and addressee on whose behalf the speaker issues the imperative. In this chapter, such distinctions are not at issue. Rather, the main concern is the commitment which the addressee takes on when s/he decides to satisfy an imperative.

is expressed by the imperative in virtue of the fact that s/he is committed to a plan which entails (given the agent's beliefs) the satisfaction of this goal.

Let us return to(10). The propositional content of this imperative is added to the commitment state of the addressee. For the sake of the argument we assume that making a cross is a basic action. This allows us to assume that the plan for satisfying the goal introduced by the imperative is identical to the propositional content of the imperative.[10] Formally, we have that $Int(c_{t_1}) = \Phi$ and $Int(c_{t_2}) = \Phi \wedge f_C(10)$.[11,12] We assume that the propositional content $f_C(10)$ corresponds with the following formula, where $occur(e, t)$ means that event e started at t:

(13) $(\forall vtt'e.(vampire(v) \wedge encounter(john, v, e) \wedge occur(e, t) \wedge successor(t', t) \wedge$
$after(t, t_{utt})) \rightarrow (\exists e'.make\_cross(john, e') \wedge occur(e', t')))$

In words, if the addressee – John – encounters a vampire at a time t after the utterance time of the imperative t_{utt}, then he makes a cross starting at the instant of time which immediately succeeds t. Let us look at two possible constraints governing the role of imperatives. Firstly, one could consider an individual imperative and demand that its content is true in the world.

(14) CONSTRAINT: TRUTH-CONDITIONAL IMPERATIVE SATISFACTION
If $f_C(\mathbf{I})$ is the content of an imperative $\mathbf{I}$ uttered at some point in time, then $f_C(\mathbf{I})$ is true in the world.

We omit the condition that this content should be made true by its addressee. We address that issue in a moment. Let us first look at a related constraint which concerns the entire commitment state of an agent. We have seen that the content of an imperative is added to the commitment state of the addressee of an imperative. Thus we can define an alternative notion of satisfaction which pertains to such commitment states:

(15) CONSTRAINT: TRUTH-CONDITIONAL COMMITMENT STATE SATISFACTION
If c is the commitment state of an agent at some point in time, then $Int(c)$ is true in the world.

The addressee of an imperative is supposed to actively make sure that the constraint (14) is satisfied. An agent who manages to live up to this expectation is said to have *complied with* the imperative. However, an agent who tries to

---

[10] For imperatives which involve composite actions, the plan or commitments which they give rise to cannot be identical to the propositional content of the imperative. The plan will have to entail the propositional content of imperative and satisfy the other conditions of (9).

[11] Where c_{t_x} stands for the commitments of the addressee at t_x.

[12] This representation does not allow for anaphoric reference to indefinite antecedents. For that we would need a dynamic system such as Discourse Representation Theory, see, Kamp and Reyle (1993).

comply with an imperative cannot address that imperative in isolation from his or her other commitments. Consider, for instance, our agent John. Suppose he is committed to encountering a vampire, because he replied *ok* to the imperative *Find a vampire*. This commitment prevents John from satisfying (10) by avoiding vampires. The question then is how an agent can make sure that all his or her commitments are true in line with (15), if it is not possible to consider them one at a time. Is there a policy which allows an agent to make sure that all his or her commitments are/become true?

Let us first try to formulate a more precise version of this question. At the basis of this section lies the idea of a model of reality. The models which we have described up till now are total in nature: such a model determines completely which states and events take place at any given instant of time/interval and who and what are involved. With respect to such a model we can check whether constraints such as (14) and (15) are satisfied. Consider a model which is just as determined as the aforementioned models except for the fact that the actions of a particular agent, say John, are not specified in this model at any interval. A policy provides us with a rule which takes such a partial model and turns it into a fully determined, i.e., total, one. Thus the policy determines which actions an agent does and does not carry out at any given instant of time.

Whether a policy is successful can now be decided by checking whether the total model which it delivers always satisfies the constraint (15). In other words, a successful policy is one which allows an agent to make sure that all his or her commitments are true.

(16) POLICY FOR ACTION: FIRST VERSION
      If at time t agent A's commitment state is c and $Int(c)$ entails that A carries out some action a at t, then A should carry out a at t. Furthermore, A should only carry out actions which are required by this policy.

For now we have assumed that the normative constraint (15) is the only constraint on our models. At the end of this chapter some further constraints are discussed, for instance, physical constraints to which any real-world events and states are subjected. Such constraints affect what actions an agent can perform at a given instant of time. A succesful policy should, of course, only suggest actions which are compatible with this kind of hard constraints.

Let us put this complication aside and look at some of the concrete predictions which the proposed policy entails. Consider an agent whose commitment state consists only of the following commitment:

(17) $(\forall vtt'e.(vampire(v) \wedge encounter(john, v, e) \wedge occur(e, t) \wedge successor(t', t) \wedge$
      $after(t, t_{utt})) \rightarrow (\exists e'.make\_cross(john, e') \wedge occur(e', t')))$

According to the policy (16), this agent will undertake no actions at all. This explains why we consider it strange for an agent to avoid vampires solely on the basis of the imperative (10). Alternatively, suppose that John's commitment state corresponds with the following formula:

150   Paul Piwek

(18) $vampire(v_1) \wedge encounter(john, v_1, e_1) \wedge occur(e_1, t_3) \wedge$
       $(\forall vtt'e.(vampire(v) \wedge encounter(john, v, e) \wedge occur(e, t) \wedge successor(t', t) \wedge$
       $after(t, t_{utt})) \rightarrow (\exists e'.make\_cross(john, e') \wedge occur(e', t')))$

In words, John is committed to v_1 being a vampire and encountering him at
t_3. John's commitment state entails that at t_4 John makes a cross. And hence,
according to policy (16), John should make a cross at t_4.[13] Finally, consider a
situation in which John is committed to not making a cross:

(19) $\neg\exists t.(make\_cross(john, e) \wedge occur(e, t)) \wedge$
       $(\forall vtt'e.(vampire(v) \wedge encounter(john, v, e) \wedge occur(e, t) \wedge successor(t', t) \wedge$
       $after(t, t_{utt})) \rightarrow (\exists e'.make\_cross(john, e') \wedge occur(e', t')))$

This commitment state entails, as is to be expected, that John should avoid
vampires:

(20) $\forall vte.(vampire(v) \rightarrow \neg(encounter(john, v, e) \wedge occur(e, t) \wedge after(t, t_{utt})))$

Let us look more closely at how successful the policy (16) is in making sure that
an agent satisfies all his or her commitments. It turns out that we need to make
a number of further assumptions to guarantee its success.

First, we need to impose a constraint on how the commitment state of an
agent changes over time. It should not be possible that an agent has a com-
mitment state c_{t_x} at t_x and c_{t_y} at t_y such that c_{t_x} and c_{t_y} are not consistent
with each other. It is impossible to satisfy both states in one and the same
world/model and therefore (15) would be violated.[14]

Second, if a commitment state c_{t_y} entails an action by an agent at t_x, then
c_{t_x} should also entail this action. Thus, in line with the policy (16), the agent
will actually carry out the action at t_x. Without this assumption, s/he would
not do so, since according to the policy an agent only carries out the actions at
time t to which s/he is committed at time t.

Third, we need to assume that we are only considering the actions which
the agent itself is supposed to carry out. Of course, s/he might also have commitments pertaining to states, events and actions by others. However, for the
moment, we need to assume that these commitments are by definition true in
the model.

Fourth, we need to assume that the agent's commitment state at each point
in time is *complete*. For instance, suppose an agent is committed only to (17).
Furthermore, suppose that in that world the agent encounters a vampire at t_4,
but does not realize this and therefore is not committed to encountering the
vampire. In that case, according to policy (16) the agent will not make a cross.

---

[13] In fact, the commitment state also needs to include the information that t_4 is the
successor of t_3. We assume that the commitment state alway contains the necessary
information to derive that one instant succeeds another.

[14] Note that the proposed assumption automatically rules out that an individual commitment state is inconsistent.

But, of course, he should have done so in order to satisfy constraint (15). In other words, for the policy to be successful the agent's commitment state should be complete in the following sense: there should be no true information which is not part of an agent's commitment state, but which if it were, would cause the agent to perform an action which s/he would not undertake if this information was not present.

Finally, we need to assume that the actions of an agent are independent of each other or that if there are any constraints governing the interactions between different actions, then these should be included in the commitment state of the agent. For instance, suppose that there is a constraint which says that if an agent does not do action a_1 at t_1, then he cannot do a_2 at t_2, such as: one cannot submit a paper without first writing it. Suppose an agent is committed to submitting a paper at t_2. If this were the only commitment that the agent maintained, then policy (16) would tell him/her to do nothing at t_1. But the aforementioned constraint would then prevent him/her from submitting a paper at t_2. Thus, the agent would not be able to live up to its commitments. To avoid such situations, an agent would need to be committed to the information expressed by the constraint. Suppose the agent were committed to the information that (1) if you do not write a paper at t_x, then you do not submit a paper at t_{x+1} and (2) the agent submits a paper at t_2. These two propositions together entail that the agent writes a paper at t_1. And, hence, at t_1 the agent has to write a paper according to (16).

According to (16) an agent will not carry out any actions which are not licensed by (16). This puts a serious constraint on the behaviour of an agent. The condition is intended to prevent an agent from performing some action which prevents him or her from carrying out some other action which s/he is committed to at a later time. For instance, one might, just for the fun of it, throw away a key, which one needs later on to open a lock. However, if we assume that an agent's commitment state captures such regularities (i.e., that the lock cannot be opened without the key), then we can formulate a more liberal policy:

(21) POLICY FOR ACTION: SECOND VERSION
      If at time t agent A's commitment state is c and $Int(c)$ entails that A carries out some action a at t, then A should carry out a at t. Furthermore, A should only carry out actions which if they were to be added to his or her commitment state would not lead to an inconsistent commitment state.

We have presented a policy and a modified version of it. Both are only successful with respect to (15) when a number of further conditions/constraints hold. Many of these constraints may be seen as too restrictive for a real-world agent. However, we hope that by making these constraints explicit we have gained a starting point for the systematic study of agent behaviour. The next step would be to investigate how an agent can make sure that as much of the constraints as possible are satisfied, for instance, by means of an active policy for gathering information, such that all true information which is relevant to the commitments is available to the agent (in other words, a policy for maintaining a complete commitment state).

We conclude this section by drawing attention to a further problem in the analysis of imperatives which goes back to Ross (1941) and which has become known as Ross' Paradox. Ross noted that whereas p entails $p \lor q$ in classical logical, the imperative p! does not entail the imperative $p \lor q$! For instance, when I tell you to *Post a letter*, then I do not tell you to *Burn it or Post it*. In my approach, we maintain the classical logical inference from *Somebody posts a letter* to *Somebody posts a letter or burns it*. However, how information affects the behaviour of an agent is regulated by (21). An agent who is committed to *Posting a letter*, as a result of accepting the imperative *Post the letter*, will in line with (21) simply post the letter, since this is a (basic) action which is entailed by his or her commitment. The entailed proposition that s/he post or burn it has no effects on his or her actions. Note that if it did, this could lead to a violation of (15). Suppose the agent had a policy of also making complex sentences true directly. Then, s/he might choose to make the disjunction true by burning the letter. But this would prevent him or her from satisfying the commitment to posting the letter.

Alternatively, a person who accepts to *Burn or post a letter* will have a commitment state which contains this proposition. From this proposition the agent can infer no action whatsoever. Here we need to invoke the completeness assumption to get the agent moving. This assumption says that there should be no true information which is not part of an agent's commitment state, but which if it were, would cause the agent to execute an action which s/he would not undertake if this information was not present. Suppose our agent considered doing nothing at first. That would mean that s/he would not burn the letter. But this information together with the commitment to burn or post it entails that the agent should post it. Alternatively, if the agent were to first consider not posting the letter, this would cause him or her to burn it. If we invoke the completeness assumption, then it turns out that that the agent either has to post the letter or burn it.

4   Conclusions and Further Issues

An analysis of imperatives has been provided which takes into account the influence of background information on the use of (complex) imperatives. In particular, we have described a model of communicating agents in which imperatives modify the commitments of these agents. We proposed to understand an agent's commitments as his or her beliefs combined with his or her (generalized) plan for action. The notion of a generalized plan was introduced as a natural extension of the traditional notion of a plan when it is looked at from a logical perspective.

The commitments are expected to influence the behaviour of the agent. We formulated a normative constraint which required that the commitments of the agent should be true. Subsequently, we examined a policy which an agent might

adopt in order to satisfy this constraint. It turned out that various further practical constraints are needed to make the policy successful, i.e., to guarantee that
all of the agents commitments are made true.

The proposed analysis of imperatives uses classical predicate logic to represent the propositional content of imperatives. We showed that such an analysis
does not need to run into certain problems which have been associated with classical logical analyses of imperatives. Therefore, we did not depart from classical
logic.[15] In this respect, my analysis of imperatives is Gricean in nature (Grice,
1975): we retain the classical logical core of the analysis and account for certain
features of the use of imperatives in terms of rules which govern the relation
between the content/information which is conveyed by imperatives and the role
which this information plays in the behaviour of the addressee. In other words,
we make a distinction between the questions 'What does the propositional content of an imperative entail?' and 'What can we conclude when somebody utters
an imperative with a particular content?'.

The work reported in this chapter can be seen as complementary to much
work in AI on planning which focuses on commitments to actions that are complex in the sense that these actions can be decomposed into a collection of sub-
actions. The actions in question are, however, typically not part of a plan which
is logically complex. In this chapter, *logically* complex commitments, which include the plans of an agent, have been at the centre of our investigation. Due
to the focus in AI on logically simple plans, much work in that tradition pays
little attention to the relation between an agent's plan and the actions which
s/he carries out on the basis of that plan. However, when we move to logically
complex plans/commitments, the relation between an agent's actions and his
plans/commitments is no longer trivial, and it is exactly that relation which has
been studied in this chapter.

Finally, let me indicate some issues for further investigation. There is, for
instance, the inherent temporal vagueness of imperatives which has not been
addressed in this chapter. Consider the simple imperative *Open the door*. A
paraphrase of this imperative might be: *Open the door as soon as possible after
now but not too long after now*. It is not immediately clear how this paraphrase
can be expressed by means of a predicate logical formula. Furthermore, a short-
coming of the current model is that it does not cater for an agent who happens
to realize that it violated one of its commitments. Suppose the commitment
was p. The realization that p is not satisfied should result in the addition of
$\neg p$ to his or her commitment state. But clearly, a strictly additive update with
this information leads to an inconsistent state. In short, a full-fledged theory of
imperatives presupposes a theory of commitment revision.

---

[15] As is, for instance, advocated in Perez Ramirez (2000).

Acknowledgments

The problems concerning the relation between imperatives and action first attracted my attention when working, from 1994 until 1998, on the DENK project (see Bunt et al., 1998). We would like to thank my colleagues on the DENK project for the stimulating environment which put me on a track which eventually led to the work which is reported in this chapter. Furthermore, thanks are due to Robbert-Jan Beun, Kees van Deemter and Miguel Perez Ramirez for commenting on earlier versions of this chapter. Naturally, we take responsibility for any remaining mistakes.

References

Ahn, R. (2000) *Agents, Objects and Events*. Ph.D. thesis, Eindhoven University of Technology.

Austin, J. (1962) *How To Do Things With Words*. Oxford: Clarendon Press.

Beun, R.J. (1992) A framework for Cooperative Dialogue. In: Taylor, M., F. Néel, and D. Bouwhuis (eds.), *The Structure of Multimodal Dialogue II*, Maratea, Italy: Proceedings of the Venaco Workshop on Multimodal Dialogue.

Beun, R.J. (1994) Mental state recognition and communicative effects. *Journal of Pragmatics* 21, 191–214.

Biber, D., S. Johansson, G. Leech, S. Conrad, and E. Finegan (1999) *Longman Grammar of Spoken and Written English*. Harlow: Longman.

Bunt, H. and A. Van Katwijk (1979) Dialogue acts as elements of a language game. In: W. Zonneveld and F. Weerman (eds.), *Linguistics in the Netherlands 1977–1979*, Dordrecht: Foris Publications, 264–282.

Bunt, H. (1989) Information Dialogues as Communicative Actions in Relation to Partner Modelling and Information Processing. In: M. Taylor, F. Néel, and D. Bouwhuis (eds.), *The Structure of Multimodal Dialogue*, Amsterdam: North-Holland, 47–74.

Bunt, H., R. Ahn, R.J. Beun, T. Borghuis, and K. van Overveld (1989) *Multimodal Cooperation with the DENK System*. In: Bunt, R.J. Beun, and T. Borghuis (eds.), *Multimodal Human-Computer Communication. Systems, Techniques, and Experiments*, Lecture Notes in Artificial Intelligence Vol. 1374. Berlin: Springer Verlag, 39–67.

Bunt, H. and W. Black (eds.) (2000) *Computational Pragmatics: Abduction, Belief and Context in Dialogue*, Amsterdam/Philadelphia: John Benjamins.

Cohen, P., J. Morgan, and M. Pollack (1990) *Intentions in Communication*. Cambridge Massachusetts: The MIT Press.

Grice, H. (1975) Logic and Conversation. In: P. Cole and J. Morgan (eds.), *Speech Acts. Syntax and semantics*, Vol. 3. 41–58, New York: Academic Press.

Grosz, B. and S. Kraus (1996) Collaborative Planning for Complex Group Action. *Artificial Intelligence* 86 (2), 269-357.

Hamblin, C. (1971) Mathematical Models of Dialogue. *Theoria* 37, 130–155.

Hamblin, C. (1987) *Imperatives*. Oxford: Blackwell.

Kamp, H. and U. Reyle (1993) *From Discourse to Logic*. Dordrecht: Kluwer Academic Publishers.

Lewis, D. (1979) Scorekeeping in a Language Game. In: Bäuerle, R., U. Egli, and A. von Stechow (eds.), *Semantics from Different Points of View*, Berlin: Springer Verlag, 172–187

Lochbaum, K. (1994) *Using Collaborative Plans to Model the Intentional Structure of Discourse*. Ph.D. thesis, Cambridge, Massachusetts: Harvard University

Parsons, T. (1990) *Events in the Semantics of English*. Cambridge, Massachusettes: The MIT Press.

Perez Ramirez, M. (2000) Imperatives, State of the Art. In: Kilgarriff, A. et al. (eds.), *Proceedings of CLUK 3*, Universities of Brighton and Sussex, 18–25.

Piwek, P. (2000) Imperatives, Commitment and Action: Towards a Constraint-Based Model. In: *LDV Forum*, Special Issue on Communicating Agents (to appear). Available at: http://www.itri.bton.ac.uk/~Paul.Piwek

Power, R. (1979) The Organisation of Purposeful Dialogues. *Linguistics* 17, 107–152.

Ross, A. (1941) Imperatives and Logic. *Theoria* 7, 53–71.

Searle, J. (1969) *Speech Acts: An Essay in the Philosophy of Language*. Cambridge: Cambridge University Press.

Stenius, E. (1967) Mood and language-game. *Synthese* 17, 254-274.

Part 3:

Multimodal Interpretation

Interpretation of Gestures and Speech: A Practical Approach to Multimodal Communication

Xavier Pouteau

IPO, Center for Research on User-System Interaction
Eindhoven, The Netherlands
xpouteau@nuance.com

Abstract. Developing multimodal interfaces is not only a matter of technology. Rather, it implies an adequate tailoring of the interface to the user's communication needs. In command and control applications, the user most often has the initiative, and in that perspective gestures and speech (the user's communication channels) have to be carefully studied to support a sensible interaction style. In this chapter, we introduce the notion of semantic *frame* to integrate gestures and speech in multimodal interfaces. We describe the main elements of a model that has been developed to integrate the use of both channels, and illustrate the model by two fully implemented systems. Possible extensions of the model are presented to improve the supported style, as technologies develop.

1 Introduction

Over the past fifteen years the concept of multimodality has emerged as important, as a result of increasing technological capabilities, more powerful theoretical models, experimental results, and the construction of proof-of-concept systems. This concept characterizes a form of communication between user and system where several channels of communication are used. Multimodality is often felt to be a chance given to the designer of an interface to improve the usability because it offers a larger 'bandwidth' to the user.

It would clearly be naive to think that a broader bandwidth allows a larger variety of styles, and thus improves the quality of the communication (see e.g. Bunt, 1998; Rasmussen, 1976). Rather, the true issue of multimodal user interface design is to tailor the interaction style supported by the system so as to actually define a usable and efficient interface.

2 Definition of an Interaction Style

2.1 Objectives and Requirements

We will consider systems with which the user can communicate by means of gestures and/or speech, while the system conveys information via the user's sight

H. Bunt and R.-J. Beun (Eds.): CMC'98, LNAI 2155, pp. 159–175, 2001.
© Springer-Verlag Berlin Heidelberg 2001

and hearing senses.[1] In this perspective, defining a 'multimodal' style consists in being able to support useful and reasonable uses of gestures and speech.

Current command and control systems are getting more and more complex, and the reaction of the user must be quick and efficient. To achieve these objectives, the *communication task* should not add too much workload to the *professional task*. The work reported in this chapter was initiated in order to try to provide more efficient interfaces, thus allowing a higher performance when working with the application. Its application areas involve highly demanding tasks, on professional consoles for applications such as the Naval Domain (Pouteau *et al.*, 1993) or Battlefield Teleoperation (Bisson *et al.*, 1995). These systems were developed on the basis of the model sketched in Section 4.

2.2   General Requirements of an Interaction Style

The characteristics of command and control applications entail the following requirements that the interface should satisfy:

-   **Access to the application.** This is mainly provided via a graphical representation of the application, representing the evolution of spatial entities in a symbolic way (e.g., use of codified iconic representations in a spatial coordinate system). In the target applications, the efficiency of the user's activity in terms of reaction delay was an important requirement. Thus, adding speech to the already employed gestural channel (through keypad buttons, and additionally mouse) was at first seen as a means to enhance the safety of the user's activity, by decreasing the reaction delay: a complex command could be performed through a single action. Furthermore, gestural interaction involves not only the hands of the operator, but also the visual perceptive channel when focusing the attention on the interaction device itself (keyboard, or graphical representation of an element of the application in case of a *reactive interface*). And in the case of a high density of elements on the screen, issues to consider are also the additional effort to accurately operate with the mouse, the additional activity (zoom/unzoom) to have easier access to objects, and the temporary loss of visual access to objects when popping up a menu or using a dialogue box. On the other hand, a 'nameable' entity would have the advantage of being easily and directly designated via speech. Of course, this theoretical 'virtue' of speech comes together with the practical problems of speech recognition errors, interpretation errors, and ambiguities. Using speech thus also presupposes that speech technologies are mature enough to envisage building such interfaces, and puts additional robustness requirements on the dialogue system.
-   **Action on the application.** The possibility of using speech to designate elements of the application also applies to the expression of commands. This

---

[1] These are the most sensible channels to consider for communication and for perception in human-computer interaction. To be more complete, we should also mention the sense of *touch*, e.g. Cadoz *et al.* (1990).

leads to the notion of a command and control language that has to be defined for the application. In fact, for professional applications it has been observed that the language used by the operator tends to have a quite stable core in normal situations (Falzon, 1983). These characteristics of human communication and activity can thus be taken as a reasonable assumption for developing multimodal interfaces, that is, in the frame of their professional activity, users employ vocal and gestural channels in a stable way. Furthermore, the fact that the users are professional makes it sensible to *define* a language that they will have to *learn*.[2] The aim is then to define a language that fits in with the actual habits of the users. The consistency of the language with the needs of the communication task and its compatibility with the users' habits can be ensured by a specification phase in which users are involved.

2.3   Guidelines for the Definition of an Interaction Style

When defining the characteristics of a multimodal communication form, some *a priori* choices have to be made. Since the new system does not yet exist, it is not possible to really establish all the features of a language that fits in both with the habits of the users and the capabilities of the technologies. To define the 'language' for the interaction, our approach has the following elements:

- **Definition of the vocabulary:** The vocabulary has to be consistent with the application, in the sense that it must cover the communication needs to allow the user to accomplish the task. This concerns the functional specification of the system, as a spin-off of the task analysis process. The next step is the choice of lexical elements, in agreement with professional users, re-using as much as possible of the existing vocabulary, and supplementing it if necessary with additional elements that have been agreed.
- **Definition of the command utterances:** None of the two applications had an existing language in the sense of a structured way of building utterances. So the actual shape of the multimodal communication had to be defined. This concerns the ways gestures would be used, speech would be used, and the two communication channels would be used together. This is discussed below.

Furthermore, though the main trend of this approach is to *a priori* define the style of the interaction, it is also necessary to make choices that integrate experimental results. From the abundant literature on experiments in multimodal

---

[2] So far, analyzes of experimental approaches (Wizard-of-Oz experiments) have shown that corpus collection and analysis could not lead to a complete coverage of the inputs used to operate the system. This is why the language has to be *learned*, which is acceptable for the professional user, since a more limited freedom can be compensated by the system being robust with respect to the user's input (with the noticeable exception of speech recognition errors, discussed in Section 5).

interaction, it is worth to cite here the well-framed Wizard-of-Oz (WOZ) experiment reported by Hauptmann and McAvinney (1993), which clearly shows a complementarity of the uses of voice and gestures for operations consisting of actions on objects and reference to objects. For the tasks presented in the experiment, this conclusion is also supported by the fact that most users actually employ voice and gestures as a subjectively optimal way of interacting with the system.

To summarize this section, we conclude that the definition of an interaction style must take into account the existing empirical material. This encompasses both results of experimental approaches, like WOZ experiments, and other empirical material. For example, when considering an application, using as much as possible of the characteristics of the professional language already applicable is a mandatory prerequisite. But those characteristics are not always observable or available, especially when one introduces voice+gesture communication in a domain where the communication task of the operator consists in using button panels, for example. In that case, the definition of an interaction style has to be situated in the context of theoretical models characterizing uses of the channels of communication, namely speech and gesture, so as to make *a priori* choices that are sensible enough to understand the main functions of both communication channels. Therefore, before presenting our model, we provide a brief overview of the uses of these channels and the related requirements on the models that will support their use.

3   Characteristics of Gestures and Speech

3.1   Use of Gesture

Gestures are already widely present in computer interfaces through the use of mouse and keyboard. However, the use of gestures in user interfaces is highly functions of gestures:

- an *epistemic* function, through the sense of touch,
- an *ergative* function, when performing operations on objects (manipulating objects),
- a *semiotic* function, involved in communication (to convey information via gestures). For example, fingers closed with thumb raised indicates agreement ("OK").

These three functions are at present only partially taken into account in user interfaces. The epistemic function is only provided by the contact with the keyboard or the mouse, and is otherwise generally further replaced by visual or audio feedback (except for example Cadoz *et al.*, 1990). For ergative and semiotic functions, the current devices and communication protocols seem to ignore the nature and use of human gestures. Buxton (1986) argues that current user interfaces characteristically make one think of a "...prevalence of our visual system over our poorly developed manual dexterity". In addition to our dexterity (involved in the ergative function), one can also argue that our communication skills are very poorly supported. Rimé and Schiaratura (1991) present a survey of studies on semiotic gestures in which they report four general categories of semiotic gestures:

- *symbolic* gestures, which in a given culture and communication context have an autonomous meaning (see the example of "OK" given above);
- *deictic* gestures, pointing at part of the spatial environment;
- *iconic* gestures, for example a hand indicating the trajectory of an object;
- *pantomimic* gestures, employed for instance when performing mime.

Of these categories, we hardly find any in user interfaces. Deictic gestures exist, in the selection of an object with a mouse, but that consists indeed of *a selection* and not of a *designation*. In other words, it is an ergative gesture that performs an operation of selection, and the result of this selection is interpreted as a designation in the frame of the system's communication protocol.

The above considerations of gestures reveal a really poor integration of semiotic gestures. But do we need more? Aren't current interfaces sufficient? Of course, our aim is not to support various uses of gestures (or speech) *per se*. In some circumstances, such interfaces have proved sufficient. They rely in most cases on a graphical metaphor, and simple physical operations (which mainly consist of selection operations) performed on objects invoke a pre-defined reaction of the system, according to the semantics inherited from the metaphorical world. In this case, the metaphor has to be simple so that the user can appropriate it. Furthermore, metaphors have been used to hide the complexity of the application area, so as to transform abstract entities from it into the concrete entities of the metaphorical world.

Why should we develop such a metaphor when the main characteristics of the application are spatial, and when the professional user is already experienced with it? Moreover, the advantage of having simple selection operations has to be paid for. We illustrate this with an example of the Battlefield Teleoperation domain.

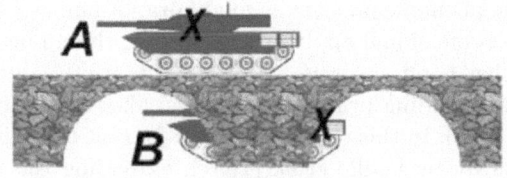

Fig. 1. The Problem of Designation.

Suppose that the user wants to have an operation performed on one of the tanks that are present (see Figure 1), for example getting some information about it like (1):

(1)   What is the speed of this tank?

We see that in the case of tank A the selection of the graphical representation is quite feasible. Tank B however is partially hidden by the bridge under which it is located. This means that the effort involved in a selection operation is quite high, which may lead to mistakes or errors. This problem is related to the combination of two facts. First, the lack of information conveyed by gestures. A gesture merely consists of a pair of spatial coordinates (x,y), which are the ones of the cursor at the mouse-click event (indicated by a cross on the picture). The second one relates to the design of a reactive interface using these events to build a semantic representation on the basis of (x,y). There is no other semantic frame to enrich the semantic content of a gestural piece of information, and since the frame of a reactive interface is rigid, only the use of artifacts (zoom/unzoom, hiding some objects, etc.) can help to resolve it.

Actually, a reactive interface implicitly tackles one problematic characteristic of gestures: it 'frames' them. Gestures generally need a frame to be interpreted, as shown in several experiments (see the debate between Feyereisen and McNeill on this issue in Feyereisen, 1987; Feyereisen *et al.*, 1988; McNeill, 1985; McNeill, 1987). Reactive interfaces provide such a frame, in a rigid way and for a tiny part of the gestural capabilities. Therefore, enhancing the supported capabilities of gestures means providing a larger and less rigid way of framing them.

3.2   Use of Speech

Another way of providing such a frame is the integrated use of speech. Speech in computer interfaces is much less present than gestures. The expected advantages of speech (hands free communication, conciseness through the expression of several semantic units at once, expression of a command in a direct way, as opposed to the n-step approach of a menu- or dialog box-based communication) come together with well-known drawbacks: speech recognition errors and the ambiguity of spoken language. Indeed, using speech also implies dealing with certain linguistic phenomena, such as anaphora (Amalberti *et al.*,, 1989). In the perspective of a professional application however, these phenomena can be handled with a rather good coverage (Gaiffe *et al.,* 1991), dealing with the most useful of them and finding practical solutions, like to the well-known *focus* concept of Sidner (1986). In this chapter, we will present the principles of the model developed primarily by Gaiffe *et al.* (1991), extending the model where necessary to taylor it to the specificities of the applications developed. To do so, we will take the basic case of a command expressed by the user through voice and/or gesture. The aim of an interpretation of such a command is then to determine:

- which action has to be performed by the system
- which elements of the application are concerned (reference solving).

In the remainder of this chapter, we will mainly present our work on the second issue in Section 4. In Section 5, we also give an outline of the mechanisms employed during the dialogue to deal with the problems of robustness and ambiguity mentioned earlier in this chapter.

4   Integrated Interpretation of Gestures and Speech

Integrated use of gestures and speech is not a new idea in the area of computer interfaces. The seminal "Put-that-there" paper (Bolt, 1980) already gave good illustrations of the possibilities of such interfaces. For the application areas that we address in this chapter, we based our model on the idea of a semantic frame provided to the interpretation of gestures, thus providing a contrast to the elements of the graphical focus of attention (Wahlster, 1991 named it the *demonstratum* in the case of a deictic gesture) to extract the right pieces of information from.

4.1   Principles of the Model

We rely on the assumption that both gestures and speech convey pieces of information, and that the right elements have to be found by interpreting the user's communicative action as a whole. Furthermore, in view of the characteristics of speech and gestures, we assume that abstract notions are provided by speech (like categories and other abstract properties of objects) and that concrete characteristics may be conveyed by gestures (e.g. position and shape). Thus, we consider the two kinds of input of the user as follows:

- **Gestural channel.** According to the semiotic functions of gestures, *shape* (orientation and direction), and the notion of *demonstratum* mentioned above.
- **Speech channel.** For clarity, we first consider the pieces of information carried by the noun phrases (NPs) of an utterance, assuming that the interpretation of the command is not ambiguous. Thus, the semantic content of an NP consists of a category (generally referring to a type of object). A variation on the example in Figure 1 is used to illustrate the case of the interpretation of the action.

4.2   Examples

A 'Classical' Example. The work reported here had to take into account various devices supporting the use of gestures: pen, digital glove, and mouse. Depending on the device actually used, part of or all of the data related to orientation, direction and position of the gesture is available. In the context of this work, modules concerned with a glove been partially developed, and supported only pointing gestures in a way robust enough to be used in the user interface. Thus, we present here the integration of voice and gestures where gestures only convey location information. As an illustration, consider the example in Figure 1. If we suppose that a designation was performed by a mouse click, the only feature of the gesture is the *demonstratum*. In other words, we consider what has been pointed at. In the remainder, we will refer to these pieces of data as Elementary Gestural Data (EGD). The content of an EGD is defined as *all visual elements possibly pointed at during the gestural designation*. Those elements which consist of *presentations* on the display, consist indeed of the following:

(2) $EGD = (time, \{(x,y), pres\text{-}1, \ldots, pres\text{-}N\})$

where time is the time the designation has been performed, (x,y) are the coordinates of the designation (position of the mouse click), and pres-i is a visual representation of an object of the application. In practice, pres-i is any presentation within a given distance to the position of the designation. The order of the sequence results from the distance of every presentation to (x,y) on the one hand, and the display precedence (foreground/background) on the other hand. When we consider the rightmost click in Figure 1, we have an EGD instance as follows:

(3) $EGD0 = (t0, \{(x0,y0), pres\text{-}b1, pres\text{-}tB\})$

together with the spoken utterance *What is the distance to this bridge.*

Here, pres-b1 is the graphical presentation of the bridge and pres-tB is the presentation of tank B. So far, gestural data only convey information related to the visual display. This means that the cross-reference (in this case a deictic reference, which Mc Kevitt (1997) calls an *exophoric* reference) has to be resolved through an adequate use of the links between the displayed presentations and a representation of the elements of the actual application. To fill the gap between visual elements and objects of the application, we developed a semantic network that takes into account the relations *is-a*, *type-of* (or *instance-of*), *represented-by* and *represents*. For example, if the bridge in Figure 1 is a viaduct, and if the viaduct has a specific type representation, we would have the following descriptions:

type	Type-viaduct
is-a	Type-bridge
represented-by	{pres-b1}
instance	br-017

type	Type-pres-viaduct-6
represents	br-017
instance	pres-b1
x	x-pres-b1
y	y-pres-b1

These representations establish a bi-directional link between the objects of the applications and the graphical presentations. Among others, it means that the system has an explicit representation of the elements that are visible and the ones that are not.

Finally, the lexicon is also supported by a semantic network. This representation fills the gap between the linguistic level and the application level by defining the scope of a linguistic category:

def	demo
category	bridge
is-a	*nil*
types	{Type-bridge}

The role of the attribute 'def'[3] is discussed further below in Example 3. From the lexical representation of the entry *bridge*, we know that we have to find an element that *is-a* Type-bridge. EGD0 is filtered accordingly, which means that only the presentations of an element that *is-a* Type-bridge are kept. In this example, only the presentation pres-b1 remains since it is the only one that *represents* an element which *is-a* Type-bridge, namely br-017.

Example 2: Designation *vs* Selection. In Section 3, we mentioned the distinction between the use of a gestural device to *select* an object and to perform a *designation*. This distinction is illustrated by the case where the use wants to refer to tank B in Figure 1. By considering designation as a gesture that points at a given area, we allow all graphical presentations in the area pointed at to be designated via gestures. We simply use EGD0 together with the representation of the elements of the application, that is, in addition to the bridge br-017.

type	Type-tank
is-a	*nil*
represented-by	{pres-tA}
instance	tank-A

type	Type-tank
is-a	*nil*
represented-by	{pres-tB}
instance	tank-B

type	Type-pres-Tank
represents	tank-A
instance	pres-tA
x	x-pres-tA
y	y-pres-tA

type	Type-pres-Tank
represents	tank-B
instance	pres-tB
x	x-pres-tB
y	y-pres-tB

category	tank
is-a	*nil*
types	{Type-tank}

---

[3] This attribute has four possible values: 'demo' in case of a demonstrative NP(*this tank*), 'def' in case of a definite NP (*the tank*), 'undef' for an undefined one (*a tank*) or 'NULL' (*tank*).

In this case, tank-A would not be considered because it is not in the demonstratum. Thus, only tank-B would be considered, and the reference would be correctly interpreted for utterance (1), *What is the speed of this tank.*

Example 3: Use of Time Information. A critical issue concerning the combined use of gestures and speech is that one has to use pieces of data processed by different modules, and generally in an asynchronous way, to build an integrated interpretation of the user's contribution. In the previous examples, we have considered the use of the mouse to produce pointing gestures. As we mentioned earlier, when using the digital glove only the possibility of pointing gestures was available. An essential distinction between mouse and glove is the possibility of segmenting the information by producing a click. For the glove, the segmentation has to be done by a module associated with the glove, and this module returns an alternative of possible sequences of EGDs, whereas the mouse returns exactly as many EGDs as mouse clicks. Thus, integrated interpretation of gestures and speech has to 'fuse' the pieces of data provided by the speech and gesture modules, combining the 'right' EGDs with the right linguistic segments (mainly noun phrases and adverbs such as *here*) of the spoken utterance. Gestural data is an alternative, and can be represented as follows:

(4)   Gdata = ((EGD-1-1, ..., EGD-n1-1) ... (EGD-k-1, ..., EGD-k-nk))

where k is the number of alternative EGDs sequences and ni the number of EGDs within the alternative sequence i.

When performing the integrated interpretation, we try first to find a solution by combining the linguistic segments that are potentially deictic with the EGDs (if any). In other words, in the situation of Figure 1, if the user utters: *Place this tank on the bridge*, we will use for each linguistic segment the value of the attribute 'def' to resolve the reference as one to a visual element together with a pointing gesture (case of a *deictic reference*); as one to the history of the dialogue (case of an *anaphor*), or as a direct reference to an element of the application.[4]

At this stage, the time of production of the EGDs and the utterance is taken into account as follows. EGDs sequences that start from the beginning of the spoken utterance are considered first, and then EGDs sequences that start slightly before the beginning of the speech (the empirical tolerance was 2 seconds). In a sequence of EGDs, we do not match EGDs and linguistic segments according to a strict overlap, but simply according to the sequentiality of both inputs. We then return a list of candidates as follows:

– successful combinations with EGDs, according to the value of 'def', where the EGD sequences start after the spoken utterance,

---

[4] The kind of preferred reference (anaphora, deixis) according to the value of the attribute 'def' has been studied in detail in Gaiffe (1992) for French. We have used this work as a source of inspiration for the development of our own models. Similar considerations apply to other languages, as may be concluded from a comparative study of Dutch and English (Piwek *et al.*, 1995).

- successful combinations with EGDs, according to the value of 'def', allowing a tolerance before the beginning of the spoken utterance,
- successful combinations with EGDs, regardless of the value of 'def',
- unsuccessful combinations (see Section 5.2).

In the current example, we consider that tank A has been pointed at by the user, and that the following sequences are returned:

(5)   Gdata = ((EGD1, EGD2, EGD3), (EGD2, EGD3))

(6)   EGD1 = (t1, {(x1,y1), pres-tA})

(7)   EGD2 = (t2, {(x2,y2)})

(8)   EGD3 = (t3, {(x3,y3)})

Of the four combination candidates listed above, only the first and the last are not empty. The first one contains the right interpretation of the utterance. This correct interpretation is made possible by the fact that we do not only try to combine the data, but rather rely on cues given by both channels to decide how to proceed to reference resolution. This point is important in the case of the use of the glove, because it can frequently overgenerate sequences of EGDs, and instead of trying to resolve a cross reference between EGD2 or EGD3 on the one hand and *the bridge* on the other hand, *the bridge* is first considered as an anaphoric or direct reference.[5] We conclude this section with an example where two cross-references between voice and gestures are performed, with the utterance:

(9)   *Place this tank here*

together with Gdata defined above. In this case, we generate two solutions resulting of the combination of *this tank* with EGD1, and of the combination of *here* with either EGD2 or EGD3. This ambiguity is dealt with at a later stage in the system, by taking dialogue mechanisms into account.

5   Characteristics of the Dialogue System

5.1   Dialogue Mechanisms: Robustness of the System

When developing an interface relying on the use of technologies such as speech or gesture processing, one has to include additional functionalities in the system to ensure the robustness of the system as a whole. As mentioned earlier, the most common kinds of robustness problems are:

---

[5] The actual way to resolve these types of references is not discussed in this chapter. The interested reader is referred to Pouteau (1995) for a complete presentation.

- speech recognition errors
- gesture processing errors
- interpretation ambiguities
- user's mistakes.

The main difficulty is that the system has no cues that *a priori* indicate whether a given input corresponds to one of those four cases, or whether the result actually fits in with the user's intention. To overcome this problem, the system systematically gives feedback to the user after each utterance. This can be in the form of a spoken message via text-to-speech synthesis, in the form of a visual feedback message, or it can be a combination of both. Deciding whether the interpretation built by the system is correct depends on the user, who can either confirm (implicitly or explicitly, as described in Pouteau *et al.*, 1997) or reject the interpretation. Looking back at Section 4, where we presented an example of multiple interpretations found by the system, the system can in the case of a rejection propose another interpretation.

The same model was used for an application of a naval domain (Pouteau *et al.*, 1993). In this application, the task of the operator is to optimize the use of various radar sensors to detect different kinds of threats approaching a ship. The application was simulated, and the aim of this prototype was to develop a console for trainees to acquire expertise. Professional domain experts participated in the definition of the system not only for the functional content, but also for the definition of the language of the application, the feedback messages and the graphical interface.

5.2   Handling of Failures and Error Messages

When no complete interpretation of a command can be found, the content of the feedback provided by the system must be to the point. To deal with this issue, we considered two cases: (1) the user's utterance is correctly interpreted but cannot be further processed by the system, and (2) no correct interpretation could be found by the system.

We give an example of the first case. The context is that the user has tuned the sensors so as to be able to detect missiles in one section (S0) and fighters and missiles in another (S1). This is represented in Figure 2. The position of the ship (in which the professional user is located) is at the center of the circle. Once the tactical situation is set, the user can access the data to read them or to modify them. For example, to optimize the use of the radar resources, it can be useful to know the settings of a given piece of radar equipment:

(10)   *What are the settings of the radar 2m*

Suppose that this utterance is interpreted correctly. The radar can be in use, and dedicated to the detection of specific threats. In this case, the system would display the parameter settings, as well as the threats tracked (for example a fighter and a missile in sector S1). But if the radar is not correctly set, or simply not activated, it will not detect any threat, and the reaction of the system to a correct interpretation of the utterance will be a message indicating that the preconditions to access the data of the radar are not met, namely:

(11)   *The radar 2m is not active*

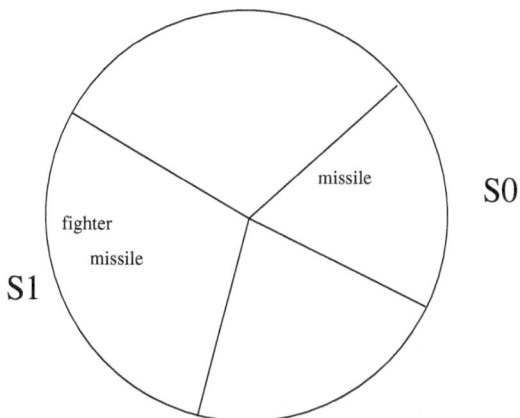

Fig. 2. Example from Naval Domain Application.

Feedback messages are also crucial to indicate that the interpretation process could not complete a correct representation of the user's contribution. We presented in Section 4 the way cross-references between gestures and speech were handled, and showed that it allowed tolerance and robustness in the pointing gestures, by an explicit representation of the pieces of data during the 'fusion' between both communication channels. Another advantage of this approach is the possibility of giving context-dependent feedback in case of a mistake. Instead of the poorly informative *Your utterance could not be interpreted*, a message indicates the user the type of failure. Indeed, it can happen that more than one reference is made in the utterance (see the famous "Put-that-there" case), and thus that more than one reference is unresolved. To give the user reasons explaining the failure in the interpretation of an utterance, the interpretation process stores for each attempt to compute a reference either the resolution, or the cues used in the attempt to resolve the reference. To do so, the feedback message will give information on one of the following ordered list of criteria (if a failure occurs for more than one criterion, only the first of the non-satisfied criteria will be mentioned in the message).

1. the utterance could not be recognized
2. the object of the command could not be found
3. a non-object referent of the command could not be found
4. all references could be resolved, but the preconditions of the task are not satisfied.

172   Xavier Pouteau

Suppose that, in the context of Figure 3, the user utters, together with a pointing gesture:

(12)   *Track this tank*

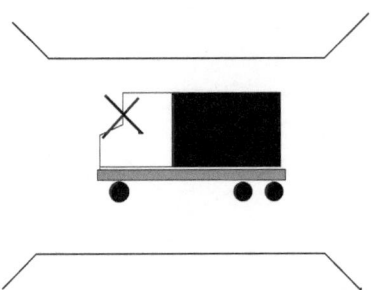

Fig. 3. Interpretation Failure.

In this example, the message of the system would be *There is no tank at the place you indicate*, which gives maximal cues to the user about why the interpretation could not be determined. According to the second and third criteria listed above, the system tries to include in its answer as much of the user's utterance as possible. We illustrate this with a more complex example.

In the context of Figure 1, consider the utterance *Put this enemy tank here.* Assume that reference resolution failed for *this enemy tank* and *here*, because there was only one EGD available (EGD0), and because tank B is not an enemy tank. According to the list above, we will generate a message corresponding to the failure to resolve the reference to the object of the command:

(13)   *There is no enemy tank at the place you indicate*

which results from the filtering of graphical data using the semantic representation of the spoken segment *this enemy tank*. For this utterance, two representations are built:

– by combining EGD0 with *this enemy tank*, with a failure for both references to *the enemy tank* and *here*,
– by combining EGD0 with *here*, leaving *this enemy tank* unspecified.

The choice we made might be viewed as debatable, since the second partial interpretation could actually be the right one (EGD0 indicates the position, and the first pointing gesture was just not detected). But the feedback message gives clues on the reason of the failure in both cases, and is a better choice than

There is no tank enemy at the place you indicate and the destination could not be recognized, or *Please indicate the position of the enemy tank,* because both of those messages would actually lead the operator to make a new attempt, and the reason of the failure (the tank is not an enemy tank) would only become clear after this new attempt.

6   Concluding Remarks

In this chapter we have suggested a set of guidelines based on literature study and used them for the definition of an 'interaction style'. We showed that this makes it possible to overcome some of the problematic limitations of reactive interfaces. Our model allows tolerance in the precision of pointing gestures, and by an explicit use of the cues used to resolve cross-references between gestures and voice it is capable of providing feedback with an improved relevance. This feature is important in virtual reality or augmented reality interfaces for at least two reasons: it allows to use 3D pointing devices, like digital gloves, and frees the user from the necessity of sitting in front of a table to operate a mouse, for example. Reported work also benefited from users' expertise in one of the two applications mentioned above. Therefore, we believe that the main characteristics that were specified and implemented are quite stable, because the presentation of the system to the users involved in the design of the system, as well as the demonstration in a professional exhibition, showed positive reactions.[6]

Finally, we would like to stress again that integration of the *uses* of the channels should be a central issue of multimodal communication, because it gives useful hints to the designer having to make *a priori* choices to define the interaction style. Furthermore, it would avoid to draw erroneous conclusions from partial studies, even if these conclusions apply in the context of the study. For example, despite the excellent quality of the work reported by Johnston *et al.* (1997), p. 285, some conclusions concerning the role of time in multimodal communication ("Empirical study on the nature of multimodal interaction has shown that speech typically follows a gesture within a window of a three to four seconds") need to be reconsidered, especially because they turn out to be false in the general case. Kendon (1986) reports in a detailed fundamental study on gestures, where the temporal relations between gestures and speech are also considered, that the *beginning* of a gesture ('preparatory phase'), not the gesture itself precedes speech, and that the gesture can end after the use of speech (in its 'retraction phase').

Though multimodal interaction is no longer a new area of research, reliable data on the feasibility of usable systems still do not seem to be available, and we believe that solutions have to rely on a sensible development of technologies and techniques. These developments should be based on hints provided by fundamental studies on the roles and use characteristics of gestures and speech,

---

[6] The 'Bourget Naval' exhibition in 1992. This exhibition takes places every two years near Paris.

providing a general framework, and on situated experimental investigations that can help us to find answers to specific questions.

Acknowledgments

This chapter reports work that was performed by the author when he was a Ph.D. student in the 'Dialogue' team of CRIN (Centre de Recherche en Informatique de Nancy, Université Henri Poincaré/Nancy I), directed by Prof. J.-M. Pierrel, and while he was employed as a research engineer in the Thomson-CSF company. The author would like to thank Mrs. Bacconnet, head of the Computer Research Group of the Central Research Laboratory of Thomson, for allowing to use the examples presented in this chapter.

References

Amalberti, R., Carbonell, N., and Falzon, P. (1989) User's representation of the machine in human-computer interaction, INRIA Research Report 1125.

Bisson, P., Kakez, S., Poulet-Mathis, C., Pouteau, X., and Cavazza, C. (1995) Augmented Reality for Telepresence, 4th Conference on Interface to Real and Virtual Worlds, Montpellier (France).

Bolt R. (1980) 'Put-That-There': Voice and Gesture at the Graphics Interface, *Computer Graphics*, 14, 262–270.

Bunt H. (1998) Issues in Multimodal Human-Computer Communication, in H. Bunt, R.J. Beun, and T. Borghuis (eds.) *Multimodal Human-Computer Communication*. Berlin: Springer, 1–12.

Buxton, W. (1986) There's More to Interaction than Meets the Eye: Some Issues in Manual Input, in D. Norman and S. Draper (eds.) (1986), *User Centered System Design: New Perspectives on Human-Computer Interaction*, Hillsdale, New Jersey: Lawrence Erlbaum Associates, 319–337.

Cadoz, C., Lisowski, L., and Florens, J.-L. (1990) A Modular Feedback Keyboard Design, *Computer Music Journal*, 4:2, 47–51.

Cadoz, C. (1992) Le geste canal de communication homme-machine, *6th Autumn School*, Thomson Campus, Jouy-en-Josas (F), September 7-11.

Falzon, P. (1983) Understanding a technical language: a schema-based approach, INRIA Research Report 237.

Feyereisen, P. (1987) Gesture and Speech, interactions and separations: A reply to McNeill (1985), in *Psychological Review*, 94:4, 493–498.

Feyereisen, P., Van de Wiele, F., and Dubois, F. (1988) The meaning of gestures: What can be understood without speech? in *Cahiers de Psychologie Cognitive*, 8:1, 3–25.

Gaiffe B., Romary L., and Pierrel J. (1991) References in a Multimodal Dialogue: Towards a Unified Process, in Proc. EUROSPEECH'91, Genova.

Gaiffe, B. (1992) Référence et dialogue homme-machine: vers un modèle adapté au multimodal, Ph.D. thesis, Université Nancy I.

Hauptmann, A. and Mc Avinney, P. (1993) Gesture with speech for graphic manipulation, *Journal of Man-Machine Studies*, 38, 231–249.

Johnston, M., Cohen, P., McGee, D., Oviatt, S., Pittman, J., and Smith, I. (1997) Unification-based Multimodal Integration, in Proc *ACL97*, Madrid, 281–288.

Kendon, A. (1986) Current issues in the study of gesture, in *The Biological Founda-tions of Gestures: Motor and Semiotic Aspects*, Nespoulos, Perron, Lecours (eds.), Hillsdale, New Jersey: Lawrence Erlbaum Associates.

Mc Kevitt, P. (1997) IntelliMedia TourGuide: understanding reference at the language/vision interface, in Proc *European Science Foundation (ESF), Network on Converging Computing Methodologies in Astronomy (CCMA)*, Sonthofen (Germany).

McNeill, D. (1985) So you think gestures are nonverbal? in *Psychological Review*, 92:3, 350–371.

McNeill, D. (1987) So you do think gestures are nonverbal? Reply to Feyereisen, in *Psychological Review*, 94:4, 499–504.

Piwek, P., Beun, R., and Cremers, A. (1995) Dutch and English demonstratives: A comparison. IPO manuscript 1134 (submitted for publication to *Computational Linguistics*).

Pouteau, X., Romary, L., and Pierrel, J. (1993) A knowledge-based approach towards operative multimodal dialogues: MELODIA experiment, in Proc *ESCA/NATO-RsG 10 Workshop on Speech Technology and its applications*, Lautrach (Germany), 183–186.

Pouteau, X. (1995) *Dialogue homme-machine multimodal: une communication na-turelle pour l'opérateur?* Ph.D. thesis, Université Henri Poincaré/Nancy I.

Pouteau, X., Krahmer, E., and Landsbergen, J. (1997) Robust Spoken Dialogue Management for Driver Information Systems, in Proc. *Eurospeech'97*, Rhodos, 2207–2210.

Rasmussen, J. (1976) *Information processing and human-machine interaction*. Amsterdam: North Holland-Elsevier.

Rimé, B. and Schiaratura, L. (1991) Gesture and Speech, in Feldman, R., Rim'e, B. (eds.) *Fundamentals of nonverbal behaviour*, Cambridge University Press, 239–281.

Sidner, C. (1986) Focusing in the comprehension of definite anaphora, in *Readings in Natural Language Processing*, Palo Alto: Morgan-Kauffman, 363-394.

Wahlster, W. (1991) User and Discourse Models for Multimodal Communication, in *Intelligent User Interfaces*, ACM Press Series, Sullivan and Tyler (eds.), Reading, Mass.: Addison-Wesley, 45-67.

Why Are Multimodal Systems so Difficult to Build? - About the Difference between Deictic Gestures and Direct Manipulation

Michael Streit

DFKI, Saarbrücken, Germany
streit@dfki.de

Abstract. By integrating conversationally used natural language with graphical interfaces, gestural interaction looses the simplicity of direct manipulation. Input in one channel may change the meaning of input in another channel rather drastically. This introduces the wait problem, i.e. the problem of when and how long the system has to wait for input in other channels, before it triggers an action. Additionally, pointing devices and feedback may cause obtrusive effects on the natural synchronisation of deictic gestures and deictic expressions. Certain uses of gestures are observed that are distinct from natural communication and direct manipulation as well, e.g. focusing gestures. The discussion of these problems is based on our experience with the multimodal prototypes MOFA and TALKY that we implemented in different variations, each showing a slightly different style of interaction. The notion of passive and active gesture forms is introduced as well as the notion of active and passive objects. Incremental natural language interpretation and the provision of incremental and preliminary feedback turn out to be important challenges for the upcoming technology of multimodal interfaces.

1 Introduction

According to Sullivan (1991) the central topic in building multimodal systems is *"to learn how linguistic notions of conversation can be incorporated into graphical user interfaces"*. Interaction in graphical user interfaces is essentially gestural. Therefore the central issue of multimodal systems is the integration of speech (or much more awkward: typed natural language with 2-D gestures.)[1] There is much effort on the side of the natural language community to integrate gestures with natural language and to apply the result to graphical interfaces. There is also growing effort on the HCI-side to integrate speech into graphical user interfaces. With the advent of practically usable speech recognisers the construction of practical multimodal interfaces becomes feasible. But also, problems become visible that have been widely ignored in the past.

---

[1] Today direct manipulation systems are usually based on 2-D gestures, e.g., mouse clicks.

H. Bunt and R.-J. Beun (Eds.): CMC'98, LNAI 2155, pp. 176–196, 2001.
© Springer-Verlag Berlin Heidelberg 2001

2 Paradigms of Multimodal Interaction

2.1 The Direct Manipulation Based Approach to Multimodal Interaction

In direct manipulation the referent of a gesture is always unambiguous: either there is one object selected or the gesture is not successful at all. In this process of selection only the gesture and the objects are involved.

The HCI community tends to use speech commands as an alternative channel for the selection of commands by manipulative gestures. But if gestural selection is replaced by speech, one is immediately confronted with the problem of ambiguity: while usually pointing gestures in a graphical user interface are unambiguously mapped to some object by standard event handling procedures, speech refers by means of a complex and context dependent inference process to the objects of the universe of discourse. Also, reference by speech is naturally not restricted to visible objects.

Since, in contrast with gestures, there are no means to relate speech directly to graphical objects, problems of ambiguity even occur with very simple speech command systems. For example, if two objects share the same name there is no simple process to distinguish them by speech. The implementation of a clarification dialogue component or a context dependent natural language interpretation component can only be avoided by putting strong restrictions on the use of speech input and also on the design of the graphical system. For example, *there are only unequivocal object names in the application* or *in any state of the application, there are only objects visible that have unequivocal names and the user is allowed to refer to visible objects only.*

Multimodal systems that are constructed along these lines are only useful in very special situations (e.g. if hands free interaction is important and the application needs only a limited set of commands). The general idea behind the direct manipulation based approach to multimodal interaction is that speech and gesture are input modalities that may substitute each other. According to Oviatt (1997), this idea belongs to the *common myths* of multimodal communication, that are not substantiated by empirical studies.

We will not elaborate further on the shortcomings of this approach. Instead, we will consider certain problems that occur when we try to implement a natural style of communication in multimodal interfaces.

2.2 The NLP-Oriented Approach to Multimodal Interaction

Multimodal systems that originate in NLP usually do not consider speech and gestures as alternative channels for the same kind of interaction. They are well aware of the complementary use of speaking and pointing, they even take into account that natural gestures may be ambiguous, and they provide inference mechanisms for context dependent interpretation of natural language. The XTRA System (see Wahlster, 1991), for example, shows all these features. But the NLP community tends to transfer too much of what they know about natural language communication into the evolving paradigm of multimodal man-machine-interaction.

In natural communication the intention of the dialogue partner is usually transferred by speech. Gestures are semantically related to speech by strict synchronisation with their linguistic counterparts, i.e., with deictic expressions. If a speaker points and speaks, she will normally not expect any reaction to her pointing gesture (except signalling awareness) before the hearer has processed the verbal utterance. Merely pointing (without speaking) is at least a strange form of communication, which is slightly more acceptable only in special situations, such as giving an answer in a clarification dialogue.

The NLP community therefore tends to follow a speech-driven interaction paradigm. If a manipulative component is considered, it is assumed to work largely independently from the conversational part. Especially, it is assumed that there is no confusion between manipulative and communicative uses of gestures.

Recently, the idea that speech-driven conversational interaction may be integrated into graphical interfaces without conflicts has become the subject of a critical discussion. For example, Oviatt et al. (1997) stated that the idea of a tight synchronisation of speech and gesture is not supported by empirical results. Streit (1997) has drawn the attention to the problem that under certain conditions manipulative and deictic uses of gestures may not easily be distinguished.

The gap between natural communication based expectations and empirical findings of multimodal interaction seems partly to result from an idealisation of natural communication, and partly from the fact that the user interacts differently with a machine than with people. But, as pointed out in the previous section, criticism on a rather *idealistic* approach to the integration of conversational interaction and graphical interfaces may not result in a direct manipulation oriented paradigm of multimodal interaction.

3   The Multimodal Systems MOFA and TALKY

Our considerations are based mainly on experience with the multimodal systems MOFA and TALKY, that we implemented in different variations, each showing a slightly different style of multimodal interaction. Our aim was to learn how multimodal systems could practically be realized that are accepted by end users. We did not perform quantitative experiments rigorously, but close observation of users was part of our work.

Mofa

The domain of MOFA is route planning. The system follows partly a direct manipulation oriented paradigm, partly it realises a conversational style of interaction. To manage these two styles, the interface of MOFA is divided into two parts.

The map information is accessible through conversational interaction. The dominant interaction style is speech-driven, but the system also accounts for a certain form of gesture-driven non-manipulative interaction: a sequence of pointing acts is interpreted as part of a route specification. Pointing gestures may also count as sufficient answers in a clarification dialogue. Due to the domain, it is very common that utterances are combined with multiple pointing gestures. Focusing gestures are not supported by the system.

Within certain limitations, the system allows for a natural style of speaking. The system may interpret a set of patterns of noun phrases and prepositional phrases, which may be freely arranged into sentences and elliptical expressions. MOFA does not handle spontaneous corrections of a request and does not allow for user-initiated sub-dialogues.

The direct manipulation part of the MOFA interface provides menus and buttons. They may also be addressed by speech - following the direct manipulation oriented paradigm of multimodality, mentioned in Section 2.1

The user does not have to explicitly change between the parts of the interface. These parts only differ with respect to their graphical objects, that behave differently with respect to pointing acts. They serve for a clear separation between manipulative and referential uses of pointing gestures.

Talky

TALKY is a prototype for calendar management. The interaction in TALKY is much more verbal than in MOFA. The task oriented robust natural language interpretation of TALKY allows for a rather free and spontaneous style of verbal communication (cf. Fig. 1).

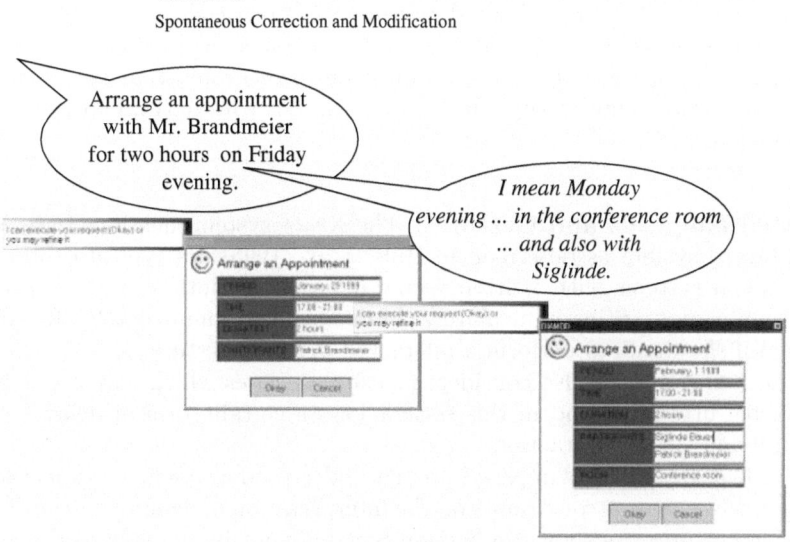

Fig. 1. Spontaneous Modification of a Task in the TALKY System.

TALKY allows for working in parallel on different tasks or task instances. The interpretation of utterances makes use of a focus stack of tasks and parts of tasks. The user may switch between tasks implicitly or explicitly. The user can leave clarification dialogues at any time and re-enter them at any time. The initiative of the user is only restricted if the clarification dialogue is concerned with acoustic recognition problems.

TALKY makes use of so-called *visual utterances* (cf. Streit, 1999b) that represent the state of a task specification and the system's comments on the last user utterance that is concerned with the task. Examples of verbal comments are questions for missing parameters. The standard representation of a verbal comment is a bubble with text. Shortcomings of speech output are discussed in Streit (1999a). In TALKY, spoken output is used only if the system wants to attract special attention.

By representing objects and stages of the discourse, visual utterances allow to use focusing gestures to navigate in the focus space. Obviously there is no comparable use of focusing gestures in natural communication. According to the laconic style of communication that users normally show with multimodal interfaces, focusing gestures are usually not accompanied by speech. In TALKY, they are the main source of long temporal gaps between gestures and parts of speech that disambiguate each other. These gaps may not be expected from the viewpoint of natural communication.

4   Problems with the Integration of Speech and Gestures

4.1   Synchronisation of Speech and Gestures

It is the *holy grail* of NLP-oriented multimodal approaches that deictic gestures are strictly synchronised with deictic natural language expressions (see e.g. Huls et al., 1995). Surprisingly, the idea of strong synchronisation is favoured by researchers who do not work with speech at all, but with natural language input by keyboard.

Written Language and Gestures. The XTRA system mentioned above and the Edward system as described in Huls et al. (1995) are typical examples of multimodal systems with written verbal interaction. Both systems expect the user to interrupt writing immediately before, during or immediately after deictic phrases if she wants to perform a referential pointing gesture.

The XTRA system also considers focusing gestures which may occur before the verbal utterance, and in this sense allows a certain form of delay between gestural and verbal interaction.

But focusing gestures in XTRA are not understood as possible referential acts by themselves, but as constraints on the interpretation of definite descriptions or pointing gestures. As shown in Section 8, it may not be possible to distinguish focusing gestures from referential ones.

Technically, the multimodal combination of written language and gestures is a little easier to handle than that of speech and gestures (even apart from problems with speech recognition). With keyboard and mouse input, events of any modality can be processed one after the other. By contrast, speech recognition results come after a little delay, and furthermore they normally don't come in a word by word mode. Therefore with speech, temporal relations between input events or even parts of input events, have to be managed explicitly.

From an ergonomic point of view, the combination of interrupted writing and pointing is a problem because it only can be performed by a highly concentrated user. Perhaps, this kind of input may be performed better with pen based systems, where the same device is used for verbal and gestural input. But this is only a speculation. In Oviatts studies this pattern is not reported and we have no experience with pen-based multimodal systems.

Speech and Gestures. In natural communication, it is strange if people do not synchronise pointing gestures with deictic expressions. But as already mentioned in Section 2.2, empirical studies show that in man-machine interaction multimodal constructions often display a different pattern.

Partly this is due to the fact that in man-machine communication deictic expressions often are dropped. Oviatt (1997) reported that only 41% of multimodal constructions did contain a deictic expression at all. But even if a deictic expression was used, they often (43%) observed a sequential pattern of interaction. In theses cases the deictic gesture was completed before the deictic term was spoken, with an average lag of ca. 1 sec.

These results impose a problem, because synchronisation of speech and gesture is important for the interpretation of multimodal utterances. For example, in natural communication we are able to distinguish (1) from (2).

(1)   *From here to there* ↗
(2)   *From here* ↗ *to there*

by merely considering temporal relations between gestures and deictic expressions (↗ represents a pointing gesture). In the first utterance the speaker refers anaphorically to the starting point and deictically to the point of destination, and vice versa in the second utterance.

In our systems we also observed gaps between parts of speech and gestures that disambiguate each other. But our conclusion is not to consider synchronisation as a concept that is not relevant for multimodal systems. Instead, we want to discuss features of multimodal systems that affect synchronisation more thoroughly. In Section 5 we will try to provide an explanation for different integration patterns in natural communication and multimodal man-machine dialogue in terms of gesture types and feedback. In Section 6 we will discuss more concretely interdependencies between the user's behaviour with respect to synchronisation and different pointing devices, feedback strategies, aspects of speech processing and the kind of natural language expressions that she uses. In the next section we will continue the discussion of problems.

4.2   Referring and Manipulative Functions of Gestures

Conflicting Interpretations with Domain Tasks. We will explain the problem with an example of the TALKY system. In TALKY, there are sheets for months and for days. The month sheets consist basically of a list of buttons representing the days of the month. The day sheets basically show the list of the appointments that are scheduled for a day.

From the viewpoint of conversational interaction the user could refer to the representation of a day in a deictic manner. If, e.g., she combines the utterance *an dem ↗ Tag geschäftlich in Kaiserslautern (in Kaiserslautern for business at this ↗ day)* with a pointing act to the graphical presentation of the day under consideration, the gesture acts only passively, supplying the spoken utterance with referential information. Besides reference, the gesture contributes nothing to the interaction.

In contrast, from the viewpoint of direct manipulation, the user will point to the representation of a day (e.g., the 1st of May) with the expectation that the sheet of the day will immediately be opened. From the viewpoint of direct manipulation, gestures are active; they are expected to trigger some action by the system.[2]

In a strictly manipulative view the user intends the gestures as a complete self-sufficient turn of the interaction. Verbal utterances that accompany or follow such manipulative gestures do not modify the meaning of the gesture. But of course, the interpretation of these utterances may depend on the gesture. For example, if in this context the user utters *um 12 Uhr in Raum 17 (at 12 o'clock in room 17)* it is most likely that she specifies an appointment on the 1st of May. In this case the elliptic verbal utterance can be resolved by the manipulative gesture. But if the user utters *on 2nd of May meeting with Mr.X* she performs an unrelated task.

How to decide between deictic and manipulative use of gestures? An ad hoc attempt to solve the problem could be: open the day sheet and then check if the day could be used to resolve a missing referent or not. But this does not help in only slightly more complicated cases.

For example, assume the user wants to enter his holidays and utters something like *holidays ↗ ↗* or *holidays from then ↗ to then ↗*, by attempting to point to two days. The user will never succeed, because the system opens the day sheet, and unmaps the month sheet, before she touches the second day.

The example depends on the semantic properties of the tasks and objects in the domain. For instance, in the example it is important that there is a manipulative object that bears a natural semantics (i.e. representing a day).

Conflicting Interpretations with Meta-tasks. Conflicting interpretations with respect to manipulation and deixis are not restricted to specific conditions as in the example in the previous section. Meta-tasks, such as asking for help, generally lead to the same problem: pointing to a manipulative object while asking for an explanation should not trigger the action which is connected with the object.

The Wait Problem. The examples discussed so far in this section have in common that the system should wait for a speech utterance that may modify the

---

[2] In the real world a gesture is a communicative act, while manipulation is basically physical. Direct manipulation may be viewed as an attempt to let a certain form of communication appear as a quasi-physical act.

gesture. Waiting is necessary, because the modification may express an intention that is not compatible with the action that would be triggered without the modification. This establishes a problem because long delays are hardly acceptable as normal behaviour of the system. We call this problem the *wait problem for multimodal systems*.

The wait problem is in principle not restricted to the change of a manipulative reading into a deictic reading of a gesture. For example, if a system is enhanced with features of natural communication, one can also think of modifying a manipulation instead of completely skipping the manipulative meaning. One could specify an action by gesture and in parallel specify by speech that the action should be performed in a certain mode (e.g., *fast* or *as usual*), thereby unfolding the hidden communicative nature of direct manipulation.

Similar problems may occur with natural gestures that play an active role in communication. Common examples of such active non-manipulative gestures are *head nodding* or *traffic control by a policeman at a street crossing*. Like manipulative gestures they may be modified by simultaneous speech.

We will discuss several approaches to resolve the wait problem, namely:

- keeping gaps short by promoting synchronisation of multimodal user utterances;
- identifying the cases where gaps are harmless;
- providing certain features to reduce the critical cases.

There is a silent assumption underlying the discussion of the wait problem. It is assumed, according to the results of Oviatt (1997), that a gesture always precedes speech or is used simultaneously with speech. Otherwise, there is the possibility that modifying speech by gesture becomes subject to the wait problem. Usually, modifying speech by gesture will not result in a complete change of the meaning of the spoken utterance, but failures with respect to reference resolution are very likely to occur. Later we will discuss cases where gestures are likely to follow speech or where gaps between gestures are relevant (see Sections 6.7 and 8.1).

5   Basic Gesture Types

5.1   Gesture Types and Gesture Forms

The wait problem basically has its origin in the fact that there are two modalities that may independently *drive* the interaction but also may *specify* each other.

To discuss the problem in a more general way we introduce some terminology and notation. By *driving the interaction* we mean that the structure in question may constitute a complete turn. In the context of task-oriented dialogue we mean by a turn an interaction that communicates an intention.

A gesture that may form a turn is called *active*. Manipulative gestures are examples of active gestures.[3] In natural communication, pointing gestures ordi-

---

[3] In direct manipulation, recognising a turn is the same task as recognising a gesture. In natural communication, a sequence of potential turns may form a complex turn. An important feature to signal the end of a turn is a gap.

narily may not be used to form a turn. Only with strong dialogue expectations as in clarification dialogues they may count as a full turn. We call these gestures *passive*.

Hence, with respect to turns we distinguish two types of gesture:

- (type A) gestures that serve as a complete turn;
- (type P) gestures that only contribute certain information to a turn.

We call gestures of type A *active* gestures, gestures of type P *passive* gestures.

Active gestures, such as manipulative gestures, need no complement to serve as a communicative act. Hence they must be recognised as an intended communicative act. By contrast, with deictic pointing gestures speech serves as a *click* which distinguishes pointing gestures as intended communication from pointing gestures that are used, e.g., for self-orientation. This motivates a second distinction:

- (form-type AF) gestures that are intended as communicative acts by virtue of their form.
- (form-type PF) gestures that are made valid as an communicative act by another event which in natural communication is usually speech.

We say that gestures of form-type AF have an *active form*,[4] while gestures of type PF have a *passive form*. Type A gestures are obviously also of form-type AF. Gestures with form-type PF obviously are of type P.

We stipulate two criteria for being an act of intended communication. First the gesture must be distinguished from unintended moves or positions, that are similar to the gesture, and secondly it must be distinguished from non-communicative uses of the gesture.[5]

The form of a gesture is constituted e.g. by body movement, posture and position, touch or mouse position, with or without button press. In the example of Section 4.2 it is assumed that gestures used for manipulation and deixis may be indistinguishable with respect to their form. Consequently the definition of type A and type P distinguishes between gestures that may share the same form.

This means there are active gesture forms that may build active as well as passive gestures. This may be viewed as being analogous to ambiguous words in natural language. Alternatively, speech may be viewed as an integral part of deictic gestures. In any case, we consider the term *gesture form* as restricted to

---

[4] As mentioned in Section 6.2, one may introduce certain stages of activity. This is common in graphical interfaces, where a double click triggers a reaction of a higher stage than a simple click.

[5] We simply declare a gesture as non-communicative if the addressee of the gesture is not the system. In fact such gestures may be used for communication with a third party. The problem to determine the addressee of an utterance is well known from speech processing. With gestures the user normally is able to distinguish between gesture forms that are used non-communicatively and gesture forms that are used to communicate with the system. With the advent of multimodal systems there is an increasing number of gestures that are used for interaction with the system. This raises the problem whether there are still non-communicative gestures available. Otherwise similar problems would occur as with speech communication.

effects that result from moving a part of the body or from assuming a certain posture.

In Section 6 we will discuss active and passive gesture forms more concretely. Later (in Section 7) we will discuss the possibilities for introducing different gesture forms for solving the wait problem.

5.2   Type-Specific Problems

Gesture types and form types are related to specific problems. The important cases are:

- active gestures (type A)
- active gesture forms, that are used passively (type P with form-type AF)
- passive gesture forms (form-type PF)

With active gestures the wait problem occurs. Ignoring a spoken modification may result in an action that contradicts the intention of the user. Therefore a user who changes a manipulative gesture into a deictic one by speech may be expected to keep gaps short. This makes this kind of gaps subject to efforts in promoting synchronisation by appropriate pointing devices.

Apart from deictically transformed manipulative gestures, active gesture forms may be used for referential gestures. For example, if a capacitive touch screen is used, the system normally provides only one gesture form which is active (cf. Section 6 and Section 7). But to refer to an object does not express any intention, thus referential gestures are passive gestures from the view point of natural communication.

Passive gestures that are made up from active gestures forms build a fuzzy region between natural communication and direct manipulation. It is mainly here that we see gaps between speech and gestures that are not expected from the viewpoint of natural communication.

With gestures of form-type PF, speech is needed as a complement of the gesture. Passive gesture forms transfer natural deixis directly to man-machine-communication. But the integration of passive gesture forms into graphical interfaces poses difficult problems for gesture recognition and is only useful under strong limitations or with certain requirements on the performance of the gesture (cf. Section 6.1).

5.3   Passively Used Active Forms: Gaps and the Role of Feedback

In our systems referential gestures are always pointing gestures, but the following considerations also apply to referential gestures with an iconic or even symbolic components such as those used in the QuickSet system (cf. Pittmann, 1996).

Gaps are well known from gestural selection in graphical interfaces. The mere selection of an object uses the same gesture that activates an menu-item or a button, i.e., an active gesture form. By *mere selection*, we mean that there is no action associated with the selection. Mere selection is a referential act that is enhanced with immediate feedback. After a mere selection, the user usually will *select* an action, but there may be an arbitrary gap between these two acts.

While in natural communication, pointing to a physical object is not expected to highlight this object, pointing in a graphical interface may highlight it. By highlighting, the system communicates that it has recognised the pointing act. Usually, as long as there is no conflicting interaction, highlighting is permanent. This communicates to the user that the system bears in mind the referent.

By feedback, in some respect, referential acts count as a full turn. But this turn is not complete with respect to the communication of an intention.[6] Presumably, the user will continue the interaction to finish her task. In natural communication a full turn that communicates no intention is rather irritating for the dialogue partner. By contrast, a machine will patiently wait till the user will continue.

Oviatt (1997) mentions a maximal gap of four seconds between gesture and speech. One may expect that sometimes even longer gaps will occur, depending on the flow of the dialogue. Further, in man machine communication the flow of the dialogue is often driven only by the user and not by the system.[7]

In the TALKY system we observed such long gaps with focusing gestures. Perhaps these slightly different findings are due to certain features of the experiment (e.g. the challenge to perform as fast as possible). Perhaps also special features of feedback may explain the differences. If feedback signals that the interpretation of the gesture is not finished, the pressure to continue may be higher than with feedback that is finally determined. In TALKY, feedback on focus gestures is vague rather than ambiguous. This may reduce the pressure to continue.

6 Multimodal Settings for Different Gesture Forms

Issues of synchronisation are difficult to discuss, because there are a lot of factors that, apart from gestural input devices, bias the behaviour of the user. These factors include the interaction habits of the user, the form of feedback that is provided by the system, the concrete form of the verbal utterance, but also certain features of speech processing. In the following we will discuss several settings for deictic pointing gestures with respect to their *synchronising* properties.

Pointing by hand is easily performed in parallel with speech. People synchronise deictic expressions and deictic pointing without any cognitive or physical stress. Pointing devices used in man-machine communication need a certain amount of mental and tactile effort, that is likely to hamper the coordination of speech and gesture.

Because synchronisation is especially important when a multimodal construction contains more than one referent, we concentrate the discussion in the following on MOFA, where multiple referents are likely to occur in one utterance. Also, in MOFA we implemented three versions of deictic pointing: click-free mouse ges-

---

[6] In certain situations, the intention may be inferred from context (cf. Section 8.1).

[7] Patiently waiting is the typical attitude of desktop programs. But systems may be designed to push the user's activity, e.g., at service access points.

tures, mouse clicks and capacitive touch screen technology, while in TALKY we used only touch screen technology and mouse clicks.

Additionally we will discuss a *mouse-wait* approach and the use of 2-D visual gesture recognition. We will touch on features of speech recognition and natural language processing that are relevant for a fluent coordination of speech and gestures. We will also consider the relations between the form of the language expression and related pointing acts. Feedback is discussed together with the pointing devices.

6.1 Click-Free Mouse Pointing

By *click-free* mouse pointing we mean that the user may point to some location without using mouse buttons, merely by moving the mouse to this location. If no further restriction is imposed on the user her effort is minimised.

Obviously this kind of click-free mouse pointing is a passive gesture form. To become a (communicative) gesture, additional information is needed. Otherwise the system could not distinguish between intended communication and other mouse moves.

In the temporal proximity of a deictic expression, the MOFA system looks for objects that semantically fit the constraints that are imposed verbally. The semantic constraints include the information given by the deictic phrase, but also information that is provided by the whole utterance, such as the information that the user is searching for a public traffic connection or for a route for the car.

But the consideration of semantic constraints depends on meaningful verbal expressions, which may not be there. In MOFA, utterances of the type *from here to there* are likely to occur. With these cases, semantic constraints are provided by pointing acts rather than by speech. For example, by pointing to a street crossing the user addresses the route planning task; by pointing to tube stations she asks for a tube connection.

Even approaches that analyse more closely the trajectory of the mouse movement to find so-called singularities (see Bellalem et al., 1995) rely on the occurrence of informative deictic phrases. To make click-free mouse pointing work we had to strongly restrict the system. The aim of this version of MOFA was not to achieve a feasible route planning system, but to provide an environment for experimenting with click-free mouse pointing.

A map provides a continuous space of locations. In principle, every location could serve as a referent for a pointing act. We first limited the information on the map. We restricted the possible referents to street crossings and also restricted their number. Additionally pointing to certain tube stations was possible.

A second problem was the use of plural deixis[8] and certain elliptical expression. These kinds of expressions are accompanied by an unknown set of pointing acts, that are scattered around the expressions. Accordingly, the second limitation was to use no plural deixis and no expressions that are elliptical with respect to deixis. The third limitation was not to use anaphoric expressions.

---

[8] Deictic expressions are often adverbs, which are not marked with respect to number. What we mean are expressions with a set denotation.

Even with these limitations there are some obstacles to achieving a successful interaction with the system, at least when multiple pointing acts are involved. With mouse pointing, the user has to move the pointer across the screen, which takes much more time than pointing by hand. For synchronisation of speech and gesture she often has to make a pause in the utterance which is not motivated by cognitive processing, but is caused by the pointing device. We sometimes observed that the pointing gesture was finished with a considerable delay after the deictic expression, which normally led to misinterpretations.

The first version of MOFA was not able to handle pauses appropriately. But the problem also occurred with later versions due to certain expectations of the user with respect to the performance of the speech processing. If users knew that they were allowed to make pauses in a verbal utterance, they performed much better with respect to synchronisation.

It is a problem in general to provide feedback on pointing gestures that are specified by speech, because speech contains information that is needed for referent resolution. With unrestricted click-free mouse pointing the speech channel is even needed to recognise the fact that a pointing gesture was performed. Therefore it is difficult to give feedback on gestural interaction before speech is processed.

We introduced a kind of feedback that is often used in graphical interfaces in a similar way. If the mouse pointer is moved across some object, the object is highlighted, but highlighting is removed when the cursor leaves the object. This is not a feedback that shows that an intended pointing act was performed. It is only shown that the user would refer to the highlighted object, if she would perform an intended pointing act. The intention to perform a pointing act is communicated by a speech click, i.e., by coincidence with an deictic expression.

The advantage of this feedback is that it may not be confused with selection. It is not permanent but vanishes. Additionally, users know that usually graphical interfaces will not trigger an action by merely moving the pointer onto an object. This prevents the user from considering this form of pointing as a more or less complete turn, that may be followed by a gap. The user understands easily that she has to speak to make the gestures valid as intended communication. The disadvantage of this feedback is that it is difficult to show ambiguity. After speech processing the system provides a final and permanent feedback which shows the objects that are selected by using speech information.

Though the system works well with respect to synchronisation, it is only of limited practical use, because it can only be used with very simple structured domains.

6.2   Click-Free Mouse Pointing with Mouse-Wait

A practical solution for click-free mouse pointing may be a procedure as is used by the visual recognition of 2-D gestures, but also in some graphical user interfaces. The system expects the user to leave the pointer for a short time on the object which she wants to refer to. We call this a *wait* or, if the mouse is used as pointing device, a *mouse wait*.

The system gives feedback to the user that it has recognised her pointing act. In contrast to the feedback procedure mentioned above, this feedback may only occur after a certain latency. With this procedure the user has to wait a short time, until she may continue the interaction. Hence the flow of communication is interrupted as it is the case with using mouse clicks (cf. next section). There is less tactile effort than with clicks but the effort with respect to visual attention is slightly higher. Still, there is a certain danger of unintentionally pointing to some object.

By waiting a certain form of *click* is introduced. This makes this gesture form a candidate for being an active form, because the gesture may be distinguished from unintended pointing without considering speech. But it may not be distinguishable from non-communicative pointing. Usually systems provide helpful information about the object that is a referent of a mouse wait, while selecting the object is done by a click.

It is debatable if this form of presenting help is active communication or not. We tend to classify it as a non-communicative effect similar to the transient highlighting of objects that is discussed above. This means that we assume that in a multimodal interface there are feedback effects that are not first-class communication. We have no theory about the nature of these effects. For example, they may be viewed as non-communicative effects in a stimulus-response manner or a as a sort of para-communication. Therefore, we are inclined to classify mouse waits as a passive form.

This topic calls for further empirical and theoretical study. Especially the appropriate form of feedback is still unclear.

6.3   Pointing with Mouse Clicks

While with a touch screen users easily understand that they may point in a natural manner, this has to be explained more explicitly if the mouse has to be used. Initially some users show an interaction style of the kind they are acquainted with for graphical user interfaces. We even observed users performing three pointing gestures and in the sequence speaking an utterance with three deictic expressions.

Even in case of multiple pointing this kind of interaction is often interpretable. The sequence of pointing acts is mapped in the same order to the sequence of deictic expressions that occur in the follow-up utterance. As long as anaphoric expressions are excluded, this approach works considerably well. But with long sequences sometimes users confused the sequential order of deictic gestures and deictic expressions.

With more than two pointing acts the sequential integration pattern becomes rather inconvenient. On the other hand, it turned out to be difficult to synchronise speech with mouse clicks. If speech processing does not allow for pauses it is almost impossible to synchronise a part of speech and a mouse click. That mouse clicks cannot be expected to be synchronised well with speech is also verified by formal ergonomic reasoning, as is presented by Faconti (1997). Nevertheless, after a certain training, users learned to perform a seamless parallelism of deictic

190   Michael Streit

expressions and pointing gestures by using appropriate speech pauses. But still, this kind of synchronisation needs rather high concentration.

6.4 Pointing with Capacitive Touch Screen

Capacitive touch screens allow for pointing by touching the screen with a finger. Performing a pointing gesture by touching an object is quite common in natural communication. This makes interaction with a touch screen intuitive.

But with a touch screen the user may be in doubt if she hits the intended object. By using the finger as pointing device the resolution of the pointing act is limited. This means that the interface needs a certain granularity to work well. Also the touch screen must be well calibrated taking into account the user's angle.

Under these conditions users performed best with respect to synchronisation with touch screen technology. Not only the coordination between speech and language worked better than with other approaches, but also sequences of pointing acts (cf. Section 6.7 and 8.1) are performed faster.

One may think about achieving a better resolution by providing a pointer as feedback. The problem with this feedback is that it is not visible in the preparation phase of the gesture, because the preparation phase of a touch (i.e. moving the finger to the screen aiming to hit a certain location) is not recognised by the touch screen.

6.5 Visual Gesture Recognition

Pointing by hand gestures that are recognised by a vision system is perhaps the most natural gestural interaction with computer systems one can think of. With vision systems it is possible to provide a pointer as feedback for the position of the finger. In contrast to touch screen technology, the pointer is visible in the preparation phase of the gesture. This allows controlling the pointing act better, but on the other hand this technique draws more attention to the gesture, which makes the gesture less casual.

Though pointing with a free hand is much more natural than pointing with a mouse, this interaction shares some problems with mouse pointing. In the SIVIT system[9] (see Kaemmerer and Maggioni, 1995), the user has to wait a short time until the system gives a prompt, indicating that it recognised an intended pointing gesture. Alternatively the user may perform certain movements to indicate a gesture, e.g. by following with the finger a graphically presented path that leads to some option. As with mouse pointing, this brings about a less fluent synchronisation of speech and gesture.

---

[9] The SIVIT System for visual recognition of 2-D gestures with a projected graphical interface is produced by the Siemens company. It is the first industrial product that uses this technology.

6.6   Speech Recognition and Natural Language Processing

With respect to synchronisation of speech and gesture the most important feature of the speech recogniser is whether it allows for pauses or not. As we have seen above, the need for pauses depends on the pointing device. But apart from the features of the pointing device, pauses originate also from cognitive processing.

In TALKY and also in later versions of MOFA we designed the recogniser's language model by means of a context-free grammar in a way that allowed for pauses. In MOFA we used a very simple method for the control of the linguistic processing with respect to pauses. The user must push a button if she starts a linguistic turn and push it again when she finishes it. The parts of speech which have been recognised in this interval are concatenated and are interpreted by the natural language analysis component.

To use *speech buttons* is very inconvenient. For TALKY, instead an incremental natural language analysis component has been developed that updates the semantic structure after every pause and shows the result via a visual utterance. TALKY provides a practically useful concept for incremental feedback by incrementally updating the visual utterance that belongs to the task specification (cf. Section 3). But to provide incremental feedback on domain presentations is a difficult and application-dependent problem which is not solved in general.

With respect to the interpretation of synchronised speech and gestures, the speech recogniser must deliver reliable time stamps at word level. The time stamps are needed to determine the temporal relations between words and gestures. In our experience speech recognisers that are on the market normally do not provide time stamps. But prototypes that provide a word-graph interface are usually augmented with time information (cf. Amtrup et al., 1996).

6.7   Dependencies between the Use of Gestures and the Structure of Related Verbal Expressions

The first obvious condition for synchronising speech and gestures is the presence of deictic expressions, i.e, adverbs as *here* and *there* or noun phrases with a demonstrative determiner.[10] As mentioned by Oviatt (1999) and also according to our experience, most users prefer a rather laconic style of verbal interaction, when they interact with a graphical interface by means of speech. This means that ellipsis is quite common and deictic expressions are often dropped.

Plural expressions may be combined with a sequence of pointing gestures. For example, the user may utter *from here ↗ to there ↗ via these crossings ↗ ↗ ↗*, combining a plural expression with a sequence of pointing acts to certain persons that are presented in a list. In a touch screen implementation of MOFA, plural deixis and deictic ellipsis could be used in this way. In natural communication this is normally avoided. Instead people prefer to use one gesture for one deictic expression. For referring to a set, either they use one vague gesture referring to

---

[10] Though there is a special demonstrative determiner in German, the definite article is used in deictic expressions as well. Therefore one need not analyse the syntactic form for deciding if an expression is used deictically or not.

a group of objects or they use as many deictic expressions as gestures: *from here* ↗ *to there* ↗ *via these crossings, this one* ↗ *this one* ↗ *and this one* ↗. This clearly shows the passive nature of deictic pointing.

Also, expressions that are elliptical with respect to deixis may be combined with a sequence of pointing acts.

From the absence of a one-to-one relation between gestures and deictic expressions it follows that passive gesture forms may not be used with plural deixis or deictic ellipsis if they need a speech click to be recognised. It may be a possibility to use mouse waits in combination with plural and elliptic deixis, because mouse waits may be recognised as an pointing act, while speech may provide a *weak* click, that justifies mouse wait to be an intended communication.

There is still another problem with multiple pointing acts that are related to a single natural language expression. Such sequences of pointing acts may occur before but also after the expression. The system has to decide when it will assume that such a sequence is finished. We discuss this question in Section 8.1.

7   Active and Passive Gesture Forms as a Solution for the Wait Problem

There is an elegant approach to solve the problems addressed in Section 4.2: If we could infer from the form of the gesture whether it is intended merely as a contribution to referent resolution or as a manipulative act, this would solve the wait problem for manipulative gestures.

Mouse Gesture Forms. The mouse is a device that provides an active and a passive gesture form. By the analysis in Section 5.1 unrestricted click-free mouse pointing is a fascinating option, but it can hardly be used now for practical systems. Perhaps by using mouse waits as a passive form it may be possible to realise a system with two forms of pointing gestures.

Touch-Screen Gesture Forms. The best performing pointing device (with respect to synchronisation) has only one pointing gesture form, that is touching the screen. What could be done is introducing double clicks for manipulative gestures, leaving single clicks for passive pointing. But performing double clicks is hard to learn for beginners. One would loose much of the naturalness that makes touch screen technology attractive for inexperienced users.

Gesture Forms with Vision Systems. In principle, vision systems are able to distinguish between different pointing gestures, e.g., systems can distinguish pointing with the finger from pointing with the full hand. But only pointing with a finger allows sufficient resolution. Perhaps the combination of a touch screen with visual 2-D gesture recognition could be a solution of the problem.

Problems with the Use of Two Different Pointing Gesture Forms.
If two different gesture forms are available, the user may employ them in an
unexpected manner. In the next section we discuss the case of applying an active
gesture form to passive objects without speaking. But also with respect to deixis,
the user may point by means of an active form instead of using a passive form,
especially if she does not expect unwanted effects.

8   Active and Passive Objects

This approach is used in MOFA as well as in TALKY. We distinguish between
passive objects which are simple objects of reference and active objects that react
actively to pointing gestures. The objects and locations on the map are passive,
while menus and buttons are active objects. This allows for a clear cut between
deictic use and manipulative use, not by the gestures form, but by virtue of a
classification of the objects. This approach is feasible if the application allows for
a design with a clear-cut distinction between active and passive objects. It is not
sufficient if there are active objects that have a semantics besides representing the
action in question, e.g. the day buttons in TALKY naturally have the semantics
of representing a certain day.

8.1   Actively Used Passive Objects

If a user uses an active gesture form for pointing to a passive object, she may
expect a reaction from the system.

First, the attempt to communicate merely gesturally with a passive object
has to be detected by the system. In MOFA it is checked if there is parallel speech
input. This introduces a new kind of wait problem. If no speech is detected during
some timeout interval, MOFA provides a reaction to the gesture. In the touch-
screen setting the timeout period must not be very long (we chose about one
second), because we do not expect long gaps between pointing and utterance.

Because in the route-planning application of MOFA it is very likely that the
user may use sequences of pointing acts as short cuts for route descriptions,
we chose in MOFA the approach of interpreting such sequences as sequences
of names of route nodes. That means we interpret gestural actions on passive
objects as if they were natural-language utterances, in contrast to the interpretation of gestures performed on active objects. The sequence of pointing to the
crossing Munich-West and to Munich's central station, for example, will basically be interpreted as the sequence of words *Munich-West, Central Station*. This
also means that sequences of such gestures exhibit the same ambiguity as corresponding sequences of names (pointing may be even more ambiguous, because
there may be a set of objects for every pointing gesture).

In TALKY we do not provide the possibility to use passive objects actively.
We interpret pointing to some passive object (e.g., an appointment field) merely
as focusing some entity.

There are two reason for a different handling. First, utterances such as
Munich-West, Central Station are common and well understandable if we are in

a route planning application. By contrast, in the calendar manager application e.g. the utterance *this appointment*, which is a possible translation of pointing to an appointment field, is much less specific with respect to any task the user may want to perform. Second, in TALKY only active gesture forms are used. In both applications pointing acts to passive objects are accepted as answers in clarification dialogues.

8.2   Passively Used Active Objects

We refer to the *holiday* example in Section 4.2. In cases where active objects are considered as semantically meaningful besides referring to some manipulative action, we also introduce a timeout handling, with an even shorter timeout. To our experience users keep gaps short when they use an active object passively.

This procedure is not necessary if there is a clear cut between passive and active gesture forms.

9   Focusing Gestures

9.1   Feedback and Focusing Gestures

Focusing gestures are a way of introducing a new topic into the conversation. In natural communication, a new topic is normally introduced verbally (explicitly or implicitly). Gestures only occur as a part of such utterances, e.g., *let's now talk about ↗ this topic*. The topic shift is performed by the verbal utterance, while the pointing act is simply deictic. In certain situations, focusing gestures may be used in isolation also in natural communication. For example, when two people discuss a list of items, it may occur that shifting from one item to another may be performed by gesture only. Sometimes the participant marks the focused item by moving an object (e.g., a pen) to the new topic of discussion. By providing a special cursor the use of focus markers was realised in the XTRA project.

Focusing is closely related to the act of selection in graphical user interfaces. In direct manipulation, selection is the counterpart of referential deictic gestures in natural communication. Highlighting serves as a marker for being selected. Apart from the tendency to interact in a laconic style, perhaps the resemblance to selection makes focusing gestures an intuitive interaction. Because focus gestures may be used without speech, an active gesture form is needed for focusing.

But focusing is not exactly the same as selection. Focusing gestures may be vague or ambiguous, like deictic gestures in natural communication. Vagueness and ambiguity cause problems for feedback that are not solved in general. The advantage of using special pointers for focusing is that they preserve vagueness. But the handling of focus pointers involves a sort of second-stage interaction, i.e. manipulating the pointer, which is not optimal. In a pen-based interface the second stage interaction may be avoided by drawing a certain marker symbol.

In the case of well-structured objects pointing is a convenient method for focusing. In TALKY focusing is used to navigate in the discourse in a task-oriented manner. Visual utterances are hierarchically structured objects, which are limited in complexity. Ambiguity in the interpretation of a pointing gesture occurs in the form of *pars pro toto* (or also *toto pro pars*) pointing. TALKY shows the vague reference of the gesture as a structured feedback by highlighting the most specific sub-structure which is met by the gesture and by highlighting in a different colour the whole visual utterance as well.

9.2 Indistinguishability of Deictic Gestures and Focusing Gestures

In TALKY the same gesture form (touch or mouse click) is used for focusing and deixis. At the moment of pointing the system cannot distinguish if the gesture is intended to be used as a focusing gesture or as a deictic gesture. But in this case no wait problem is introduced, because focusing does not trigger any action which may conflict with a speech specification.

Therefore focusing gestures are employed in three ways:

- the gesture provides a background for the interpretation of follow-up utterances, e.g. for the interpretation of elliptic utterances,
- the gesture provides a referent that is referred to later by anaphoric expressions,
- the gesture is used deictically.

10   Conclusion

By integrating conversationally used natural language with graphical interfaces gestural interaction looses the simplicity of direct manipulation. Certain uses of gestures are introduced that are distinct from natural communication and direct manipulation as well. Important examples for such gestures are focusing gestures and the use of gestures with elliptic deixis and plural deixis. The integration of different paradigms together with the interdependencies of gestural and spoken interaction introduce the wait problem. Pointing devices cause obtrusive effects on synchronisation.

There is no single cure for the problems discussed. We showed a range of possibilities that can be used to reduce these problems as appropriate pointing devices and gesture forms and the provision of appropriate feedback. Incremental natural language interpretation and the provision of incremental or provisional feedback turn out to be important challenges for the upcoming technology of multimodal interfaces. Also the improvement of passive mouse gestures or the introduction of passive vs. active pointing facilities into touch screen or vision technology may improve multimodal interaction technology.

The development of a multimodal system involves many design parameters. Beyond the pioneering work of Oviatt and Cohen, there is a need for further empirical studies that consider the different parameters of multimodal systems in detail.

196   Michael Streit

References

Amtrup, J.W., H. Heine, and U. Jost (1996) Whats in a Word Graph, Evaluation and Enhancement of Word Lattices, Verbmobil Report 186. Universität Hamburg.

Bellalem, N. and L. Romary (1995) Reference interpretation in a multimodal environment combining speech and gestures". In *Proc. First International Workshop on Intelligence and Multimedia Interfaces: Research and Applications*. Edinburgh University.

Faconti, G.P. and M. Massink (1997) A Syndetic Approach to Referring Phenomena in Multimodal Interaction. In *Proceedings of the Workshop 'Referring Phenomena in a Multimedia Context and Their Computational Treatment'*, ACL/EACL 1997, Madrid.

Huls, C., E. Bos, and W. Claassen (1995) Automatic Referent Resolution of Deictic and Anaphoric Expressions, *Computational Linguistics* 21(1): 59–79.

Kaemmerer, B. and Ch. Maggioni (1995) Gesture Computer - from Research to Practice. In *Proc. Conference on Real and Virtual Worlds*, 1995.

Oviatt, S.L., A. DeAngeli, and K. Kuhn (1997) Integration and Synchronization of Input Modes during Multimodal Human-Computer Interaction. In *Proc. Conference on Human Factors in Computing Systems: CHI'97*. NewYork: ACM Press.

Oviatt, S.L. A. DeAngeli, and K. Kuhn (1999) Ten Myths of Multimodal Interaction. *Communications of the ACM* Vol. 42, No. 11.

Pittmann, J.A., I.Smith, P. Cohen, S. Oviatt, and T. Yang (1996) QuickSet: A Multimodal Interface for Military Simulation. In *Proc. 6th Conference on Computer-Generated Forces and Behavioral Representation,* University of Central Florida, 217-224.

Streit, M. and A. Krüger (1996) Eine agentenorientierte Architektur für multimediale Benutzerschnittstellen. In *Online 96 - Congressband VI*, Hamburg.

Streit, M. (1997) Active and Passive Gestures - Problems with the Resolution of Deictic and Elliptic Expressions in a Multimodal System. In *Proceedings of the Workshop 'Referring Phenomena in a Multimedia Context and Their Computational Treatment'*, ACL/EACL 1997, Madrid.

Streit, M. (1999a) The Interaction of Speech, Deixis, and Graphics in the Multimodal Office Agent TALKY. In *Proceedings of the ESCA Workshop on Interactive Dialogue in Multi-Modal Systems,* ESCA and Center for PersonKommunikation Aalborg University, Aalborg, Denmark.

Streit, M. (1999b) Interaction of Speech, Deixis, and Graphical Interface, Proceedings of the Workshop on Deixis, Demonstration and Deictic Belief. In *Proc. 11th European Summer School in Logic, Language and Information*, Utrecht.

Sullivan, J.W. and S.W. Tyler (eds.) (1991) *Intelligent User Interfaces*. Frontier Series, New York: ACM Press.

Wahlster, W. (1991) User and Discourse Models for Multimodal Communication. In J.W. Sullivan and S.W. Tyler (eds.) *Intelligent User Interfaces*. New York: ACM Press, 45–67.

Multimodal Cooperative Resolution of Referential Expressions in the DenK System

Leen Kievit[1], Paul Piwek[2], Robbert-Jan Beun[3], and Harry Bunt[1]

[1] Computational Linguistics and AI Group
Tilburg University, Tilburg, The Netherlands
bunt@kub.nl,l.kievit@chello.nl
[2] ITRI, University of Brighton, Brighton, UK
Paul.Piwek@itri.brighton.ac.uk
[3] Department of Computer Science, University of Utrecht
Utrecht, The Netherlands
rj@cs.uu.nl

Abstract. We present an approach to the resolution of multimodal referential expressions in a cooperative human-machine communication setting, provided by the DenK system. We discuss how references involving multiple modalities are resolved, and we also indicate how the system can respond cooperatively in case the resolution process fails.

1 Introduction

In this chapter we present an approach to the resolution of multimodal referential expressions, designed and implemented in the DenK system. This is a multimodal dialogue system that instantiates a generic cooperative multimodal user interface architecture based on the formal and computational modelling of fundamental principles of communication, knowledge representation, and language understanding.[1] The architecture that was developed in the DenK project is inspired by a view on human-machine interaction called the 'cooperative assistant' metaphor. A system that interacts with a user according to this metaphor presents itself as an 'electronic assistant' who is knowledgeable in the application domain and who interacts in a competent and cooperative way with the user, while at the same time providing visual feedback about the current state of the domain (see further Bunt, 1998). The DenK system has the use of an electron microscope as its application domain, and is generic in that both its architecture and also the modelling formalisms developed and incorporated in the various modules should be applicable over a wide range of application domains and tasks.

---

[1] The DenK project is a long-term collaborative research activity of the universities of Tilburg and Eindhoven, which has received support from Philips Research and Philips Electron Optics; see Ahn et al. (1995); Bunt et al. (1998), and http://let.kub.nl/research/ti/denk. DenK is a semi-acronym derived from 'Dialoogvoering en Kennisopbouw', which is approximately equivalent to 'Dialogue Modelling and Knowledge Acquisition'. The word *denk* in Dutch means *think*.

H. Bunt and R.-J. Beun (Eds.): CMC'98, LNAI 2155, pp. 197–214, 2001.
© Springer-Verlag Berlin Heidelberg 2001

The top-level design of the DENK system reflects the underlying metaphor in that it has two main components:

1. The *cooperative assistant*, which supports symbolic interaction; it interprets messages in natural language from the user (using a parsing and interpretation system based on HPSG and the use of underspecified semantic representations; see Verlinden, 1999 and Kievit, 1998); it is capable of reasoning about various aspects of the application and the user; and it produces communicative behaviour adequate with respect to (its model of) the user's beliefs and goals through a dialogue management module (see Piwek, 1998) that oversees the interaction with the user and can generate responses to the user's utterances, including requests for clarification;
2. The *application model*, in this case a formal model of the working of an electron microscope (Ahn, 1995), implemented by means of an object-oriented animation system which incorporates spatio-temporal components and graphical tools for representation, visualisation and manipulation (Peeters, 1995). The user can see a schematic representation of an electron microscope, in particular see the (simulated) events that take place, and can directly operate on certain parts of the microscope with graphical actions.

The interaction between the user and the system can thus be seen to take place in a 'trialogue' rather than a dialogue system, as depicted in Figure 1, which shows the user communicating with the assistant in natural language and interacting visually and graphically with the application. Note that the interaction along these two lines must be integrated in order to fully grasp the communication; the user may for instance point at an object in the application domain while talking about it to the assistant, and the assistant may for instance answer a question with text plus highlighting of an element on the display.

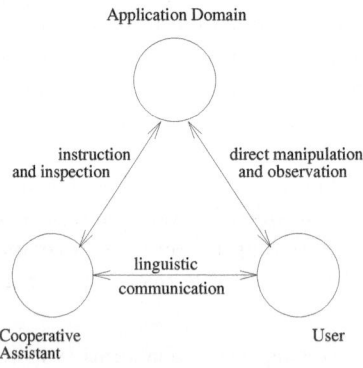

Fig. 1. The DENK *'triangle view'* of Interaction: User, Cooperative Assistant, and Application Domain.

Because of the different modalities involved in the interaction, the system is suited to handle multimodal references to objects: a user can select an object and use a deictic term, or can refer to something that is visible on the screen by means of a pronoun. Conversely, if the system wants to identify an object to the user, there is a choice of modality. The system can highlight the object or describe it in natural language. The generation of referring expressions will not be taken up here.

In this chapter we consider the submodule of the cooperative assistant that finds referents for referring expressions, and we look at the options of the dialogue manager in case a referential expression cannot be resolved. This chapter is organised as follows. In the next section we will introduce the format that is used for the semantic representation of the user's utterances, and the different sources of information that the assistant uses in interpretation (in particular, reference resolution). In Section 3 we will describe the multimodal resolution algorithm and the way the dialogue manager can respond to cases where a referent cannot be identified. Section 4 resents some data on the evaluation of the resolution algorithm. Section 5 briefly compares our work with related research, and we end with some concluding remarks.

2   Contexts in Dialogue

When interacting with the DENK system, the user communicates with the cooperative assistant via typed input (possibly combined with object selection using the mouse) and observes the (changing) state of the application domain on the visual display. The assistant responds to the user's communicative actions on the basis of the actions themselves and the context in which the actions are performed. A response is computed roughly in two stages: the *interpretation* and the *reaction* stage. In the interpretation stage, a formal representation of the user's utterance is computed that indicates how the utterance is intended to change the current dialogue context, notably the current state of the application domain. This representation is determined on the basis of the input and the (previous) context. In the reaction stage, a reaction in English is computed from the formal representation of the user's utterance and the current context.[2]

The design of both stages is based on a context-change approach to interpretation and dialogue management developed in *Dynamic Interpretation Theory* (DIT, see Bunt 1991; 1994; 2000). In this approach, a dialogue utterance is interpreted as a set of context-changing operations, called *dialogue acts*. A dialogue act is semantically structured into a *semantic content*, which is roughly speaking the information that is entered into the current context, and a *communicative function* that specifies in what way the current context is to be updated with the semantic content. For example, the statement *The lens is on* and the question *Is the lens on?* on this analysis both have the same semantic content (namely the proposition that the lens is on), but the statement has a communicative

---

[2] In the reaction stage the system also determines whether the user's utterance counts as a direct or an indirect speech act. For details, see Beun and Piwek (1997).

function specifying that this content is to be added to the representation of the beliefs of the speaker, whereas the question has a communicative function specifying that this content should be added to the representation of those potential beliefs of which the speaker has the goal to know whether they are true. The notion of context that is used in DIT consists of a variety of information types, including dialogue participants' beliefs about the domain of discourse and their recursive beliefs about each other beliefs (called the 'semantic context'); the previous discourse ('linguistic context'); the status of their understanding and further processing ('processing status' or 'cognitive context'); the current pressures or inhibitions to say certain things ('social context'), and the availability of visual or auditory information ('physical and perceptual context').

The reaction stage has as its main goal to compute a dialogue act to continue the dialogue. This is the task of the Dialogue Manager module, that uses the representation in the current context of goals and beliefs to determine a dialogue act that would contribute to the satisfaction of these goals. Of particular importance in this process is that part of the context representation that contains the goals and beliefs that have emerged in the dialogue and that have not yet been dealt with (answered, or accepted, or discarded); this part of the context is called the *pending context*. The dialogue acts that are computed by the Dialogue Manager are subsequently expressed in English using a simple generator that uses standard phrases for the various dialogue act types. We consider the interpretation and reaction stages in a little more detail.

Interpretation. The output of the interpretation stage is a so-called *annotated segment* (Piwek 1995), a pair consisting of a type-theoretical segment and an annotation. Type-theoretical segments are expressions of the language of Constructive Type Theory (CTT, see e.g., Barendregt 1992; De Bruijn 1980; Martin-Löf 1984).

A CTT-segment is a sequence of expressions, called *introductions*, of the form $O : T$, where O is an object and T is the type of the object. Both objects and types can be either atomic or complex terms. One way to build up complex terms is by applying functions to an argument. For instance, the sentence *A lens is on* can be represented as the segment $[x : lens, y : on(x)]$. The first of these introductions presents an object x of type *lens*; the y in the second introduction stands for a proof of the proposition $on(x)$. This proposition is represented by a complex term formed by applying the predicate *on* to the object x.

In CTT, a proposition corresponds to the set of all proofs of that proposition. Proofs are explicitly represented in the CTT language and can fulfil a similar role as discourse referents in Discourse Representation Theory (DRT; Kamp and Reyle 1993). Ahn and Kolb (1990) have demonstrated that CTT can be seen as a higher-order generalisation of DRT (see also Ahn, 2000).

To form an annotated segment, a CTT segment is paired with an annotation in the form of a set of feature-value pairs. The annotation contains, among other things, information about the information in the utterance that is represented which contributes to the determination of its communicative functions.

For instance, the representation of the question *Which lens is on?* contains the CTT-segment $[x : lens, y : on(x)]$, which is the same as for *A lens is on* and the annotation $ri = [[x]]$, which says that x carries the feature ri ('requested information'). In the reaction stage, this information tells the Dialogue Manager that it should attempt to generate an answer to what was apparently a wh-question; in this case it should tell the user which lens (if any) is on. To construct such annotated segments, the string that the user typed in has to be interpreted using contextual information. We will focus on one specific part of this process: the resolution of referential expressions.

The semantic representations that are constructed in the DENK system may be underspecified in some respects.[3] Annotations are also used in annotated segments to indicate underspecified parts of a segment that require further specification in order to get a sufficiently specified representation of what the user means. Consider, for instance, the utterance *The lens is on* containing the referential *The lens*. Before reference resolution we have a segment $[x : lens, y : on(x)]$ and the the the annotation $rb = [[x]]$, where the feature rb stands for 'requires binding'. In words, an object has to be found in the context which can be substituted for x.

Here, the context encompasses the linguistic context (the dialogue history), the physical and perceptual context (what the user can see in the application domain) and the shared beliefs in the semantic context (information the system believes to share with the user); to the latter part we will refer as the *common context*. The question thus arises, first, in which contexts to look for the object, and second, which object the user meant if there is more than one candidate object satisfying the predicate *lens*. For the latter purpose, we invoke the notion of *salience*. For instance, the salience of an object in the linguistic context depends on how recently the object was mentioned: the most recently mentioned objects are more salient than those mentioned some time back. In the physical and perceptual context, an object that is currently visible in a window on the screen is more salient than one that is hidden.

It should be noted that, formally, both the linguistic context and the common context are represented using CTT enriched with annotations and that both are internal to the cooperative assistant. By contrast, the physical and perceptual context is *external* to the assistant module. It is a simulation in an object-oriented graphical language of the electron microscope which the user can see and which the assistant module can access to verify propositions; the assistant can for instance look for lenses in the domain.

Reaction. We have already introduced the common context, the linguistic context and the physical and perceptual context as sources of information that are important for the interpretation of user utterances. Two other important contextual information sources are the assistant's *private* context, which contains information that the system thinks it does not share with the user, and the

---

[3] For discussions of the use of underspecification in computer interpretation of natural language see Kievit (1998); Bunt and Muskens (1999); Pinkal (1999).

pending context, that we already came across. The pending context is a list containing utterances of user or system that still have to be dealt with, for example a command which still needs to be reacted to. In the reaction stage, the representation of the user's utterance is added to the pending context, but only after all utterances have been removed that at that point are no longer under discussion. For instance, consider the following dialogue fragment (1).

(1) a.   U: Switch on the lens.
     b.   S: OK (does it).
     c.   U: Now, increase its excitation.

When utterance (c) is interpreted, the pending context is the stack $[b, a]$. From the interpretation of (c), the system can infer that the user is satisfied with the system's response to (a). This means that both (a) and (b) have been processed successfully and can be removed from the pending context. Utterance (c) is then added and the new pending context is now $[c]$. Furthermore, the linguistic context is updated with the objects that have been mentioned. In the case of utterance (c) there is a reference to the lens (introduced in (a)) and its excitation; representations of both objects are added to the linguistic context.

After the pending context has been updated, the system examines its top element and computes a reaction to it. We distinguish three possibilities:

1. The formal representation of the utterance is unambiguous, enabling the system to generate an appropriate response. If the communicative function of the utterance is a question, the system will base its response on its *private* context, in order to provide the user with information that he does not know. In the DENK system, the private context of the cooperative assistant constitutes the system's permanent knowledge about the application; typically, this concerns information about regularities in the domain that the user is not familiar with, for instance, *If the diffraction lens is off then the microscope is in imaging mode.* The response that the cooperative assistant computes input is communicated and simultaneously added to the pending context - which allows a subsequent reaction from the user to be interpreted in the light of the preceding utterance of the system.

2. The formal representation is not fully unambiguous. In particular, the system may not have been able to resolve all the underspecified referential material in the user's utterance. In that case, the system can generate a clarification question, as in (2b).

(2) a.   U: Switch on the lens.
     b.   S: Which lens?
     c.   U: The condenser lens.
     d.   S: Ah, OK (does it).

(iii) The representation of the user's utterance provides insufficient information for computing a response of the kind that the user would like to have (like an answer to a question) or for generating a clarification question. For instance, some of the words in the user's utterance are not in the system's lexicon. In such cases, the system generates an error message, stating that it does not understand the user and why, as illustrated in (3b).

(3) a.   U: Switch on the magnation lens.
     b.   S: I do not know the word *"magnation"*.

In the next section we will see how the resolution algorithm and the dialogue manager use the different contexts in the DENK system that we have seen to be involved in interpretation and reaction: the private and common context that together make up the semantic context, the physical and perceptual context (the application domain as simulated on the screen), the linguistic context (dialogue history), and the pending context.

3   Multimodal Cooperative Reference Resolution

The DENK resolution algorithm is based on the following assumptions:

- Referents for referential expressions can come from different contexts available to the dialogue partners.
- The intended referent for an expression is the *most salient fitting object*.
- Exactly when an object is fitting and when it is salient, depends on the kind of referential expression.
- When no fitting salient object can be found, or several objects are fitting and equally salient, the algorithm should terminate and report the outcome.

Given these considerations, the algorithm is constructed as a guided search through the available contexts. For each kind of referential expression, a search strategy is defined, consisting of one or more *resolution steps*. Each resolution step in turn consists of four elements:

- The selection of possible objects (candidate referents) from a single context.
- The application of a number of filters on the set of candidates.
- The ordering of the candidates by decreasing saliency.
- An evaluation of the result.

So each step is a sequence **selection-filtering-ordering-evaluation**. The selection and filtering make sure that the remaining candidates are fitting objects; the ordering allows us to make use of their saliency. The algorithm terminates as soon as one of the resolution steps results in a unique object (positive outcome) or produces several objects and is unable to determine which of those is the intended one (negative outcome). This means that not all resolution steps are necessarily always performed. This guarantees that we use the least possible effort to find the intended referent, but care must be taken not to make a premature choice. The precise order of the resolution steps is therefore a matter of careful consideration and is subject to empirical testing.

The current version of the resolution strategies is based on (Beun and Kievit, 1995). Rather than describing the entire algorithm in detail, we consider a number of representative examples of how it finds the intended referent in various situations and discuss the specific resolution steps involved.

Take dialogue (1) above. The first sentence contains the referential expression *the lens* of type def_art (noun phrase with definite article). The annotated segment representing this expression is (4).

(4) $< [x : lens, y : on(x)], [rb = [[x]], mt = [x : def\_art, ra = [[y]] >$

(where the feature mt stands for 'marker type', which refers to the definiteness of the noun phrase; ra stands for 'requested action').

Figure 2 shows the resolution strategy for expressions of type def_art. Each step in the strategy is defined in terms of:

1. The context from which candidate objects are selected;
2. The set of filters which are applied to the candidate objects;
3. An ordering algorithm for the filtered set of candidates;
4. A set of evaluation clauses for the ordered and filtered set of candidates.

Suppose (1a) is the start of the dialogue. The first resolution step yields no candidates, because the list called 'hypothetical' which is used in that step, which corresponds to objects introduced in the antecedent part of 'if...then'-sentences, is empty. Next, in the second step, candidates are taken from the private context. This yields five candidates, as the system knows five different lenses. However, since the referent in the case of this utterance should be part of the common context and this context is empty, none of these pass the prove(common) filter which is applied in this step. In such cases, the filter observe is tried next. This one allows all the candidates to pass, since the only requirement is that they are lenses. The same goes for the final filter, prove(private). So after filtering we still have all the lenses as possible referents. These are now ordered. Since there has been no dialogue yet, ordering by dialogue recency has no effect. Note that in the evaluation we require the dialogue position of whatever lens happens to be first in the candidate list to be less than 10 objects ago[4]. Objects that do not appear in the dialogue get assigned the position 1000. Given the evaluation criteria for this resolution step, like the first step it fails to deliver any candidates, but the algorithm stores the results it has computed, so that if all else fails, the system can use these objects to offer the user a choice.

The third resolution step starts with getting candidates from the domain. This again yields all five lenses, but now we have a filter (same_window) that checks which of the lenses is visible in the currently active window and which might allow some of the lenses to pass while blocking the others. This is then an instance of taking multimodality into account: a visual clue may influence the saliency of objects referred to in a natural language utterance.

---

[4] The value of the length parameter, that has been fixed here at 10, should be determined empirically.

```
res_step( candidates(hypothetical),
          filters([prove(basic+hypothetical)]),
          ordering([]),
          evaluation([ length>1 means fail,
                       length=1 means succeed,
                       otherwise continue ])
        ),
res_step( candidates(private),
          filters([prove(common),
                   observe,
                   prove(private)]),
          ordering([dialogue]),
          evaluation([ length=0 means continue,
                       dialogue_pos_first<10 means succeed,
                       otherwise store ])
        ),
res_step( candidates(domain),
          filters([prove(common),
                   observe,
                   prove(private),
                   same_window]),
          ordering([distance]),
          evaluation([ length>0 means succeed,
                       otherwise continue ])
        ),
res_step( candidates(focus_association),
          filters([]),
          ordering([]),
          evaluation([ length=1 means succeed,
                       otherwise continue ])
        ),
res_step( candidates(accommodation),
          filters([]),
          ordering([]),
          evaluation([ length=1 means succeed,
                       otherwise continue ])
        ),
res_step( candidates(storage),
          filters([]),
          ordering([]),
          evaluation([ length>0 means succeed,
                       otherwise fail ])
        )
```

Fig. 2. Resolution Strategy for Noun Phrases with a Definite Article.

Suppose only one lens is visible in the active window: the so-called 'mini condenser' lens. The CTT representation for this lens is $\texttt{mini\_condensor(m1):lens}^5$, then this will be the referent that needs to be substituted for x. The resulting annotated segment is (5).

$$(5) \quad < [y : exc(mini\_condensor((m1)))], [ra = [[y]] >$$

In the reaction stage of computing a response, the system will make sure the ra annotation is taken care of by exciting (switching on) the lens. The system will then respond OK, as in the second sentence of the first dialogue.

In the third sentence of the same dialogue, we see the possessive pronoun *its*. The annotated segment for the sentence is (6).[6] Figure 3 shows the resolution strategy for pronouns.

$$(6) \quad < [t : *, x : t, y : increase(exc(x))], [rb = [[x, t]], mt = [x : pronoun], ra = [y],$$
$$tr = [t \leq lens]] >$$

```
res_step( candidates(hypothetical),
          filters([type_restrictions,not_generalized_subject]),
          ordering([]),
          evaluation([ length=1 means succeed,
                       length>1 means fail,
                       otherwise continue ])
        ),
res_step( candidates(dialogue),
          filters([type_restrictions]),
          ordering([dialogue]),
          evaluation([ length=0 means continue,
                       dialogue_pos_first<10 means succeed,
                       otherwise continue ])
        ),
res_step( candidates(accommodation),
          filters([]),
          ordering([]),
          evaluation([ length=1 means succeed,
                       otherwise fail ])
        )
```

Fig. 3. Resolution Strategy for Pronouns.

---

[5] The CTT predicate corresponding to the word *"condenser"* is consistently spelled "$\texttt{condensor}$". The CTT representation given here for the mini condenser is in fact slightly simplified.

[6] The annotation $tr = [t \leq lens]$, where tr stands for 'translation', is used to restrict the variable type t to values consistent with the type $lens$. This makes sure that the application is allowed of the function exc, which gives for each lens its excitation, and is the translation of the word *excitation* in conjunction with the use of the possessive.

Again, the `hypothetical` context is empty, so the first resolution step does not provide an answer. The second step starts by getting candidates from the dialogue, which means that the last 10 objects are considered that were mentioned. This yields the list $[act54 : on(mini\_condensor(m1)), mini\_condensor(m1) : lens]$. The $act54$ object was created by the system when it executed the command to switch *the lens* on, and was added to the dialogue context to allow reference to events.

The filter `type_restrictions` checks the types of both candidate objects by comparing them with the tr annotation. Only the second object survives, resulting in a candidate list containing just the mini condenser. Since it has dialogue position 2, it is acceptable and selected as the intended object. This also results in the binding of t to the type *lens*. The resulting annotated segment is thus (7).

(7) $< [y : increase(exc(mini\_condensor(m1)))], [ra = [y]] >$

Finally, we look at dialogue (2) and examine the states of the pending context as they develop during the dialogue. The annotated segment (8), corresponding to the first utterance, *Switch on the lens*, is put on the pending context.

(8) $< [x : lens, y : on(x)], [rb = [[x]], mt = [x : def\_art], ra = [y]] >$

In the interpretation stage, the resolution algorithm tries to fill in the rb ('requires binding') gaps in the annotated segment. In this case, the resolution algorithm fails. The fact that the resolution algorithm does not succeed is stored in a feature in the annotated segment called '*error*', so that we obtain the representation (9).

(9) $< [x : lens, y : on(x)], [rb = [[x]], mt = [x : def\_art], ra = [y],$
$error = [uo(x, [])]] >$

The error feature contains the item $uo(x, [])$, which signifies that x is an *unresolved object*; the empty list '$[]$' indicates that the algorithm did not find suitable candidates for x.

In the generation stage, the system looks at the top of the pending context and tries to generate a response to the utterance it finds there. In this particular case, the system produces a clarification question and constructs the annotated segment (10) which represents it:

(10) $< [x : lens, y : on(x)], [cl\_ri = [x], ra = [y], mean = [pos]] >$

This annotated segment can be paraphrased as: *Which lens do you ask me to switch on?* In fact, the system produces the elliptical utterance *Which lens?* and adds the annotated segment (10) to the pending context.[7] So now we have a

---

[7] More precisely, the pending context consists of indices that represent utterances. These indices have several features, including one for the annotated segment and another one which records the speaker of the utterance.

pending context containing the user's initial utterance and the system's clarification question: [1, 2].

Subsequently, the user's answer to the clarification question is added to the pending context: [1, 2, 3]. The annotated segment (11) corresponds to the answer (with index 3).

$$(11) < [z : lens, p : condensor(z)], [rb = [[z]], mt = [z : def\_art]] >$$

Before the resolution algorithm is applied, the pending context is first updated. The system tries to unify the representations of the utterances 1 and 3.[8] In this case, it succeeds. The clarification question and the answer to it are removed from the pending stack and the revised version 1' of the user's original question, with representation (12), is put in its place.

$$(12) < [x : lens, p : condensor(x), y : on(x)], [rb = [[x]], mt = [x : def\_art],$$
$$ra = [y]] >$$

The system now applies the resolution algorithm to this representation. Due to the extra information $(p : condensor(x))$, the algorithm succeeds.

In the reaction stage, the system looks at the pending context, and finds an annotated segment with the ra ('requested action') feature:

$$(13) < [y : on(condensor(m1))], [ra = [y]] >.$$

In other words, the system has to execute an action such that a proof for the proposition $on(condenser(m1)))$ comes into existence. Since all problems are resolved, the system produces the action in question, i.e., it switches on the condenser lens and reports this to the user saying *OK*. Simultaneously, the system updates the pending context with a representation of the feedback utterance *OK*. So now we have: [1', 4]. In fact, the system also maintains a record of the relation between utterances, In this case $acknowledge(1', 4)$. If the next utterance of the user is a new (non-clarification) question or command, 1' and 4 are removed from the pending context. Furthermore, the common context is updated with the information that the user and the system both know that the condensor lens has been switched on.

4   Evaluation

The DENK resolution algorithm has been evaluated using a corpus of 523 referring acts, obtained from four dialogue experiments which were collected to investigate the linguistic and multimodal communicative behaviour in various

---

[8] If the user's response to the clarification question cannot be unified with the user's original utterance, the system asks the user to reformulate the answer or to stop, as in the following interaction: U: *Is this lens on?* S: *Which lens?* U: *The magnation lens.* S: *I do not know the word "magnation"; try again or stop.* U: *I mean the magnification lens.* S: *Yes, the magnification lens is on.*

cooperative tasks. Each of the four dialogue situations is in some respects comparable to the DENK situation. The evaluation was carried out by a student at the University of Amsterdam, who had no involvement in the DENK project, as part of a master's thesis (see Verbeem, 1996).

The dialogue situations of the corpus data were as follows.

1. The world under consideration is a world of toy blocks. Two subjects are seated side by side at a table, separated by a screen. To avoid communication other than by spoken language and gestures, they can only see each other's hands, and only when these are above the table. One of the participants plays the role of 'instructor'; the other, the 'builder', is meant to construct a replica of an example blocks building that is only visible to the instructor. This experiment was performed in two variations:
   (a) the participants are allowed to freely talk about the building process and to gesticulate in the building domain; only the builder is allowed to manipulate blocks;
   (b) the participants communicate via keyboard and computer monitor rather than via speech, with the same possibilities to gesticulate.
   For more details about these experiments see Cremers (1992; 1993).
2. In a second set of dialogue experiments, one participant (A) is examining the functioning of an electron microscope in the presence of another person (B). While examining the microscope, A explains to B what she is doing. B asks questions and gives comments on the actions and utterances of A. Both participants can see the microscope; participant A is allowed to physically manipulate the device. Some objects are not observable (such as magnetic lenses and electric currents) and cannot be manipulated directly, therefore the participants often talk about objects that are invisible and cannot be touched or pointed to. These experiments were performed under two conditions:
   (a) participant A is an expert concerning the working of electron microscopes;
   (b) participant A is not an expert concerning the working of electron microscopes.

Table 1 summaries the results of applying the DENK resolution algorithm to the referential expressions occurring in the dialogues obtained under these conditions. The column labelled 'Resolved' in this table contains the numbers and percentages of the correctly resolved referring expressions; the column 'Misresolved' contains those cases where the resolution algorithm produced a referent, but not the correct one; the column 'Ambiguous' contains the cases where the algorithm found several possible referents, among which it was unable to make a choice, or no referent at all.

We see that the resolution algorithm produces an incorrect interpretation of a referring expression in 5% of the cases. The 'ambiguous' cases are not necessarily incorrect; sometimes a human understander is also faced with a genuine ambiguity problem or is unable to find a suitable referent for a referring expression. The cases in this column where therefore analysed for the difficulties that

Table 1. Evaluation Data.

Condition	Resolved		Misresolved		Ambiguous		Total
1A	132	(80%)	11	(7%)	23	(13%)	166
1B	90	(81%)	7	(6%)	14	(13%)	111
2A	123	(87%)	6	(4%)	12	(9%)	141
2B	87	(83%)	0		18	(17%)	105
TOTAL	431	(82%)	24	(5%)	68	(13%)	523

the dialogue participants might have had to resolve them. This analysis revealed that there were 4 out-of-domain references (which could be resolved because the participants shared the necessary out-of-domain knowledge); that in 9 cases the dialogue participant who had to resolve the expression had a problem in doing so, and that in 18 cases it was not clear whether successful resolution actually occurred or not. If we leave the 4 out-of-domain references and the 18 unclear cases out of consideration, and distinguish the 'ambiguous' cases between 'correctly ambiguous' (i.e. also ambiguous for a human dialogue participant) and 'incorrectly ambiguous', the bottom line of Table 1 changes into that of Table 2.

Table 2. Corrected Evaluation Data.

Correctly resolved		Incorrectly resolved		Correctly ambiguous		Incorrectly ambiguous		Total
431	(86%)	24	(5%)	9	(2%)	37	(7%)	501

Altogether, this means that the algorithm can be said to have performed correctly in 88% of the cases; moreover, in another 7% of the cases, where it encountered an ambiguous situation, this resulted in a dialogue with the user in an attempt to resolve the ambiguity. In only 5% of the cases did the algorithm clearly fail. For a more detailed analysis and discussion see Verbeem (1996).

5   Related Research

We briefly compare our approach to reference resolution with some of the most influential proposals found in the literature.

Centering Theory and Discourse Structure. In Grosz et al. (1983), anaphora resolution is tied to the notions of *forward-* and *backward-looking centers*. Centers are (intensional) objects in the world, that may be *realized* by noun phrases, i.e. noun phrases may be used to refer to these objects.

The approach taken in the DENK system uses some results from centering theory. For instance, there is a filter on candidates for pronouns through which those candidates pass that were referred to using a pronoun the previous time. However, contrary to centering theory, we do not assume that every sentence has a single backward-looking center. Utterances may be linked to the preceding dialogue by any number of anaphoric expressions. Moreover, since links to the 'preceding context' in a multimodal system may exist in multiple modal dimensions, it may be that an utterance has no link at all with the preceding utterance. Also, we assume that every object that is mentioned is a forward-looking center, except in some cases such as universally quantified objects or objects in *if...then* constructions.

Grosz and Sidner (1986) presents a far richer theory than we use in the DENK system, to account for possible topic changes in discourse and resulting problems for reference. Although we agree that discourse structure should play a role in reference resolution in general, we feel that for contemporary human-machine interfaces there is no need for this. Users of such interfaces will have a strong tendency to stay on topic, e.g. since the interface will have a domain-specific, limited vocabulary. If the role of discourse structure is taken away from Grosz and Sidner's theory, what remains is a theory of reference based on focus spaces. These focus spaces can be identified with the dialogue context and the pending context in our system. As a result, similar predictions will be made by Grosz and Sidner's model and by our model, as far as references to objects introduced in previous dialogue are concerned.

The CAPTURE *System.* The way reference resolution is performed in the DENK system is in some ways similar to what was done in the CAPTURE system (Alshawi 1987). In CAPTURE, noun phrase reference resolution is also performed by first selecting a set of entities that satisfy the constraints found in the linguistic expression, and subsequently filtering this set until a unique referent is found (in the case of singular noun phrases). Also, in both systems, some constraints are dropped if they are so strong as to discard all candidates.

A difference with Alshawi's system is the use of constraints coming from predicates. In CAPTURE, a predicate imposes sortal constraints on its arguments, which can be used to filter the candidate set. In the DENK system, the user is not expected to be an expert in the domain of discourse, hence he may not be aware of some of the constraints on predicates. In such cases, if the system used these constraints it might select the wrong referent. Since we allow the reference resolution to fail, and have equipped the dialogue manager with ways to handle such situations, we prefer resolution failure above possibly selecting the wrong referent.

The above is also true in case the constraints are not strong enough to identify a unique referent. In Alshawi's system, the algorithm makes an arbitrary choice; in our case, the system is more cautious and the dialogue manager reports an interpretation problem.

The MMI² System. In the MMI² system (Multi Modal Interaction with Man Machine Interfaces for knowledge based systems; Binot et al. 1992), a different approach to multimodal reference is taken. There is no context representation for dialogue history. Every interaction, be it linguistically expressed, visual or otherwise, is added to the general interaction history without extracting specific

212   Leen Kievit et al.

context updates. The extraction of relevant information is performed only when it is needed by some module, for instance reference resolution.

While this has the advantage of saving time, a lot of the work that is needed for extracting context-relevant information from an utterance has to be done anyway in order to be able to determine the meaning of the utterance with sufficient precision to be able to compute a meaningful response.

Another difference between the DENK system and the MMI[2] system is that the latter ignores the differences between modalities for the purpose of reference resolution. The DENK system, by contrast, initially limits its search space to certain contexts, depending on the kind of referential marker that is used.

6   Concluding Remarks

The DENK system operates in a setting where multimodal interaction is natural: the use of an electronic device which has a physical reality and allows physical operations, while being functionally complex and inviting explanation, exploration and discussion of its functions. The system is multimodal in that it allows the user to type text and to point (using the mouse) to entities in the visual representation on the screen, and in that it can both generate text and highlight elements on the screen. The system is cooperative in that it builds up a representation of what it believes the user does and does not know, and acts accordingly. One of the many interesting and complex aspects of building such a system is how it can deal in a contextually appropriate way with the user's multimodal referring 'expressions'.

The DENK resolution algorithm, as we have seen, can look for objects in the different (sub-)contexts that are present in such a setting. In this respect, our approach extends much of the research on resolution of referential expressions, which concentrates mostly on language-only discourse. The system is furthermore equipped with mechanisms to provide cooperative feedback through clarification questions and to re-evaluate ambiguous utterances on the basis of the user's reply. Evaluation of the DENK resolution algorithm indicates that it resolves referring expressions correctly 88% of the time, enters into a clarification subdialogue 7% of the time (where it would ideally have performed a correct resolution), and fails in the sense of assigning an incorrect referent 5% of the time. As a whole, the strong context-driven approach of the algorithm seems to be a fruitful one for reference resolution in multimodal dialogue systems.

A question that naturally arises, from a context-change point of view, is whether the approach taken in interpretation could also be of interest for generation. Assuming that, in general, a dialogue participant's interpretation can be viewed as reconstructing what she would have said in the context ascribed to her dialogue partner, the question arises whether the resolution algorithm could in some sense be reversed in order to generate contextually appropriate multimodal referring expressions. This question is the focus of currently ongoing follow-up research of the DENK project; initial findings, reported by Van der Sluis and Krahmer (2000) suggest that this is indeed a promising way to go for multimodal generation.

References

Ahn, R. (2000) *Agents, Objects and Events. A computational approach to knowledge, observation and communication.* Ph.D. thesis, Eindhoven University of Technology.

Ahn, R. (1995) *Logical Model of the Electron Microscope.* DENK Report 95/16, SOBU, Tilburg.

Ahn, R., Beun, R.J., Borghuis, T., Bunt, H.C., and Van Overveld C. (1995) The DENK - architecture: A fundamental approach to user interfaces, *Artificial Intelligence Review 8 (3),* 431–445.

Ahn, R. and Kolb, H.-P. (1990) Discourse Representation meets Constructive Mathematics, in László Kálmán and László Pólos (eds), *Papers from the Second Symposium on Logic and Language,* Akademiai Kiadó, Budapest, 105–124.

Alshawi, H. (1987) *Memory and context for language interpretation,* Studies in Natural Language Processing, Cambridge University Press, Cambridge, UK.

Barendregt, H.P. (1992) Lambda Calculi with Types, in S. Abramsky, D. Gabbay, and T. Maibaum (eds), *Handbook of Logic in Computer Science,* Oxford University Press, Oxford.

Beun, R.-J. and Kievit, L.A. (1995) *Resolving definite expressions in* DENK, DENK report 95/16, SOBU, Tilburg.

Beun, R.J. and Piwek, P. (1997) *Pragmatische features in* DENK: *PRAGTAGS,* DENK Report 97/29, SOBU, Tilburg.

Binot, J.L., Debille, L., Sedlock, D., and Vandecapelle, B. (1992) Multimodal Integration in MMI^2: Anaphora Resolution and Mode Selection, in H. Luczak, A. Cakir, and G. Cakir (eds.), *Work With Display Units–WWDU'92.* Technische Universität Berlin, Institut für Arbeitswissenschaften.

Bunt, H.C. (1991) DIT - Dynamic Interpretation in Text and Dialogue. In: L. Kálm'an and L. Pólos (eds.) *Papers from the Second Symposium on Logic and Language,* Budapest: Akademiai Kiadó, 67–104.

Bunt, H.C. (1994) Context and Dialogue Control. *THINK Quarterly 3(1),* 19-31.

Bunt, H.C. (1998) Issues in Multimodal Human-Computer Communication. In H.C. Bunt, R.-J. Beun, and T. Borghuis (eds.) *Multimodal Human-Computer Communication.* Springer Verlag, Berlin, 1–12.

Bunt, H.C. (2000) Dialogue Pragmatics and Context Specification. In: H.C. Bunt and W.J. Black (eds.) *Abduction, Belief and Context in Dialogue. Studies in Computational Pragmatics,* Benjamins, Amsterdam, 81–150.

Bunt, H.C., Ahn, R., Beun, R.J., Borghuis, T., and Van Overveld C. (1998) Multimodal Cooperation with the DENK System. In H.C. Bunt, R.-J. Beun and T. Borghuis (eds) *Multimodal Human-Computer Communication.* Springer Verlag, Berlin, 39–67.

Bunt, H.C. and Muskens, R.M. (1999) Computational semantics. In H.C. Bunt and R.M. Muskens (eds.) *Computing Meaning, Vol. 1.* Kluwer Academic Publishers, Dordrecht, 1–32.

De Bruijn, N.G. (1980) A Survey of the Project Automath, in J.R. Seldin and J.P. Hindley (eds), *To H.B. Curry: Essays on Combinatory Logic, Lambda Calculus and Formalisms,* Academic Press, New York, 589–606.

Cremers, A. (1992) Transcripties dialogen blokken-experiment. IPO Report 889, IPO, Eindhoven.

Cremers, A. (1993) Transcripties terminal-dialogen blokken-experiment. IPO Report 1049. IPO, Eindhoven.

Grosz, B.J., Joshi, A.K., and Weinstein, S. (1983) Providing a Unified Account of Definite Noun Phrases in Discourse, in *21st Annual Meeting of the Association for Computational Linguistics / Proceedings of the Conference.*

214   Leen Kievit et al.

Grosz, B.J. and Sidner, C.L. (1986) Attention, Intentions and the Structure of Discourse, *Computational Linguistics 12 (3)*, 175–204.
Kamp, H. and Reyle, U. (1993) *From Discourse to Logic: Introduction to Model-theoretic Semantics of Natural Language, Formal Logic and Discourse Representation Theory*, Kluwer Academic Publishers, Dordrecht.
Kievit, L. (1998) *Context-driven Natural Language Interpretation*. Ph.D. thesis, Tilburg University.
Martin-Löf, P. (1984) *Intuitionistic Type Theory*, Bibliopolis, Naples.
Peeters, E. (1995) *Design of an Object-Oriented, Interactive Animation System*. Ph.D. thesis, Eindhoven University of Technology.
Pinkal, M. (1999) On semantic underspecification. In H.C. Bunt and R.M. Muskens (eds.) *Computing Meaning, Vol. 1*. Dordrecht: Kluwer Academic Publishers, 33–55.
Piwek, P. (1995) *Annotated Type Theory for Information Representation*, DENK Report 95/17, SOBU, Tilburg.
Piwek, P. (1998) *Logic, Information and Conversation*. Ph.D. thesis, Eindhoven University of Technology.
Van der Sluis, I. and Krahmer, E. (2000) Efficient generation of referring expressions in a multimodal context. Presented at the *11th Computational Linguistics in the Netherlands Conference*, Tilburg, November 2000.
Verbeem, M. (1996) *An evaluation of Resolve*, DENK Report 96/28, SOBU, Tilburg.
Verlinden, M. (1999) *A Constraint-Based Grammar for Dialogue Utterances*. Ph.D. thesis, Tilburg University.

Part 4:

Multimodal Platforms
and Test Environments

The IntelliMedia WorkBench –
An Environment for Building Multimodal
Systems

Tom Brøndsted, Paul Dalsgaard, Lars Bo Larsen,
Michael Manthey, Paul Mc Kevitt*,
Thomas B. Moeslund, and Kristian G. Olesen

Institute for Electronic Systems (IES)
Aalborg University, Aalborg, Denmark
mmui@cpk.auc.dk

Abstract. Intelligent MultiMedia (IntelliMedia) focuses on the computer processing and understanding of signal and symbol input from at least speech, text and visual images in terms of semantic representations. We have developed a general suite of tools in the form of a software and hardware platform called "CHAMELEON" that can be tailored to conducting IntelliMedia in various application domains. CHAMELEON has an open distributed processing architecture and currently includes ten agent modules: blackboard, dialogue manager, domain model, gesture recogniser, laser system, microphone array, speech recogniser, speech synthesiser, natural language processor, and a distributed Topsy learner. Most of the modules are programmed in C and C++ and are glued together using the DACS communications system. In effect, the blackboard, dialogue manager and DACS form the kernel of CHAMELEON. Modules can communicate with each other and the blackboard which keeps a record of interactions over time via semantic representations in frames. Inputs to CHAMELEON can include synchronised spoken dialogue and images and outputs include synchronised laser pointing and spoken dialogue.
An initial prototype application of CHAMELEON is an *IntelliMedia Work-Bench* where a user will be able to ask for information about things (e.g. 2D/3D models, pictures, objects, gadgets, people, or whatever) on a physical table. The current domain is a *Campus Information System* for 2D building plans which provides information about tenants, rooms and routes and can answer questions like *Whose office is this?* and *Show me the route from Paul Mc Kevitt's office to Paul Dalsgaard's office.* in real time. CHAMELEON and the IntelliMedia WorkBench are ideal for testing integrated signal and symbol processing of language and vision for the future of SuperinformationhighwayS.

* Paul Mc Kevitt was also a British Engineering and Physical Sciences Research Council (EPSRC) Advanced Fellow at the University of Sheffield, England for five years under grant B/94/AF/1833 for the Integration of Natural Language, Speech and Vision Processing and recently took up appointment as Chair in Digital MultiMedia at The University of Ulster (Magee), Northern Ireland (p.mckevitt@ulst.ac.uk).

H. Bunt and R.-J. Beun (Eds.): CMC'98, LNAI 2155, pp. 217–233, 2001.
© Springer-Verlag Berlin Heidelberg 2001

1   Introduction

IntelliMedia, which involves the computer processing and understanding of perceptual input from at least speech, text and visual images, and then reacting to it, is complex and involves signal and symbol processing techniques from not just engineering and computer science but also artificial intelligence and cognitive science (Mc Kevitt 1994, 1995/96, 1997). With IntelliMedia systems, people can interact in spoken dialogues with machines, querying about what is being presented and even their gestures and body language can be interpreted.

People are able to combine the processing of language and vision with apparent ease. In particular, people can use words to describe a picture, and can reproduce a picture from a language description. Moreover, people can exhibit this kind of behaviour over a very wide range of input pictures and language descriptions. Although there are theories of how we process vision and language, there are few theories about how such processing is integrated. There have been extensive debates in psychology and philosophy with respect to the degree to which people store knowledge as propositions or pictures (Kosslyn and Pomerantz 1977, Pylyshyn 1973). Other recent moves towards integration are reported in Denis and Carfantan (1993), Mc Kevitt (1994, 1995/96) and Pentland (1993).

The Institute for Electronic Systems at Aalborg University, Denmark has expertise in the area of IntelliMedia and has already established an initiative called IntelliMedia 2000+ funded by the Faculty of Science and Technology. IntelliMedia 2000+ coordinates research on the production of a number of real-time demonstrators exhibiting examples of IntelliMedia applications, a new Master's degree in IntelliMedia, and a nation-wide MultiMedia Network (MMN) concerned with technology transfer to industry. A number of student projects related to IntelliMedia 2000+ have already been completed and currently five student groups are enrolled in the Master's conducting projects on multimodal interfaces, billiard game trainer, virtual steering wheel, audio-visual speech recognition, and face recognition. IntelliMedia 2000+ is coordinated from the Center for PersonKommunikation (CPK) which has a wealth of experience and expertise in spoken language processing, one of the central components of IntelliMedia, but also in radio communications which would be useful for mobile applications (CPK Annual Report, 1998). IntelliMedia 2000+ involves four research groups from three departments within the Institute for Electronic Systems: Computer Science (CS), Medical Informatics (MI), Laboratory of Image Analysis (LIA) and Center for PersonKommunikation (CPK), focusing on platforms for integration and learning, expert systems and decision taking, image/vision processing, and spoken language processing/sound localisation respectively. The first two groups provide a strong basis for methods of integrating semantics and conducting learning and decision taking while the latter groups focus on the two main input/output components of IntelliMedia, vision and speech/sound. More details on IntelliMedia 2000+ can be found at http://www.cpk.auc.dk/imm.

2   CHAMELEON and the IntelliMedia WorkBench

IntelliMedia 2000+ has developed the first prototype of an IntelliMedia software and hardware platform called CHAMELEON which is general enough to be used for a number of different applications. CHAMELEON demonstrates that existing software modules for (1) distributed processing and learning, (2) decision taking, (3) image processing, and (4) spoken dialogue processing can be interfaced to a single platform and act as communicating agent modules within it. CHAMELEON is independent of any particular application domain and the various modules can be distributed over different machines. Most of the modules are programmed in C++ and C. More details on CHAMELEON and the IntelliMedia WorkBench can be found in Brøndsted et al. (1998).

2.1   IntelliMedia WorkBench

An initial application of CHAMELEON is the *IntelliMedia WorkBench* which is a hardware and software platform as shown in Figure 1. One or more cameras and lasers can be mounted in the ceiling, and a microphone array placed on the wall, and there is a table where things (objects, gadgets, people, pictures, 2D/3D models, building plans, or whatever) can be placed. The current domain is a *Campus Information System* which at present gives information on the architectural and functional layout of a building. 2-dimensional (2D) architectural plans of the building drawn on white paper are laid on the table and the user can ask questions about them. At present the plans represent two floors of the 'A' (A2) building at Fredrik Bajers Vej 7, Aalborg University.

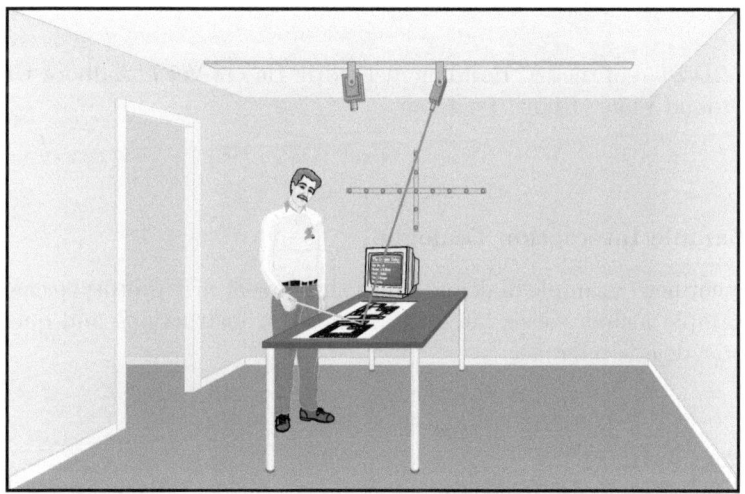

Fig. 1. Physical Layout of the IntelliMedia WorkBench.

Presently, there is one static camera which calibrates the plans on the table and the laser, and interprets the user's pointing while the system points to locations and draws routes with a laser. Inputs are simultaneous speech and/or pointing gestures and outputs are synchronised synthesised speech and pointing. We currently run all of CHAMELEON on a 200 MHz Intel pentium computer (r2d2) which handles input for the Campus Information System in real-time.

The 2D plan, which is placed on the table, is printed out on A0 paper having the dimensions: 84x118cm. Due to the size of the pointer's tip (2x1cm), the size of the table, the resolution of the camera and uncertainty in the tracking algorithm, a size limitation is introduced. The smallest room in the 2D plan, which is a standard office, can not be less than 3cm wide. The size of a standard office on the printout is 3x4cm which is a feasible size for the system. The 2D plan is shown in Figure 2.

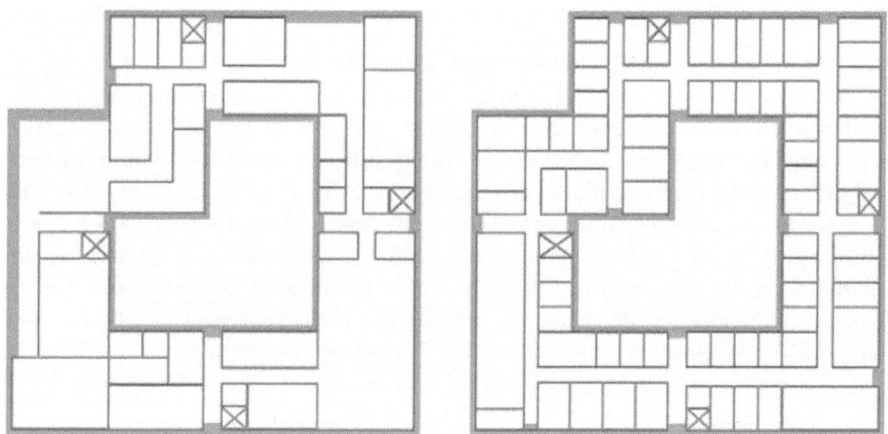

Fig. 2. 2D Plan of the 'A' Building at Fredrik Bajers Vej 7, Aalborg University. Left: Ground Floor; Right: 1st Floor.

2.2   Sample Interaction Dialogue

We present here a sample dialogue which the current first prototype can process. The example includes user intentions which are instructions and queries, and exophoric/deictic reference.

```
USER:       Show me Tom's office.
CHAMELEON:  [points]
            This is Tom's office.
USER:       Point to Thomas' office.
CHAMELEON:  [points]
            This is Thomas' office.
```

```
USER:        Where is the computer room?
CHAMELEON:   [points]
             The computer room is here.
USER:        [points to instrument repair]
             Whose office is this?
CHAMELEON:   [points]
             This is not an office, this is instrument repair.
USER:        [points]
             Whose office is this?
CHAMELEON:   [points]
             This is Paul's office.
USER:        Show me the route from Lars Bo Larsen's office to
             Hanne Gade's office.
CHAMELEON:   [draws route]
             This is the route from Lars Bo's office to Hanne's office.
USER:        Show me the route from Paul Mc Kevitt's office
             to instrument repair.
CHAMELEON:   [draws route]
             This is the route from Paul's office to instrument repair.
USER:        Show me Paul's office.
CHAMELEON:   [points]
             This is Paul's office.
```

2.3   Architecture of CHAMELEON

CHAMELEON has a distributed architecture of communicating agent modules processing inputs and outputs from different modalities and each of which can be tailored to a number of application domains. The process synchronisation and intercommunication for CHAMELEON modules is performed using the DACS (Distributed Applications Communication System) Inter Process Communication (IPC) software (see Fink et al. 1996) which enables CHAMELEON modules to be glued together and distributed across a number of servers. Presently, there are ten software modules in CHAMELEON: blackboard, dialogue manager, domain model, gesture recogniser, laser system, microphone array, speech recogniser, speech synthesiser, natural language processor (NLP), and Topsy as shown in Figure 3. Information flow and module communication within CHAMELEON are shown in Figures 4 and 5. Note that Figure 4 does not show the blackboard as a part of the communication but rather the abstract flow of information between modules. Figure 5 shows the actual passing of information between the speech recogniser, NLP module, and dialogue manager. As is shown all information exchange between individual modules is carried out using the blackboard as mediator.

As the intention is that no direct interaction between modules need take place the architecture is modularised and open but there are possible performance costs. However, nothing prohibits direct communication between two or more modules if this is found to be more convenient. For example, the speech recogniser and NLP modules can interact directly as the parser needs every recognition

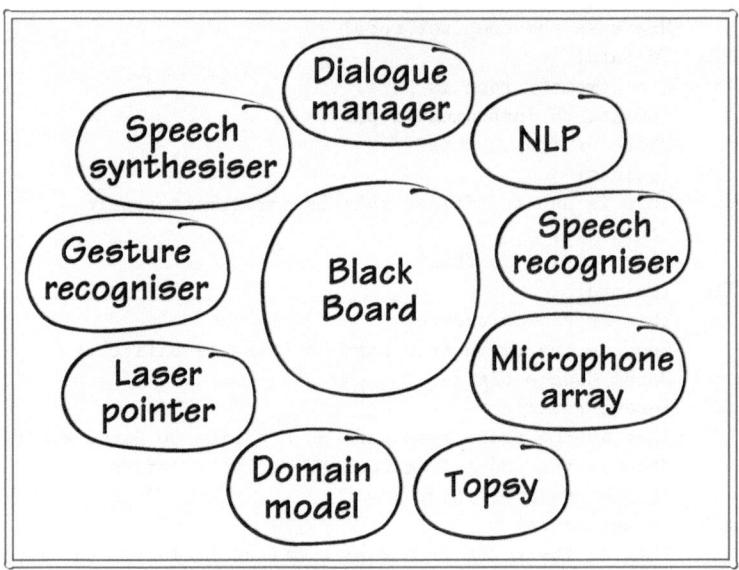

Fig. 3. Architecture of CHAMELEON.

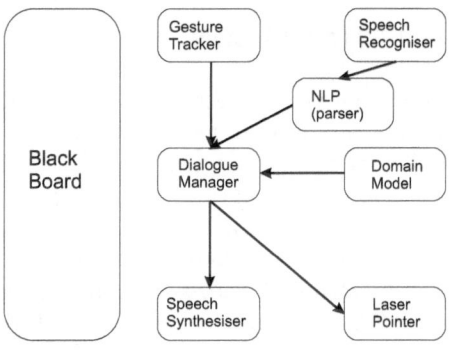

Fig. 4. Information Flow and Module Communication.

result anyway and at present no other module has use for output from the speech recogniser. The blackboard and dialogue manager form the kernel of CHAMELEON. We shall now give a brief description of each module.

The **blackboard** stores semantic representations produced by each of the other modules and keeps a history of these over the course of an interaction. All modules communicate through the exchange of semantic representations with each other or the blackboard. Semantic representations are frames in the spirit of Minsky (1975) and our frame semantics consists of (1) input, (2) output, and (3) integration frames for representing the meaning of intended user input and

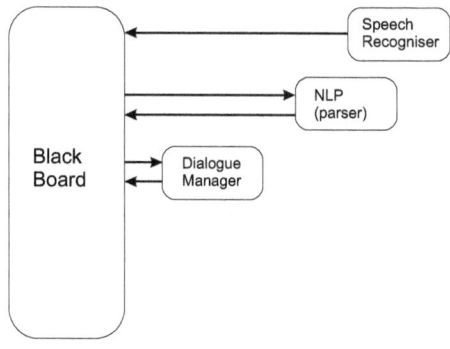

Fig. 5. Information Flow with the Blackboard.

system output. The intention is that all modules in the system will produce and read frames. Frames are coded in CHAMELEON as messages built of predicate-argument structures following the BNF definition given in Appendix A. The frame semantics was presented in Mc Kevitt and Dalsgaard (1997) and for the sample dialogue given in Section 2.2. CHAMELEON's actual blackboard history in terms of frames (messages) is shown in Appendix B.

The **dialogue manager** makes decisions about which actions to take and accordingly sends commands to the output modules (laser and speech synthesiser) via the blackboard. At present the functionality of the dialogue manager is to integrate and react to information coming in from the speech/NLP and gesture modules and to sending synchronised commands to the laser system and the speech synthesiser modules. Phenomena such as managing clarification sub-dialogues where CHAMELEON has to ask questions are not included at present. It is hoped that in future prototypes the dialogue manager will enact more complex decision taking over semantic representations from the blackboard using, for example, the HUGIN software tool (Jensen (F.) 1996) based on Bayesian Networks (Jensen (F.V.) 1996).

The **domain model** contains a database of all locations and their functionality, tenants and coordinates. The model is organised in a hierarchical structure: areas, buildings and rooms. Rooms are described by an identifier for the room (room number) and the type of the room (office, corridor, toilet, etc.). The model includes functions that return information about a room or a person. Possible inputs are coordinates or room number for rooms and name for persons, but in principle any attribute can be used as key and any other attribute can be returned. Furthermore, a path planner is provided, calculating the shortest route between two locations.

A design principle of imposing as few physical constraints as possible on the user (e.g. data gloves or touch screens) leads to the inclusion of a vision based **gesture recogniser**. Currently, it tracks a pointer via a camera mounted in the ceiling. Using one camera, the gesture recogniser is able to track 2D pointing gestures in real time. Only two gestures are recognised at present: pointing and not-pointing. The recognition of other more complex kinds of gestures like marking an area and indicating a direction (with hands and fingers) will be incorporated in the next prototype.

The camera continuously captures images which are digitised by a frame-grabber. From each digitised image the background is subtracted leaving only the motion (and some noise) within this image. This motion is analysed in order to find the direction of the pointing device and its tip. By temporal segmenting of these two parameters, a clear indication of the position the user is pointing to at a given time is found. The error of the tracker is less than one pixel (through an interpolation process) for the pointer.

A **laser system** acts as a 'system pointer'. It can be used for pointing to positions, drawing lines and displaying text. The laser beam is controlled in real-time (30 kHz). It can scan frames containing up to 600 points with a refresh rate of 50 Hz thus drawing very steady images on surfaces. It is controlled by a standard Pentium PC host computer. The pointer tracker and the laser pointer have been carefully calibrated so that they can work together. An automatic calibration procedure has been set up involving both the camera and laser where they are tested by asking the laser to follow the pointer.

A **microphone array** (Leth-Espensen and Lindberg 1996) is used to locate sound sources, e.g. a person speaking. Depending upon the placement of a maximum of 12 microphones it calculates sound source positions in 2D or 3D. It is based on measurement of the delays with which a sound wave arrives at the different microphones. From this information the location of the sound source can be identified. Another application of the array is to use it to focus at a specific location thus enhancing any acoustic activity at that location. This module is in the process of being incorporated into CHAMELEON.

Speech recognition is handled by the grapHvite real-time continuous speech recogniser (Power et al. 1997). It is based on HMMs (Hidden Markov Models) of triphones for acoustic decoding of English or Danish. The recognition process focuses on recognition of speech concepts and ignores non content words or phrases. A finite state network describing phrases is created by hand in accordance with the domain model and the grammar for the natural language parser. The latter can also be performed automatically by a grammar converter in the NLP module. The speech recogniser takes speech signals as input and produces text strings as output. Integration of the latest CPK speech recogniser (Christensen et al. 1998) which is under development is being considered.

We use the Infovox Text-To-Speech (TTS) **speech synthesiser** which at present is capable of synthesising Danish and English (Infovox 1994). It is a rule based formant synthesiser and can simultaneously cope with multiple languages, e.g. pronounce a Danish name within an English utterance. Infovox takes text as input and produces speech as output. Integration of the CPK speech synthesiser (Nielsen et al. 1997) which is under development for English is being considered.

Natural language processing is based on a compound feature based (so-called unification) grammar formalism for extracting semantics from the one-best utterance text output from the speech recogniser (Brøndsted 1998). The parser carries out a syntactic constituent analysis of input and subsequently maps values into semantic frames. The rules used for syntactic parsing are based on a subset of the EUROTRA formalism, i.e. in terms of lexical rules and structure building rules (Bech 1991). Semantic rules define certain syntactic subtrees and which frames to create if the subtrees are found in the syntactic parse trees. The natural language generator is currently under construction and at present generation is conducted by using canned text.

The basis of the Phase Web paradigm (Manthey 1998), and its incarnation in the form of a program called "Topsy", is to represent knowledge and behaviour in the form of hierarchical relationships between the mutual exclusion and co-occurrence of events. In AI parlance, Topsy is a distributed, associative, continuous-action, dynamic partial-order planner that learns from experience. Relative to MultiMedia, integrating independent data from multiple media begins with noticing that what ties otherwise independent inputs together is the fact that they occur simultaneously. This is also Topsy's basic operating principle, but this is further combined with the notion of mutual exclusion, and thence to hierarchies of such relationships (Manthey 1998).

2.4   DACS

DACS is currently the communications system for CHAMELEON and the Intelli-Media WorkBench and is used to glue all the modules together enabling communication between them. Applications of CHAMELEON typically consist of several interdependent modules, often running on separate machines or even dedicated hardware. This is indeed the case for the IntelliMedia WorkBench application. Such distributed applications have a need to communicate in various ways. Some modules feed others in the sense that all generated output from one is treated further by another. In the Campus Information System all modules report their output to the blackboard where it is stored. Although our intention is currently to direct all communication through the blackboard, we could just as well have chosen to simultaneously transfer output to several modules. For example, utterances collected by the speech recogniser can be sent to the blackboard but also sent simultaneously to the NLP module which may become relevant when efficiency is an important issue.

Another kind of interaction between processes is through remote procedure calls (RPCs), which can be either *synchronous* or *asynchronous*. By synchronous RPCs we understand procedure calls where we want immediate feedback, that is, the caller stops execution and waits for an answer to the call. In the Campus Information System this could be the dialogue manager requesting the last location to which a pointing event occurred. In the asynchronous RPC, we merely submit a request and carry on with any other task. This could be a request to the speech synthesiser to produce an utterance for the user or to the laser to point to some specific location. These kinds of interaction should be available in a uniform way in a heterogeneous environment, without specific concern about what platform the sender and receiver run on.

All these facilities are provided by the Distributed Applications Communication System (DACS) developed at the University of Bielefeld, Germany (Fink et al. 1995, 1996), where it was designed as part of a larger research project developing an IntelliMedia platform (Rickheit and Wachsmuth 1996) discussed further in the next section. DACS uses a communication demon on each participating machine that runs in user mode, allows multiple users to access the system simultaneously and does not provide a virtual machine dedicated to a single user. The demon acts as a router for all internal traffic and establishes connections to demons on remote machines. Communication is based on simple asynchronous message passing with some extensions to handle dynamic reconfigurations of the system during runtime. DACS also provides on top more advanced communication semantics like RPCs (synchronous and asynchronous) and *demand streams* for handling data parts in continuous data streams. All messages transmitted are recorded in a Network Data Representation which includes type and structure information. Hence, it is possible to inspect messages at any point in the system and to develop generic tools that can handle any kind of data. DACS uses Posix threads to handle connections independently in parallel. A database in a central name service stores the system configuration to keep the network traffic low during dynamic reconfigurations. A DACS Debugging Tool (DDT) allows inspection of messages before they are delivered, monitoring configurations of the system, and status on connections.

3   Relation to Other Work

Situated Artificial Communicators (SFB-360) (Rickheit and Wachsmuth 1996) is a collaborative research project at the University of Bielefeld, Germany which focuses on modelling that which a person performs when with a partner he cooperatively solves a simple assembly task in a given situation. The object chosen is a model airplane (Baufix) to be constructed by a robot from the components of a wooden building kit with instructions from a human. SFB-360 includes equivalents of the modules in CHAMELEON although there is no learning module competitor to Topsy. What SFB-360 gains in size it may loose in integration, i.e. it is not clear yet that all the technology from the subprojects have been fitted together and in particular what exactly the semantic representations passed between the modules are. The DACS process communication system currently used in CHAMELEON is a useful product from SFB-360.

Gandalf is a communicative humanoid which interacts with users in MultiModal dialogue through using and interpreting gestures, facial expressions, body language and spoken dialogue (Thórisson 1997). Gandalf is an application of an architecture called *Ymir* which includes perceptual integration of multimodal events, distributed planning and decision making, layered input analysis and motor-control with human-like characteristics and an inherent knowledge of time. Ymir has a blackboard architecture and includes modules equivalent to those in CHAMELEON. However, there is no vision/image processing module in the sense of using cameras since gesture tracking is done with the use of a data glove and body tracking suit and an eye tracker is used for detecting the user's eye gaze. However, it is anticipated that Ymir could easily handle the addition of such a vision module if one were needed. Ymir has no learning module equivalent to Topsy. Ymir's architecture is even more distributed than CHAMELEON's with many more modules interacting with each other. Ymir's semantic representation is much more distributed with smaller chunks of information than our frames being passed between modules.

AESOPWORLD is an integrated comprehension and generation system for integration of vision, language and motion (Okada 1997). It includes a model of mind consisting of nine domains according to the contents of mental activities and five levels along the process of concept formation. The system simulates the protagonist or fox of an Aesop fable, "The Fox and the Grapes", and his mental and physical behaviour are shown by graphic displays, a voice generator, and a music generator which expresses his emotional states. AESOPWORLD has an agent-based distributed architecture and also uses frames as semantic representations. It has many modules in common with CHAMELEON although again there is no vision input to AESOPWORLD which uses computer graphics to depict scenes. AESOPWORLD has an extensive planning module but conducts more traditional planning than CHAMELEON's Topsy.

The INTERACT project (Waibel et al. 1996) involves developing MultiModal Human Computer Interfaces including the modalities of speech, gesture and pointing, eye-gaze, lip motion and facial expression, handwriting, face recognition and tracking, and sound localisation. The main concern is with improving recognition accuracies of modality-specific component processors as well as developing optimal combinations of multiple input signals to deduce user intent more reliably in cross-modal speech acts. INTERACT also uses a frame representation for integrated semantics from gesture and speech and partial hypotheses are developed in terms of partially filled frames. The output of the interpreter is obtained by unifying the information contained in the partial frames. Although Waibel et al. present sophisticated work on multimodal interfaces it is not clear that they have developed an integrated platform which can be used for developing multimodal applications.

4   Conclusion and Future Work

We have described the architecture and functionality of CHAMELEON: an open, distributed architecture with ten modules glued into a single platform using the DACS communication system. We described the IntelliMedia WorkBench application, a software and physical platform where a user can ask for information about things on a physical table. The current domain is a *Campus Information System* where 2D building plans are placed on the table and the system provides information about tenants, rooms and routes and can answer questions like *Whose office is this?* in real time. CHAMELEON fulfils the goal of developing a general platform for integration of at least language/vision processing which can be used for research but also for student projects as part of the Master's degree education. More details on CHAMELEON and the IntelliMedia WorkBench can be found in Brøndsted et al. (1998).

There are a number of avenues for future work with CHAMELEON. We would like to process dialogue that includes examples of (1) spatial relations and (2) anaphoric reference. It is hoped that more complex decision taking can be introduced to operate over semantic representations in the dialogue manager or blackboard using, for example, the HUGIN software tool (Jensen (F.) 1996) based on Bayesian Networks (Jensen (F.V.) 1996). The gesture module will be augmented so that it can handle gestures other than pointing. Topsy will be asked to do more complex learning and processing of input/output from frames. The microphone array has to be integrated into CHAMELEON and set to work. Also, at present CHAMELEON is static and it might be interesting to see how it performs whilst being integrated with a web-based virtual or real robot or as part of an intellimedia videoconferencing system where multiple users can direct cameras through spoken dialogue and gesture. A miniature version of this idea has already been completed as a student project (Bakman et al. 1997).

Intelligent MultiMedia will be important in the future of international computing and media development and IntelliMedia 2000+ at Aalborg University, Denmark brings together the necessary ingredients from research, teaching and links to industry to enable its successful implementation. Our CHAMELEON platform and IntelliMedia WorkBench application are ideal for testing integrated processing of language and vision for the future of SuperinformationhighwayS.

Acknowledgements

This opportunity is taken to acknowledge support from the Faculty of Science and Technology, Aalborg University, Denmark and Paul Mc Kevitt would also like to acknowledge the British Engineering and Physical Sciences Research Council (EPSRC) for their generous funded support under grant B/94/AF/1833 for the Integration of Natural Language, Speech and Vision Processing (Advanced Fellow). `

References

Bakman, L., M. Blidegn, T.D. Nielsen, and S. Carrasco Gonzalez (1997) *NIVICO - Natural Interface for VIdeo COnferencing*. Project Report (8th Semester), Department of Communication Technology, Institute for Electronic Systems, Aalborg University, Denmark.

Bech, A. (1991) Description of the EUROTRA framework. In *The Eurotra Formal Specifications, Studies in Machine Translation and Natural Language Processing*, C. Copeland, J. Durand, S. Krauwer, and B. Maegaard (Eds), Vol. 2, 7-40. Luxembourg: Office for Official Publications of the Commission of the European Community.

Brøndsted, T. (1998) *nlparser*. http://www.kom.auc.dk/~tb/nlparser

Brøndsted, T., P. Dalsgaard, L.B. Larsen, M. Manthey, P. Mc Kevitt, T.B. Moeslund, and K.G. Olesen (1998) *A platform for developing Intelligent MultiMedia applications.* Technical Report R-98-1004, Center for PersonKommunikation (CPK), Institute for Electronic Systems (IES), Aalborg University, Denmark, May.

Christensen, H., B. Lindberg, and P. Steingrimsson (1998) *Functional specification of the CPK Spoken LANGuage recognition research system (SLANG).* Center for PersonKommunikation, Aalborg University, Denmark, March.

CPK Annual Report (1998) *CPK Annual Report.* Center for PersonKommunikation (CPK), Fredrik Bajers Vej 7-A2, Institute for Electronic Systems (IES), Aalborg University, DK-9220, Aalborg, Denmark.

Denis, M. and M. Carfantan (Eds.) (1993) *Images et langages: multimodalité et modelisation cognitive.* Actes du Colloque Interdisciplinaire du Comité National de la Recherche Scientifique, Salle des Conférences, Siège du CNRS, Paris, April.

Fink, G.A., N. Jungclaus, H. Ritter, and G. Sagerer (1995) A communication framework for heterogeneous distributed pattern analysis. In *Proc. International Conference on Algorithms and Applications for Parallel Processing*, V. L. Narasimhan (Ed.), 881-890. IEEE, Brisbane, Australia.

Fink, G.A., N. Jungclaus, and F. Kummert, H. Ritter, and G. Sagerer (1996) A distributed system for integrated speech and image understanding. In *Proceedings of the International Symposium on Artificial Intelligence*, Rogelio Soto (Ed.), 117-126. Cancun, Mexico.

Infovox (1994) *INFOVOX: Text-to-speech converter user's manual (version 3.4).* .Solna, Sweden: Telia Promotor Infovox AB

Jensen, F.V. (1996) *An introduction to Bayesian Networks.* London, England: UCL Press.

Jensen, F. (1996) Bayesian belief network technology and the HUGIN system. In *Proceedings of UNICOM seminar on Intelligent Data Management*, Alex Gammerman (Ed.), 240-248. Chelsea Village, London, England, April.

Kosslyn, S.M. and J.R. Pomerantz (1977) Imagery, propositions and the form of internal representations. In *Cognitive Psychology*, 9, 52-76.

Leth-Espensen, P. and B. Lindberg (1996) Separation of speech signals using eigenfiltering in a dual beamforming system. In *Proc. IEEE Nordic Signal Processing Symposium (NORSIG)*, Espoo, Finland, September, 235-238.

Manthey, M.J. (1998) The Phase Web Paradigm. In *International Journal of General Systems, special issue on General Physical Systems Theories*, K. Bowden (Ed.). in press.

Mc Kevitt, P. (1994) Visions for language. In *Proceedings of the Workshop on Integration of Natural Language and Vision processing*, Twelfth American National Conference on Artificial Intelligence (AAAI-94), Seattle, Washington, USA, August, 47-57.

Mc Kevitt, P. (Ed.) (1995/1996) *Integration of Natural Language and Vision Processing (Vols. I-IV).* Dordrecht, The Netherlands: Kluwer-Academic Publishers.

Mc Kevitt, P. (1997) SuperinformationhighwayS. In *"Sprog og Multimedier" (Speech and Multimedia)*, Tom Brøndsted and Inger Lytje (Eds.), 166-183, April 1997. Aalborg, Denmark: Aalborg Universitetsforlag (Aalborg University Press).

Mc Kevitt, P. and P. Dalsgaard (1997) A frame semantics for an IntelliMedia TourGuide. In *Proceedings of the Eighth Ireland Conference on Artificial Intelligence*

(AI-97), Volume 1, 104-111. University of Uster, Magee College, Derry, Northern Ireland, September.

Minsky, M. (1975) A framework for representing knowledge. In *The Psychology of Computer Vision*, P.H. Winston (Ed.), 211-217. New York: McGraw-Hill.

Nielsen, C., J. Jensen, O. Andersen, and E. Hansen (1997) *Speech synthesis based on diphone concatenation.* Technical Report, No. CPK971120-JJe (in confidence), Center for PersonKommunikation, Aalborg University, Denmark.

Okada, N. (1997) Integrating vision, motion and language through mind. In *Proceedings of the Eighth Ireland Conference on Artificial Intelligence (AI-97), Volume 1*, 7-16. University of Uster, Magee, Derry, Northern Ireland, September.

Pentland, A. (Ed.) (1993) *Looking at people: recognition and interpretation of human action.* IJCAI-93 Workshop (W28) at The 13th International Conference on Artificial Intelligence (IJCAI-93), Chambéry, France, August.

Power, K., C. Matheson, D. Ollason, and R. Morton (1997) *The grapHvite book (version 1.0).* Cambridge, England: Entropic Cambridge Research Laboratory Ltd..

Pylyshyn, Z. (1973) What the mind's eye tells the mind's brain: a critique of mental imagery. In *Psychological Bulletin*, 80, 1-24.

Rickheit, G. and I. Wachsmuth (1996) Collaborative Research Centre "Situated Artificial Communicators" at the University of Bielefeld, Germany. In *Integration of Natural Language and Vision Processing, Volume IV, Recent Advances*, Mc Kevitt, Paul (ed.), 11-16. Dordrecht, The Netherlands: Kluwer Academic Publishers.

Thórisson, K.R. (1997) Layered action control in communicative humanoids. In *Proceedings of Computer Graphics Europe '97*, June 5-7, Geneva, Switzerland.

Waibel, A., M.T. Vo, P. Duchnowski, and S. Manke (1996) Multimodal interfaces. In *Integration of Natural Language and Vision Processing, Volume IV, Recent Advances*, Mc Kevitt, Paul (Ed.), 145-165. Dordrecht, The Netherlands: Kluwer Academic Publishers.

Appendix A

Syntax of Frames

The following BNF grammar defines a predicate-argument syntax for the form of messages (frames) appearing on CHAMELEON's implemented blackboard.

```
FRAME           ::= PREDICATE

PREDICATE       ::= identifier(ARGUMENTS)

ARGUMENTS       ::= ARGUMENT
                |   ARGUMENTS, ARGUMENT

ARGUMENT        ::= CONSTANT
                |   VARIABLE
                |   PREDICATE
```

```
CONSTANT        ::= identifier
                |  integer
                |  string


VARIABLE        ::= $identifier
```

FRAME acts as start symbol, CAPITAL symbols are non-terminals, and terminals are lower-case or one of the four symbols ( ) , and $. An *identifier* starts with a letter that can be followed by any number of letters, digits or _, an *integer* consists of a sequence of digits and a *string* is anything delimited by two "'s. Thus the *alphabet* consists of the letters, the digits and the symbols ( ) , _ and $. A parser has been written in C which can parse the frames using this BNF definition.

Appendix B

Blackboard in Practice

Here we show the complete blackboard (with all frames) as produced exactly by CHAMELEON for the example dialogue given in Section 2.

```
Received: nlp(intention(instruction(pointing)),location(person(tb),
type(office)),time(889524794))
which is passed on to dialog_manager
Received: dialog_manager(output(laser(point(coordinates(249,623))),
speech_synthesizer(utterance("This is Toms office"))))
Calling laser: laser(point(coordinates(249,623)))
Calling speech_synthesizer:
speech_synthesizer(utterance("This is Toms office"))
Received: nlp(intention(instruction(pointing)),location(person(tbm),
type(office)),time(889524818))
which is passed on to dialog_manager
Received: dialog_manager(output(laser(point(coordinates(278,623))),
speech_synthesizer(utterance("This is Thomass office"))))
Calling laser: laser(point(coordinates(278,623)))
Calling speech_synthesizer:
speech_synthesizer(utterance("This is Thomass office"))


Received: nlp(intention(query(where)),location(place(a2_221)),
time(889524831))
which is passed on to dialog_manager
Received: dialog_manager(output(laser(point(coordinates(132,500))),
speech_synthesizer(utterance("computer room is here"))))
Calling laser: laser(point(coordinates(132,500)))
Calling speech_synthesizer:
speech_synthesizer(utterance("computer room is here"))
```

```
Received: nlp(intention(query(who)),location(this($Deixis),
type(office)),time(889524864))
which is passed on to dialog_manager
Received: dialog_manager(output(laser(point(coordinates(658,546))),
speech_synthesizer(
utterance("This is not an office, this is instrument repair"))))
Calling laser: laser(point(coordinates(658,546)))
Calling speech_synthesizer:
speech_synthesizer(
utterance("This is not an office, this is instrument repair"))


Received: nlp(intention(query(who)),location(this($Deixis),
type(office)),time(889524885))
which is passed on to dialog_manager
Received: dialog_manager(output(laser(point(coordinates(223,568))),
speech_synthesizer(utterance("This is Pauls office"))))
Calling laser: laser(point(coordinates(223,568)))
Calling speech_synthesizer:
speech_synthesizer(utterance("This is Pauls office"))


Received: nlp(intention(instruction(show_route)),
source(location(person(lbl),type(office))),
destination(location(person(hg),type(office))),time(889524919))
which is passed on to dialog_manager
Received: dialog_manager(output(laser(route(
coordinates(278,585,278,603,249,603,220,603,197,603,197,623))),
speech_synthesizer(
utterance("This is the route from Lars Bos office to Hannes office"))))
Calling laser:
laser(route(
coordinates(278,585,278,603,249,603,220,603,197,603,197,623)))
Calling speech_synthesizer:
speech_synthesizer(
utterance("This is the route from Lars Bos office to Hannes office"))


Received: nlp(intention(instruction(show_route)),
source(location(person(pmck),
type(office))),destination(location(place(a2_105))),time(889524942))
which is passed on to dialog_manager
Received:
dialog_manager(output(laser(route(
coordinates(174,453,153,453,153,481,153,500,153,510,153,
540,153,569,153,599,153,603,184,603,197,603,220,603,249,
603,278,603,307,603,330,603,330,655,354,655,911,655,884,
```

```
655,884,603,810,603,759,603,717,603,717,570,696,570))),
speech_synthesizer(
utterance("This is the route from Pauls office to instrument repair"))))
Calling laser:
laser(route(coordinates(174,453,153,453,153,481,153,500,153,
510,153,540,153,569,153,599,153,603,184,603,197,603,220,603,
249,603,278,603,307,603,330,603,330,655,354,655,911,655,884,
655,884,603,810,603,759,603,717,603,717,570,696,570)))
Calling speech_synthesizer:
speech_synthesizer(
utterance(
"This is the route from Pauls office to instrument repair"))


Received: nlp(intention(instruction(pointing)),location(person(pd),
type(office)),time(889524958))
which is passed on to dialog_manager
Received: dialog_manager(output(laser(point(coordinates(220,585))),
speech_synthesizer(utterance("This is Pauls office"))))
```

A Unified Framework for Constructing Multimodal Experiments and Applications

Adam Cheyer[1], Luc Julia[1], and Jean-Claude Martin[2]

[1] SRI International, Menlo Park, Ca., USA
{cheyer,julia}@speech.sri.com
[2] LIMSI-CNRS, Orsay, France
martin@limsi.fr

Abstract. Inspired by a Wizard of Oz (WOZ) simulation experiment, we developed a working prototype of a system that enables users to interact with a map display through synergistic combinations of pen and voice. To address many of the issues raised by multimodal fusion, our implementation employed a distributed multi-agent framework to coordinate parallel competition and cooperation among processing components. Since then, the agent-based infrastructure has been enhanced with a collaboration technology, creating a framework in which multiple humans and automated agents can naturally interact within the same graphical workspace.

Our current endeavour is the leveraging of this architecture to create a unified implementation framework for simultaneously developing both WOZ simulated systems and their fully-automated counterparts. Bootstrapping effects made possible by such an approach are illustrated by an experiment currently under way in our laboratory: as a naive subject draws, writes, and speaks requests to a (simulated) interactive map, a hidden Wizard responds as efficiently as possible using our best fully-automated system, through either standard graphical interface devices or multimodal combinations of pen and voice. The input choices made by both subject and Wizard are invaluable, and the data collected from each can be applied directly to evaluating and improving the automated part of the system.

1 Introduction

Wizard of Oz (WOZ) simulations have proven an effective technique for discovering how users would interact with systems that are beyond the current state of the art (see Oviatt, 1996; Oviatt, De Angeli, and Kuhn, 1997). However, WOZ systems are costly to build from scratch and are rarely reusable across domains. Furthermore, it is often difficult to evaluate how lessons learned from the experiment directly impact the design and effectiveness of a real application.

In this chapter, we will first describe a fully-automated prototype (presented at the CMC'95 conference and described in Cheyer and Julia, 1998b) that was inspired by a multimodal WOZ simulation (of Oviatt, 1996), and then explain how its functionality evolved as the application was used. We then describe how the system was enhanced to serve as a hybrid WOZ simulation where the actions of both the naive subject and the expert Wizard are objects of the

H. Bunt and R.-J. Beun (Eds.): CMC'98, LNAI 2155, pp. 234–242, 2001.
© Springer-Verlag Berlin Heidelberg 2001

experiment. The approach is put forth as a general-purpose, unified framework for simultaneously constructing multimodal WOZ experiments and their fully-functional versions, such that the two synergistically improve each other. We call this methodology a WOZZOW experiment, for reasons which we shall explain in the text.

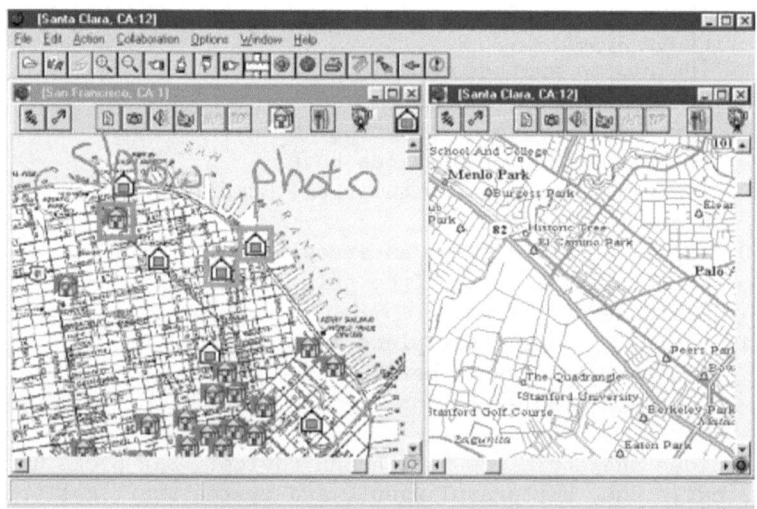

Fig. 1. A Multimodal Map Application.

2   A Fully-Automated Multimodal Map Application

2.1   Description

Our multimodal map application provides an interactive interface on which the user may draw, write, or speak. In a travel planning domain (Figure 1), available information includes data about hotels, restaurants, and tourist sites that have been retrieved by distributed software agents from commercial Internet World Wide Web sites. The types of user interactions and multimodal issues handled by the application can be illustrated by a brief scenario featuring working examples taken from the current system.

Sara is planning a business trip to San Francisco, but would like
to schedule some activities for the weekend while she is there.
She turns on her laptop PC, executes a map application, and
selects San Francisco.

Ex1.1   [Speaking] Where is downtown?
         Map scrolls to appropriate area.
Ex1.2   [Speaking + drawing region] Show me all hotels near here.
         Icons representing hotels appear.

236 Adam Cheyer, Luc Julia, and Jean-Claude Martin

Ex1.3   [Writes on a hotel] Info?
        A textual description (price, attributes, etc.) appears.
Ex1.4   [Speaking] I only want hotels with a pool.
        Some hotels disappear.
Ex1.5   [Crosses out a hotel that is too close to a highway]
        Hotel disappears
Ex1.6   [Speaking and circling] Show me a photo of this hotel.
        Photo appears.
Ex1.7   [Points to another hotel]
        Photo appears.
Ex1.8   [Speaking] Price of the other hotel?
        Price appears for previous hotel.
Ex1.9   [Speaking and drawing an arrow] Scroll down.
        Display adjusted.
Ex1.10 [Speaking and drawing an arrow toward a hotel]
        What is the distance from this hotel to Fisherman's wharf?
        Distance displayed.
Ex1.11 [Pointing to another place and speaking]
        And the distance to here?
        Distance displayed.

Sara decides she could use some human advice. She picks up the
phone, calls Bob, her travel agent, and writes Start collaboration
to synchronize his display with hers. At this point, both are
presented with an identical map, and the input and actions of one
will be remotely seen by the other.

Ex2.1   [Sara speaks and circles two hotels]
        Bob, I'm trying to choose between these two hotels.
        Any opinions?
Ex2.2   [Bob draws an arrow, speaks and points]
        Well, this area is really nice to visit. You can walk
        there from this hotel.
        Map scrolls to indicated area. Hotel selected.
Ex2.3   [Sara speaks] Do you think I should visit Alcatraz?
Ex2.4   [Bob speaks] Map, show video of Alcatraz.
        Video appears.
Ex2.5   [Bob speaks] Yes, Alcatraz is a lot of fun.

   For this system, the main research focus is on how to generate the most
appropriate interpretation for the incoming streams of multimodal input. Our
approach employs an agent-based framework to coordinate competition and cooperation among distributed information sources, working in parallel to resolve
the ambiguities arising at every level of the interpretation process:

 — *low-level processing* of the data stream: Pen input may be interpreted as a
   gesture (e.g., Ex1.5: crossout, Ex1.9: arrow) by one algorithm, or as handwriting by a separate recognition process (e.g., Ex1.3: info?). Multiple hypotheses may be returned by a modality recognition component.

- *anaphora resolution*: When resolving anaphoric references, separate information sources may contribute to resolving the reference:

  - *Context by object type*: For an utterance such as show photo of the hotel, the natural language component can return a list of the last hotels talked about.
  - *Deictic*: In combination with a spoken utterance like show photo of this hotel, pointing, circling, or arrow gestures might indicate the desired object (e.g., Ex1.7). Deictic references may occur before, during, or after an accompanying verbal command.
  - *Visual context*: Given the request display photo of the hotel, the user interface agent might determine that only one hotel is currently visible on the map, and therefore this might be the desired reference object.
  - *Database queries*: Information from a database agent can be combined with results from other resolution strategies. Examples are show me a photo of the hotel in Menlo Park and Ex1.2.
  - *Discourse analysis*: Discourse can provide a source of information for phrases such as No, the other one (or Ex1.8).

  This list is by no means exhaustive. Examples of other resolution methods include spatial reasoning (*the hotel between Fisherman's Wharf and Lombard Street*) and user preferences (*near my favourite restaurant*).
- *cross-modality influences*: When multiple modalities are used together, one modality may reinforce or disambiguate the interpretation of another. For instance, the interpretation of an arrow gesture may vary when accompanied by different verbal commands (e.g., *scroll left* vs. *show info about this hotel*). In the latter example, the system must take into account how accurately and unambiguously an arrow selects a single hotel.
- *addressee*: With the addition of collaboration technology, humans and automated agents all share the same workspace. A pen doodle or a spoken utterance may be meant for either another human, the system (Ex2.1), or both (Ex2.2).

A first version of this prototype system was presented at the CMC'95 conference (see Cheyer and Julia, 1995; 1998b); the system has evolved since then in several ways. First, the user interface was redesigned with an eye toward practicality (Figure 1). Whereas the design for the user interface of the original system was patterned directly after that of the WOZ experiments, which for obvious reasons encourages the user to produce strictly pen/voice input, the redesign provides standard GUI devices (e.g., scrollbars, toolbars, menus, dialogue boxes) if that is the most efficient means of expressing the intent. The human-human collaboration mode is new. The map interface has also been augmented to accommodate multiple windows, each representing a workspace with a separate context (e.g., city, viewport position, zoom factor, shared vs. private space) The distributed multimodal interpretation process, as described above, has evolved considerably, particularly with respect to cross-modality ambiguity resolution. Finally, the multimodal map has been applied to a number of applications outside of the travel planning domain (see Moran et al., 1997).

2.2 Implementation

The map application is implemented within a multiagent framework called the Open Agent Architecture (OAA)[1]. The OAA provides a general-purpose infrastructure for constructing systems composed of multiple software agents written in different programming languages and running on different platforms. Similar in spirit to distributed object frameworks such as OMG's CORBA or Microsoft's DCOM, agent interactions are more flexible and adaptable than the tightly bound object method calls provided by these architectures, and are able to exploit parallelism and dynamic execution of complex goals. Instead of preprogrammed single method calls to known object services, an agent can express its requests in terms of a high-level logical description of what it wants done, along with optional constraints specifying how the task should be performed. This specification request is processed by one or more Facilitator agents, which plan, execute and monitor the coordination of the subtasks required to accomplish the end goal (first detailed in D. Martin, Cheyer and Moran, 1999).

The core services of the OAA are implemented by an agent library working closely with a Facilitator agent; together, they are responsible for domain-independent coordination and routing of information and services. These basic services can be classified into three areas: agent communication and cooperation, distributed data services, and trigger management. For details on these topics and information about how to build applications using the OAA, refer to D. Martin, Cheyer and Moran, 1998. SRI has recently made OAA openly available for non-commercial use: a Facilitator agent, libraries for several programming languages, runtime and debugging tools, and a sample application can be freely downloaded from http://www.openagent.com.

The map application is composed of 10 or more distributed agents that handle database access, speech recognition (Nuance Communications Toolkit or IBM's VoiceType), handwriting (by CIC or Vadem Paragraph) and gesture (in-house algorithms) recognition, natural language interpretation, and so forth. As mentioned in the previous section, these agents compete and cooperate to interpret the streams of input media being generated by the user. More detailed information regarding agent interactions for the multimodal map application and the strategies used for modality merging can be found in Cheyer and Julia, 1998b and Julia an Cheyer, 1997a].

In addition to the system described in this chapter, the OAA has been used to construct more than 30 different applications, integrating various technologies in many domains: multirobot control and coordination (see Guzzoni et al., 1997), office automation and unified messaging (Cohen et al., 1998), front ends (Julia et al., 1997b) and back ends (D. Martin et al., 1997) for the Web, and development tools (D. Martin, Cheyer and Lee, 1996) for creating and assembling new agents within the OAA. Other agent-base multimodal applications are described in Cheyer (1998a), Moran et al. (1997), and Moore et al. (1997).

---

[1] Open Agent Architecture and OAA are trademarks of SRI International. Other brand names and product names herein are trademarks and registered trademarks of their respective holders.

3   A Hybrid Approach: The WOZZOW Experiment

For any WOZ experiment, the runtime environment must generally provide the following facilities:

1. An interface, for the subject, which will accept user input (without processing it), transmit the input to a hidden Wizard, and then display the results returned by the Wizard.
2. An interface, for the Wizard, which provides a means for viewing the subject's input, and for rapidly taking appropriate action to control the subject's display.
3. Automated logging and playback of sessions to facilitate the data analysis process.

The multimodal map application already possesses two qualities that help the fully-automated application function part of a WOZ experiment: the system allows multiple users to share a common workspace in which the input and results of one user may be seen by all members of the session – this will enable the Wizard to see the subject's requests and remotely control the display; the user interface can be configured on a per-user basis to include more or fewer GUI controls – the Wizard can lay out all GUI command options, and still work on the map by using pen and voice (Figure 2). Conversely, the subject will be presented with a map-only display (Figure 3).

To extend the fully-automated map application to be suitable for conducting WOZ simulations, we added only three features: a mode to disable the interpretation of input for the subject, domain-independent logging and playback functions that leverage the agent collaboration services, and a separate message agent for sending WOZ-specific instructions (e.g., *Please be more specific*) to the user with text-to-speech and graphics.

The result is a hybrid WOZ experiment: While a naive user is free to write, draw, or speak to a map application without constraints imposed by specific recognition technologies, the hidden Wizard must respond as quickly and accurately as possible using any means at his or her disposal. In certain situations, a scrollbar or dialogue box might provide the fastest response, whereas in others, some combination of pen and voice may be the most efficient way of accomplishing the task.

In a single 'WOZZOW' experiment, we simultaneously collect data input from both an unconstrained new user (unknowingly) operating a simulated system (the Wizard-of-Oz simulation or 'WOZ' part of WOZZOW), and from an expert user (under duress) making full use of our best automated system (the 'ZOW' part of WOZZOW). The 'WOZ' side of the experiment provides data about how pen and voice are combined in the most natural way possible, while the 'ZOW' side clarifies how well our real system performs and lets us make comparisons between the roles of a standard GUI and a multimodal interface.

We expect that this data will prove invaluable from an experimental standpoint, and that since all interactions are logged electronically, both sets of data can be directly applied to evaluating and improving the automated processing. How well did the real system perform for the Wizard? How well would the fully-automated system have fared on the actual data produced by the new user if

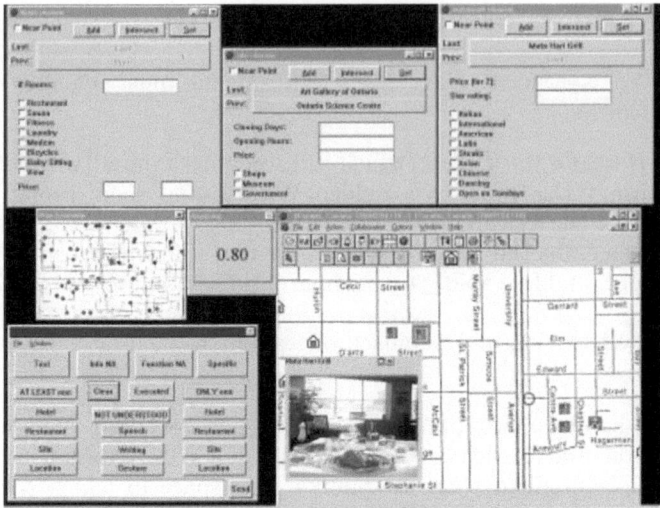

Fig. 2. The Wizard Interface.

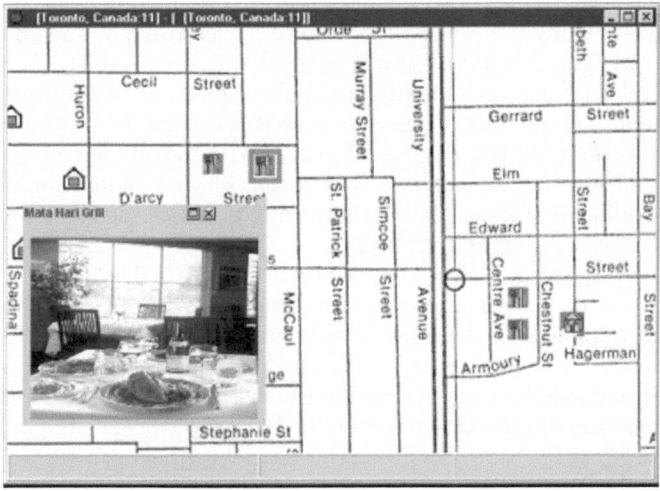

Fig. 3. The Subject Interface.

there were no Wizard? Are there improvements that could be made to the speech grammar, modality merging process, or other aspects of the system that would significantly increase overall performance? How much do the changes actually improve the system?

Performing such experiments and evaluations in a framework where a WOZ simulation and its corresponding fully-functional end-user system are tightly intertwined produces a bootstrap effect: as the automated system is improved to better handle the corpus of subject interactions, the Wizard's task is made easier and more efficient for future WOZ experiments. The methodology promotes an incremental way of designing an application, testing the design through semiautomated user studies, gradually developing the automated processing to implement appropriate behaviour for input collected from subjects, and then testing the finished product while simultaneously designing and collecting data on future functionality – all within one unified implementation. The system can also be used without a Wizard, to log data about how real users make use of the finished product.

4   Conclusions and Future Work

We have described a framework and a novel approach for simultaneously developing a WOZ simulation and a working prototype for multimodal applications. This integration encourages bootstrap effects: data and results obtained from the user experiment can directly improve the automated processing components, making the Wizard's responses more efficient. The architecture is generic, allowing an application/experiment developer to freely select programming languages, input and output modalities, third-party recognition engines, and modality combination technologies (e.g., neural nets, slot-based approaches, temporal fusion).

We are currently in the process of applying the framework described in this chapter to conduct a data collection effort, of approximately 30 subjects, that focuses on spatial references in multimodal map-based tasks. The data is being analysed along a several dimensions by using TYCOON, a theoretical framework for evaluating multimodal user studies, as described in J.C. Martin, Julia and Cheyer (1998). Initial findings from these experiments are available in Kehler et al., 1998, and we expect to publish more detailed results in the near future.

Acknowledgements

This chapter was supported in part by National Science Foundation/Advanced Research Project Agency Grant IRI-9619126. We would like to thank Andy Kehler, Jerry Hobbs, and John Bear for valuable discussions and comments on earlier drafts. Thanks also to Wayne Chambliss for his excellent Wizardry.

References

Cheyer, A. (1998) MVIEWS: Multimodal tools for the video analyst. In: *Proceedings of IUI'98,* San Francisco (USA), 55–62.

Cheyer A. and Julia L. (1995) Multimodal maps: An agent-based approach. In: *Proceedings of the International COnference on Cooperative Multimodal Communication CMC'95*, Eindhoven (The Netherlands), May 1995, 103–113.

Cheyer A. and Julia L. (1998) Multimodal maps: An agent-based approach. In: H. Bunt, R.J. Beun, and T. Borghuis (eds.), *Multimodal Human-Computer Communication; Systems, Techniques and Experiments*. Lecture Notes in Artificial Intelligence 1374, Berlin: Springer, 111–121.

References

Cheyer, A. (1998) MVIEWS: Multimodal tools for the video analyst. In: *Proceedings of IUI'98*, San Francisco (USA), 55–62.

Cheyer A. and Julia L. (1995) Multimodal maps: An agent-based approach. In: *Proceedings of the International COnference on Cooperative Multimodal Communication CMC'95*, Eindhoven (The Netherlands), May 1995, 103–113.

Cheyer A. and Julia L. (1998) Multimodal maps: An agent-based approach. In: H. Bunt, R.J. Beun, and T. Borghuis (eds.), *Multimodal Human-Computer Communication; Systems, Techniques and Experiments*. Lecture Notes in Artificial Intelligence 1374, Berlin: Springer, 111–121.

Cohen, P., Cheyer, A., Wang, M., and Baeg, S. (1998) An Open Agent Architecture. In: M.N. Huhns and M.P. Singh (eds.), *Readings in Agents*, San Francisco: Morgan Kaufmann Publishers, 197–204.

Guzzoni, D., Cheyer, A., Julia, L., and Konolige, K. (1997) Many robots make short work. AI Magazine, Vol. 18, No. 1, Spring 1997, 55–64.

Julia, L. and Cheyer, A. (1997) Speech: a privileged modality. In: *Proceedings of EuroSpeech'97*, Rhodes (Greece), vol. 4, 1843–1846.

Julia, L., Cheyer, A., Neumeyer, L., Dowding, J., and Charafeddine, M. (1997) http://WWW.SPEECH.SRI.COM/DEMOS/ATIS.HTML. In: *Proceedings of AAAI'97*, Stanford (USA), 72–76.

Kehler A., Martin J.C., Cheyer A., Julia L., Hobbs J., and Bear J. (1998) On representing Salience and Reference in Multimodal Human-Computer Interaction. In: *Proceedings of AAAI'98 (Representations for Multi-Modal Human-Computer Interaction)*, Madison (USA), 33–39.

Martin, D., Cheyer, A., and Moran, D. (1999) The Open Agent Architecture: A framework for building distributed software systems. *Applied Artificial Intelligence: An International Journal. (13,1–2)*.

Martin, D., Cheyer, A., and Moran, D. (1998) Building Distributed Software Systems with the Open Agent Architecture. See http://www.ai.sri.com/~oaa and "Publications", 1998.

Martin, D., Cheyer, A., and Lee, GL. (1996) Agent development tools for the Open Agent Architecture. In: *Proceedings of the International Conference on the Practical Application of Intelligent Agents and Multi-Agent Technology*, London, April 1996.

Martin, D., Oohama, H., Moran, D., and Cheyer, A. (1997) Information brokering in an agent architecture. In: *Proceedings of the Second International Conference on the Practical Application of Intelligent Agents and Multi-Agent Technology*, London, April 1997.

Martin, J.C., Julia, L., and Cheyer, A. (1998) A theoretical framework for multimodal user studies. In: *Proceedings of the Second International COnference on Cooperative Multimodal Communication CMC/98*, Tilburg (The Netherlands), January 1998, 104–110.

Moore, R., Dowding, J., Bratt, H., Gawron, J.M., and Cheyer, A. (1997) CommandTalk: A spoken-language interface for battlefield simulations. In: *Proceedings of Fifth Conference on Applied Natural Language Processing*, Washington, D.C., April 1997.

Moran, D., Cheyer, A., Julia, L., and Park, S. (1997) Multimodal user interfaces in the Open Agent Architecture. In: *Proceedings of IUI'97*, Orlando (USA), 61–68.

Oviatt, S. (1996) Multimodal interfaces for dynamic interactive maps. In: *Proceedings of CHI'96*, April 13-18, 1996. 95–102.

Oviatt, S., De Angeli, A., and Kuhn, K. (1997) Integration and synchronization of input modes during multimodal human-computer interaction. In: *Proceedings of the workshop "Referring Phenomena in a Multimedia Context and their Computational Treatment"*, ACL/EACL'97 (Madrid), 1–13.
Also: http://www.dfki.uni-sb.de/imedia/workshops/mm-references.html

Index

Author Index

Lecture Notes in Artificial Intelligence (LNAI)

Lecture Notes in Computer Science